ESSENTIAL FIRST STEPS TO DATA ANALYSIS

ESSENTIAL FIRST STEPS TO DATA ANALYSIS

Scenario-Based Examples Using SPSS

CAROL S. PARKE
Duquesne University, Pittsburgh, PA

Los Angeles | London | New Delhi
Singapore | Washington DC

Los Angeles | London | New Delhi
Singapore | Washington DC

FOR INFORMATION:

SAGE Publications, Inc.
2455 Teller Road
Thousand Oaks, California 91320
E-mail: order@sagepub.com

SAGE Publications Ltd.
1 Oliver's Yard
55 City Road
London EC1Y 1SP
United Kingdom

SAGE Publications India Pvt. Ltd.
B 1/I 1 Mohan Cooperative Industrial Area
Mathura Road, New Delhi 110 044
India

SAGE Publications Asia-Pacific Pte. Ltd.
3 Church Street
#10-04 Samsung Hub
Singapore 049483

Acquisitions Editor: Vicki Knight
Associate Editor: Lauren Habib
Editorial Assistant: Kalie Koscielak
Production Editor: Eric Garner
Copy Editor: Liann Lech
Typesetter: C&M Digitals (P) Ltd.
Proofreader: Laura Webb
Indexer: Jeanne Busemeyer
Cover Designer: Candice Harman
Marketing Manager: Nicole Elliott
Permissions Editor: Adele Hutchinson

Printed in the United States of America

Library of Congress Cataloging-in-Publication Data

Parke, Carol S.

Essential first steps to data analysis: scenario-based examples using SPSS / Carol S. Parke.

pages cm
Includes bibliographical references and index.

ISBN 978-1-4129-9751-5 (pbk.)

1. SPSS (Computer file) 2. Social sciences--Statistical methods—Data processing. I. Title.

HA32.P37 2013
300.72'7—dc23   2012043929

This book is printed on acid-free paper.

SUSTAINABLE FORESTRY INITIATIVE

Certified Chain of Custody
Promoting Sustainable Forestry
www.sfiprogram.org
SFI-01268

SFI label applies to text stock

12 13 14 15 16 10 9 8 7 6 5 4 3 2 1

Brief Contents

Detailed Contents

Preface

S tudents in social sciences, behavioral sciences, and education learn how to design studies and carry out descriptive and inferential analysis in their research and statistics courses. However, they often struggle when faced with analyzing real data for a class project or for research in which they are involved. They are unsure about what should be done first and typically have the misconception that statistics can be conducted immediately to answer their research questions. Without guidance, these students may perform inappropriate procedures and obtain erroneous output, not realizing that their results are invalid.

Purpose △

The purpose of this book is to provide instruction and guidance on preparing quantitative data sets prior to answering a study's research questions. Preparation may involve data management and manipulation tasks; data organization; structural changes to data files; or conducting preliminary analysis such as examining the scale of a variable, the validity of assumptions, or the nature and extent of missing data. The "results" from these essential first steps can also help guide a researcher in selecting the most appropriate statistical tests for his or her study.

The book is intended to serve as a supplemental text in statistics or research courses offered in graduate programs in education, counseling, school psychology, behavioral sciences, and social sciences as well as undergraduate programs that contain a heavy emphasis on statistics. The content and issues covered are also beneficial for faculty and researchers who are knowledgeable about research design and able to use a statistical software package, but are unsure of the first steps to take with their data. Increasingly, faculty are forming partnerships with schools, clinics, and other institutions to help them analyze data in their extensive databases. This book can serve as a reference for helping them get existing data files in an appropriate form to run statistical analysis.

This book is not a replacement for a statistics textbook. It assumes that readers have some knowledge of basic statistical concepts and use of statistical software, or that they will be learning these concepts and skills concurrently throughout the course. IBM SPSS Statistics* was chosen to illustrate the preparation, evaluation, and manipulation of data. However, students or researchers who do not use SPSS will benefit from the content because the overall structure and pedagogical approach of the book focuses heavily on the data issues and decisions to be made.

△ Goals

The book was conceptualized with two goals in mind. One goal is to provide students and researchers with in-depth scenarios that illustrate common data issues to consider, evaluations to perform, and decisions to be made prior to embarking on the main analysis. It is a practical book that focuses on critical thinking. Many other resources on data preparation describe the procedures without any context and are essentially "how-to" books. Although they may use real-world data sets, there is often no discussion of the reasons *why* a researcher would want (or need) to recode a variable, transform a variable, examine outliers, aggregate cases, restructure a file, and so on. The strength of this book is that it makes the necessity of these steps and procedures transparent to the researcher. It does not read like a manual; rather, "stories" are told about researchers who thoroughly examined their data and the decisions they made along the way.

The second goal is a broader one, which is to raise awareness of these essential first steps in the research process. Getting from Point A (the raw data file) to Point B (ready for analysis of the research questions) is not always straightforward. With the pedagogical approach taken here, the intended outcome is for students and researchers to appreciate the amount of time, patience, and thoughtfulness that must go into the preparation phase of data analysis in order to ensure accurate and meaningful results.

△ Structure and Organization

Twelve modules are used to present the content. Each module contains a detailed scenario that illustrates how a researcher deals with specific issues related to his or her data file. The structure of each module is as follows:

- **Description of Researcher's Study**
  The scenario is placed in a context.
- **A Look at the Data**
  The data file's cases, variables, and other relevant attributes are described.

*IBM SPSS Statistics was formerly called PASW® Statistics.

- **Planning and Decision Making**
  The issues the researcher needs to address are described, and explanations of why the issues are important are also given.
- **Using SPSS to Address Issues and Prepare Data**
  The detailed steps the researcher took to address the issues are presented. SPSS dialog boxes, tables of output, and figures are included.
- **Reflection and Additional Decision Making**
  The researcher's reflections on the process and, in some cases, descriptions of further data manipulations or file preparation are described.
- **Writing It Up**
  A summary of the procedures and outcomes from his or her data preparation is provided.

With regard to the last bullet, it is important to see how a researcher communicates and summarizes his or her issues, decisions, and findings in words. Published journal articles and technical reports often include summaries of preliminary data preparation and analysis that describe, for example, how model assumptions were evaluated and how the results influenced the type of data analysis conducted.

Modules are not necessarily grouped by difficulty, but rather by the nature of their content into five sections that somewhat follow the research process (evaluating a sample, organizing and recoding variables, examining the variables' distributions, evaluating assumptions, identifying missing data, and working with multiple data files). The sections are not dependent on each other, meaning that knowledge of prior modules is not necessary. Within each section, however, it would be best to read the modules in the order in which they are presented. Each section begins with a cover page that briefly introduces the topic of each module and ends with a page that lists additional resources on the topic.

Section 1: The Sample

Two modules describe how researchers evaluated the representativeness of a sample using chi-square analysis, created ranks and standardized values for the sample, and prepared the data file for analyzing targeted subsets of cases. This section also includes information on best practices for assigning variable and file names as well as documenting their attributes.

Section 2: Nature and Distribution of Variables

Three modules describe the process of recoding and computing new variables, determining the scale of measurement for variables, and identifying outliers. They incorporate the use of visual displays of data (histograms, stem-and-leaf plots, and boxplots).

Section 3: Model Assumptions

Two modules describe how a researcher evaluated model assumptions for t-tests, analysis of variance, and multiple regression. Visual inspections of data include histograms, normal probability plots, scatterplots, and standardized residual plots. This section also describes how the researcher used alternative procedures to further examine the validity of results, including modifications of the test statistic, use of nonparametric tests, and a data transformation. These are the longest modules in the book due to the extensive nature of the statistical content.

Section 4: Missing Data

A basic introduction to missing data is provided in this section. Two modules describe how researchers quantified missing data in their data files, determined its nature, and diagnosed patterns. The section does not address procedures for replacing missing values. Data replacement is quite complex and thus goes beyond the scope of this book. However, several excellent references are provided for further reading.

Section 5: Working With Multiple Data Files

The three modules in this section describe how a researcher incorporated information from multiple files in a database to answer the questions in her study. In this age of maintaining comprehensive longitudinal databases in school districts, clinics, and institutions, it is necessary that researchers know how to combine data from several files. These modules demonstrate how the researcher merged variables from two files, aggregated coursework data to obtain mean grades, used longitudinal information to identify a student cohort, and restructured a file so that all data for each student are contained in one row.

△ Special Features

Two instructional features occur throughout the book. First, each module includes "asides" from the researcher who is conducting the study. The purpose is to provide commentary that the researcher wants to share with the reader. For example, Dr. Salerno might describe why she made a particular decision, or she might describe an alternate path she could have taken to deal with the data issue. These appear in a text box in the margin of the page and begin with "Dr. Salerno says. . . ." Each module also includes SPSS tips that serve the purpose of further explaining SPSS procedures and the various options within them. Similar to the "asides," these are placed in a text box on the relevant page. The tips are procedural in nature, whereas the "asides" are context related and more substantive.

Other formatting conventions used across all modules help the reader easily identify variable names (*italicized*), SPSS procedures and options (**bolded**), and paths for obtaining dialog boxes (e.g., **Transform** → **Compute Variable).** Names of the data files are also italicized and always begin with the module number so they can be easily associated with their research scenario. They are available on the book's companion website at **www.sagepub.com/parke**. Version 20 of SPSS was used in the creation of this book. Previous versions of the software execute the procedures in a similar fashion.

A set of specific learning objectives is provided at the beginning of each module. They indicate what the reader should be able to do after he or she reads the scenario and uses the files to carry out the data preparation, manipulation, or evaluation. A set of reflective questions is included at the end of each module to help evaluate the knowledge and skills gained. Finally, extensions are provided that are specific to each module. Some provide starting points for further discussion of the research or statistical concepts included in the research scenario. Other extensions include suggestions for additional practice of the procedures and analyses demonstrated in the modules.

How to Use the Book ∆

Instructors may find it useful to determine the best fit for each module in their course syllabus. For instance, the module on the nature of a variable's distribution would most naturally fit within instruction on determining the scale of measurement for variables (nominal, ordinal, interval, ratio) or when learning how to decide which statistical tests are appropriate for analyzing data.

Although each module focuses on a particular data preparation issue, other statistical concepts naturally come into play because the content is presented using research scenarios. Instructors can take advantage of these teachable moments to reinforce content that was already taught or to introduce the new concepts to students. As an example, a discussion of Type I error and power can occur when using the module that evaluates assumptions for tests of mean differences.

Finally, the scenarios can become a springboard for specific discussions of students' and instructors' own data sets. It is impossible for one research scenario to cover all situations a researcher may encounter within a topic. Therefore, it would be beneficial to examine additional data sets so that students can practice what was learned in the module and make their own decisions along the way. Instructors or students may want to share data sets they have used or are currently using in their own research. Another option is to obtain public-use data files from educational institutions, government, and other entities. The intention is that these in-depth discussions of data will lead to lively interactions among students and teachers about very practical issues.

△ Acknowledgments

I extend my deepest gratitude to Dr. Rick McCown, then-chair of the Department of Educational Foundations and Leadership at Duquesne University, who encouraged me to pursue my idea for this book and pointed me toward the appropriate outlet for it. I thank him for generously permitting me the time to conceptualize, develop, and write this book.

My thanks are also due to all the graduate students I have taught, students on whose dissertation committees I have served, and my fellow faculty members for providing the stimulating intellectual atmosphere that provided the inspiration for this book and helped to make clear to me the need for it. Also, special thanks to Dr. Laura M. Crothers (Duquesne University) for the use of her data set in Module 6.

And, certainly, I must extend warm appreciation to my SAGE editor, Vicki Knight, who was always available, always supportive, always encouraging and knowledgeable. From the start, she provided the encouragement and feedback necessary to turn my nugget of an idea into a finished, useful work.

I also want to acknowledge the reviewers and thank them for their insightful comments and suggestions throughout the process: Julie Alonzo (University of Oregon), Stephanie A. Bennett (The College of St. Rose), Paul R. Brandon (University of Hawaii at Manoa), Derek Briggs (University of Colorado at Boulder), Christina M. Bruhn (Aurora University), Carrie L. Cook (Georgia College & State University), David W. Eccles (Florida State University), Kathy Boone Ginter (Indiana State University), David K. Griffin (Nova Southeastern University), Elizabeth Harwood (Rivier College), Leslie

R. Hinkson (Georgetown University), Amy B. Jessop (The University of the Sciences in Philadelphia), Karen H. Larwin (Youngstown State University), Tera D. Letzring (Idaho State University), Min Li (University of Washington at Seattle), Christopher J. Maglio (Truman State University), Claudette M. Peterson (North Dakota State University), Steven Pulos (University of Northern Colorado), Philip C. Rodkin (University of Illinois at Urbana–Champaign), Claude Rubinson (University of Houston–Downtown), Youngyol Yim Schanz (Slippery Rock University), Jason F. Sikorski (Central Connecticut State University), Homer Tolson (Texas A&M University), Deanna L. Trella (Northern Michigan Univeristy), Kyle M. Woosnam (Texas A&M University), and Mary Ann Zager (Florida Gulf Coast University).

I am, of course, eternally grateful to my family, who sacrificed so much of their time to allow me to work on this book from concept to development to writing to final editing. I can't thank you enough.

About the Author

Carol S. Parke, PhD, is an associate professor in the Department of Educational Foundations and Leadership at Duquesne University in Pittsburgh, PA. She teaches statistics, research, and measurement courses to students in master's and doctoral programs in the School of Education. Her educational background includes a PhD in Research Methodology and an MA in Mathematics/Statistics from the University of Pittsburgh as well as a BS in Secondary Mathematics Education from Indiana University of Pennsylvania.

Dr. Parke's 20 years of research span a broad range from the design and analysis of large-scale, long-term state and national assessment projects to working intimately with teachers in the classroom to show them how to collect and use data to make decisions and real-time, real-world improvement. Her work has appeared in research and practitioner journals in measurement, assessment, mathematics education, and statistics and includes *Using Assessment to Improve Middle-Grades Mathematics Teaching and Learning*, a book for teachers on using performance assessment in mathematics classrooms published by the National Council of Teachers of Mathematics.

INTRODUCTION TO
SECTION 1

The Sample

The two modules in this section focus on a few of the first steps researchers encounter after they collect their sample (Module 1) or obtain their data from an already existing source (Module 2).

Module 1: Checking the Representativeness of a Sample △

In the first module, Dr. Porter is planning to evaluate a new initiative intended to support students with disabilities. His target population consists of all schools in three rural counties in the region. Due to time, monetary, and traveling constraints, it was not possible to include the entire population in his study. Therefore, he identified a sample of schools using the cluster sampling approach. This module describes how he examined the representativeness of his sample in terms of student distribution by county and by disability type. Dr. Porter used chi-square tests to obtain statistical evidence regarding how well his sample represents the population.

Module 2: Splitting a File, Selecting Cases, △
and Creating Standardized Values and Ranks

The scenario in the second module differs from the first in that the researcher, Dr. Baird, is conducting an exploratory study on data she downloaded from an existing source. She is interested in comparing the number of librarians and guidance counselors employed in public schools across all 50 states in the United States and Washington, DC. Each case in her file represents a state or DC, and the variables represent total frequencies for each state. After extracting the data from a public national database, she finalized her exploratory research questions and identified the preliminary procedures she needed to conduct before answering them. The module describes how she created new variables containing standardized values and ranks for the ratios of librarians and counselors per school. It also describes how she split the file to analyze subsets of states by geographic region. Finally, Dr. Baird further refined her sample by selecting only those states in her specific area of the nation for a more focused analysis.

Checking the Representativeness of a Sample

⊰⊱
DATA FILES FOR THIS MODULE

module1_county_weighted.sav
module1_disability_standard.sav

⊰⊱

KEY LEARNING OBJECTIVES

The student will learn to

- use the weighted cases approach to conduct a one-sample chi-square test that determines how well the sample generalizes to the population
- use the standard approach to conduct a one-sample chi-square test that determines how well a subgroup of students that participates in a particular aspect of the study generalizes to all students in the sample.

A. Description of Researcher's Study △

Dr. Porter is an educator and researcher who was asked to evaluate the first year of an initiative that provides support to students with Individual Education Plans (IEPs) in three rural counties. Support during the first year focused on students whose primary disability was either learning, mental, or emotional. Dr. Porter created a comprehensive evaluation plan involving quantitative and qualitative data analysis. Data were collected from school records, artifacts, questionnaires, and interviews.

The evaluation required that Dr. Porter travel across the three counties. Due to the time-intensive nature of collecting the data as well as the time and monetary expenses involved in visiting schools that are widespread across the rural region, it was not feasible to travel to all schools. Therefore, Dr. Porter used a cluster sampling approach to obtain his sample. Using this approach, the schools in each county were considered to be the "clusters." His first step was to randomly select half of all schools in each county, and then he contacted each school to seek permission from the administrators. He received permission to collect evaluation data from all but two schools. In these two cases, he randomly chose another school in the same county. Ultimately, the sample consisted of 7 of the 14 total schools in the three counties. In addition, within each school, parents or guardians of students in the initiative were asked to provide consent for their child to be interviewed. In all, 87% of parents/guardians in the sample agreed to allow their child to participate in this portion of the evaluation study.

This module describes how Dr. Porter examined the representativeness of his sample in terms of student distribution by county and by disability type using two forms of a one-sample chi-square analysis.

△ B. A Look at the Data

The entire population of students with IEPs who have a learning, mental, or emotional disability as their primary type was 463 across the three counties. Table 1.1 shows the total number of districts and schools in each county as well as the frequencies of students.

Table 1.1 Frequencies in the Population by County

	Districts (*n*)	Schools (*n*)	Students (*n*)
County 1	1	2	191
County 2	2	7	203
County 3	4	5	69
Total	7	14	463

Dr. Porter's sample contained 190 students across seven schools. This sample represents 41% of the total population of students with IEPs[1] and learning, mental, or emotional disabilities. Table 1.2 shows the number of districts, schools, and students in his sample by county.

Table 1.2 Frequencies in the Sample by County

	Districts (*n*)	Schools (*n*)	Students (*n*)
County 1	1	1	31
County 2	2	3	115
County 3	3	3	44
Total	6	7	190

In addition to the aggregated data, Dr. Porter also has a data file that includes the primary disability (learning, mental, emotional) for each of the 165 students in the sample whose parents provided permission for interviews. It also includes the county in which they reside. Codes for the two variables in the file are listed in Table 1.3.

Table 1.3 Variables in the Disability File

Type of Disability by County for the Sample	
Variable Name	**Description**
county	codes of 1, 2, and 3 for each county
disability	indicates type of disability for each student (1 = learning; 2 = mental; 3 = emotional)

The variable names Dr. Porter created for his two variables, *county* and *disability,* are succinct and adequate descriptors. In early versions of SPSS, variable names were limited to eight characters, but now they can be up to 64 characters in length. However, the best practice is to keep them as short and simple as possible. There are several rules for naming variables in SPSS. For example, each name must be unique, spaces are not allowed, and the first character cannot be a number or certain symbols such as % or &. An underscore, _, is useful for separating letters, numbers, or words in a variable name, but it is best to avoid ending a variable name with this symbol. A combination of upper- and lowercase letters may be used. For a complete description of the rules, go to the **Help menu** in SPSS and select **Topics**. Then, in the **Index tab,** type "variable names" and click on **rules**.

Researchers often develop their own naming conventions and try to follow them as closely as possible. For demographic or background variables, they may use one word that best describes the variable, and whenever that variable appears in another data file, they are consistent in assigning the same name. This practice is beneficial if a study involves merging multiple data files (see Section 5). Consistency is also useful for variables that represent responses on a questionnaire or scores on a test. Using names such as *q1, q2, q3,* and so on allow for easy identification of these variables.

Another best practice is to document all pertinent information about the attributes of each variable. This is sometimes called a data dictionary. Brief descriptions for each variable, or at least for those variables needing additional explanation, should be created. In addition, numerical codes (e.g., 1, 2, and 3) for each categorical variable should be defined by creating value labels (a word or two) that describe each category. In SPSS, assigning variable descriptions and value labels can be performed in the **Variable View** window of the **Data Editor**. Other variable attributes in this window include data type (numeric, string, date, etc.); number of decimal places; user-defined missing values; and measurement level (scale, ordinal, nominal). Custom variable attributes can also be created. For further information on variable attributes and their default settings, go to the **Help menu** in SPSS and select **Topics**. Then, type "variable view" in the **Index tab** and select **Customizing Variable View**.

Some researchers choose to develop and maintain a data dictionary for their variables in a word processing program, especially if they need to document further information specific to their study. The format is typically a table containing the variable name, description, and categorical value labels, as well as other important information such as the source of the data (e.g., existing data from a school district's database versus data obtained from questionnaires administered as part of the study) and when the data were obtained (month and year). Creating and maintaining a data dictionary is not only helpful when conducting analysis for the current study, it is also beneficial if the researcher needs to use, or refer to, the data file in the future.

The file is available on the website and is called *module1_disability_standard.sav*. The naming convention for all data files in the book is to begin with the word "module" and its number (e.g., module 1) followed by a descriptive word or two about the file. The descriptors are separated by an underscore, _. For example, the file *module1_disability_standard.sav* indicates that the file is for use with module 1, it contains disability information, and it's used to illustrate the standard approach to conduct a one-sample chi-square test. Although there are no specific rules with regard to naming files, it is important to create your own naming conventions for data files that are used within a research project. Keep the file names as short as possible, and be diligent about sticking to the conventions you created.

It is also useful to write a brief description of each data file. This is possible in SPSS by selecting **Data File Comments** under the **Utilities menu**. The dialog box in Figure 1.1 will open, and comments can be typed in the **Comments** box. After **OK** is clicked, the comments will be saved with the file. At any point, comments can be viewed by opening the dialog box or displaying them in the output file by selecting **Display comments in output**.

Figure 1.1   Utilities → Data File Comments

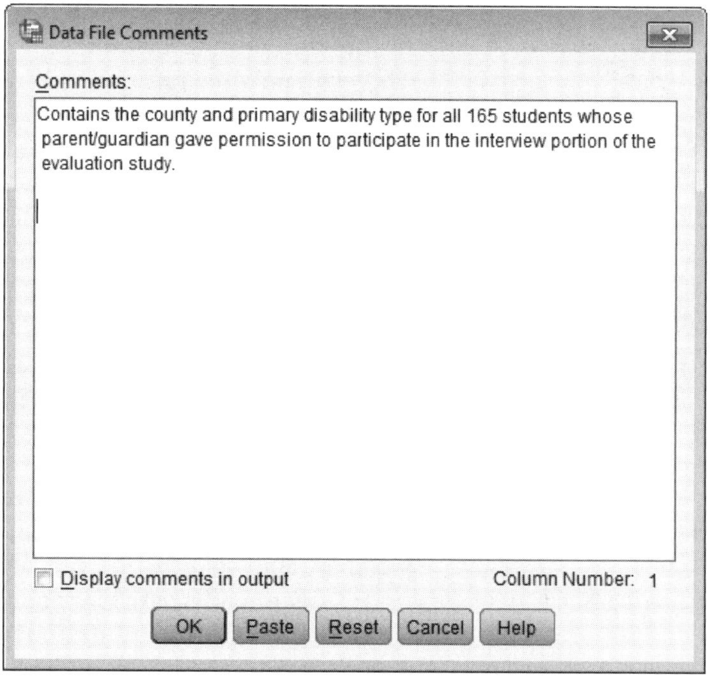

C. Planning and Decision Making △

Working with the data available to him, Dr. Porter decided to check the representativeness of his sample in two ways. ****Dr. Porter(1)** First, he wanted to know how well the sample he obtained using the cluster method reflected the population with regard to student distribution by county. Using the frequencies in Tables 1.1 and 1.2, he will need to create a data file and

**1 Dr. Porter says: "I had access to certain variables for my sample but not the entire population. For example, I knew the disability types for all sample students but not for all students in the population. In addition, some of my data were in aggregate form (e.g., the frequencies in Table 1.1 for the population), and other data were at the student level (e.g., the data file containing the primary disability type for sample students). Therefore, the data available to me and [their] format guided my planning and approach to evaluating the representativeness of the sample."

**2 Dr. Porter says: "Some people refer to this statistical test as a chi-square goodness-of-fit test because it reflects whether empirical distributions match (or 'fit') theoretical distributions. I prefer to call it the one-sample chi-square test because it examines frequencies/proportions for one variable. There is another type of chi-square test available to examine frequencies/proportions across categories for two variables. It is called the two-sample chi-square test or the chi-square test of association because it evaluates whether the two variables are correlated or associated with each other."

then conduct a one-sample chi-square test. **Dr. Porter(2)** This type of statistical test allows for examining whether the proportions of the sample students in each county are similar to, or significantly different from, the hypothesized proportions. In his situation, the hypothesized proportions are the population proportions of students in each county.

Dr. Porter also wanted to determine whether the group of students whose parents provided permission for interviews was representative of all students in the sample in terms of disability type. The participation rate for the interview collection data was quite high (87%), but he wanted to have statistical evidence that would support representativeness. Therefore, Dr. Porter will conduct another one-sample chi-square test using the *module1_disability_standard.sav* data file.

In order to conduct a one-sample chi-square test in SPSS, data must be represented in one of two ways. The most common is the standard method, which requires that the number of cases in the data file is equal to the number of subjects. In other words, there is a row for each student and a variable that contains a value or code for each student. The second way to conduct a one-sample chi-square test does not require a student-level data file. Rather, only the total frequencies in each category of the variable are necessary. This approach is called the weighted cases method. The data file is structured so that the total number of rows equals the total number of categories in the variable of interest. Typically, the file contains two variables. One variable lists the codes for each category (e.g., 1, 2, 3), and the other variable indicates the observed total frequencies for each category.

To summarize, Dr. Porter will use two types of chi-square analysis. The first analysis involves the weighted cases method to determine the extent to which his sample (n = 190) generalizes to the population (N = 463) in terms of the distribution of students across the three counties. The second chi-square analysis uses the standard method to determine the extent to which the distribution of disability types for the 165 students whose parents/guardians provided permission for interviews generalizes to the distribution of disability types for all 190 students in the sample. **Dr. Porter(3)**

**3 Dr. Porter says: "For the first analysis, I could use the frequencies in the county categories to create a file that has the same number of rows as students (n = 190) so that the standard method for the chi-square test could be conducted. However, I chose to use the weighted cases method because it is more efficient. It is not necessary to spend time entering data for 190 students into a data file, and data entry error is also reduced."

D. Using SPSS to Address Issues and Prepare Data △

First Chi-Square Analysis—Weighted Approach

To examine how well the sample generalizes to the population in terms of distribution of students across the three counties, Dr. Porter used the weighted cases approach to conducting the one-sample chi-square test.

His first step was to create a file with 3 cases (rows) and 2 variables. The file is on the website and is called *module1_county_weighted.sav*. The variables are *county* and *IEP_students*. **SPSS Tip 1** Values for *county* represent the county numerical codes. Values for *IEP_students* represent the frequency of students in each county in the sample obtained from Table 1.2. In order to conduct the chi-square test using the weighted cases approach, SPSS requires that the frequencies for each category be listed in the data file from lowest to highest. Therefore, Dr. Porter's file contains *county* values of 1, 3, and 2, and *IEP_students* values of 31, 44, and 115. Not following this rule will lead to an inaccurate chi-square result.

Now, Dr. Porter needs to weight the three cases in his file so that SPSS will know that, for example, 31 is not a value for one student, but instead represents 31 students in County 1. Under the **Data menu**, Dr. Porter selected **Weight Cases** and obtained the SPSS dialog box shown in Figure 1.2. He

SPSS Tip 1: The *county* variable is not absolutely necessary in the file because SPSS needs only the frequency variable (*IEP_students*) to calculate the chi-square test. However, placing *county* in the file will make it easier for Dr. Porter to associate the frequencies with their corresponding county codes.

Figure 1.2   Data → Weight Cases

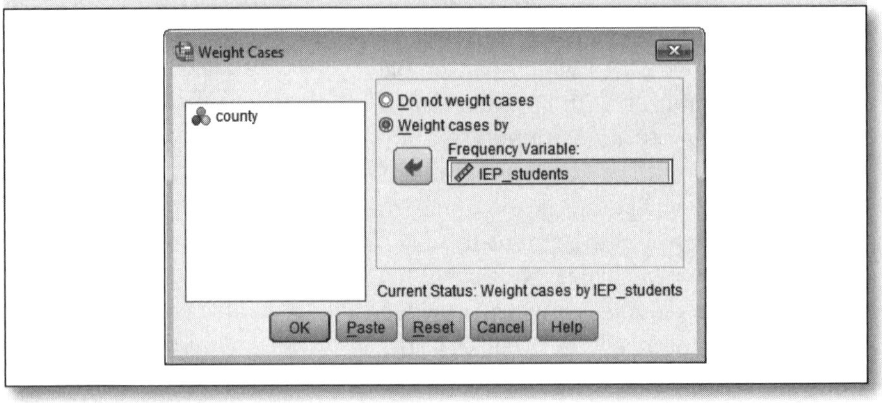

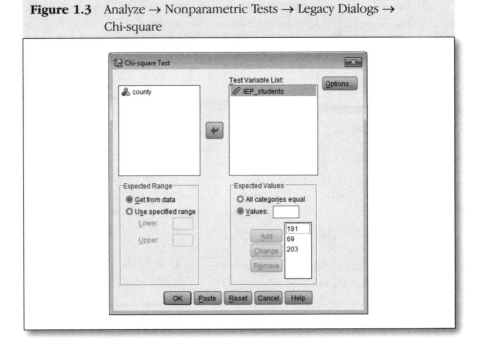

selected the **Weight cases by** button and placed the variable containing the frequencies of students (*IEP_students*) in the **Frequency Variable** box and clicked **OK**. This essentially tells SPSS that there are actually 31 students in County 1, 44 students in County 3, and 115 students in County 2.

Dr. Porter is now ready to conduct the one-sample chi-square test. Under the **Analyze menu**, he selected **Nonparametric Tests**, **Legacy Dialogs**, and **Chi-square** in order to get the dialog box shown in Figure 1.3. The frequency variable of interest, *IEP_students*, is placed in the **Test**

Figure 1.3   Analyze → Nonparametric Tests → Legacy Dialogs → Chi-square

Variable List box. The *county* variable is not placed in the box. Recall that the only purpose of this variable is to help Dr. Porter remember which frequencies are associated with each county.

In the **Expected Values** box, the population frequencies for each county (from Table 1.1) must be entered by selecting the **Values** button, typing in the frequency, and clicking **Add.** If an error is made, the **Remove** or **Change** buttons can be used. It is extremely important to remember that the order of the counties was from the smallest sample (observed frequency) to the largest sample (observed frequency) (i.e., counties 1, 3, and 2). Therefore, the population frequencies must be entered in the same order. ****SPSS Tip 2**

There is also an **Expected Range** box. This allows you to select only some of the categories to include in the chi-square analysis. Because Dr. Porter's analysis incorporated all three categories of his county variable, he did not need to use this box. He used the default option (**Get from data**), which means that all categories will be used in the analysis. ****SPSS Tip 3**

After he clicked **OK**, the output showed two tables. In Table 1.4, the

SPSS Tip 2: The expected values could also be equal. For example, suppose a researcher needed to sample an equal number of participants from each category of a variable. To examine whether his final sample statistically had the same frequency of participants across categories, he would simply select "All categories equal" and SPSS would calculate the Expected Values to be the total number of cases divided by the total number of categories.

SPSS Tip 3: An example of when the Expected Range box might be helpful is if an ethnicity variable contains five categories but the analysis only focuses on the first three categories because they contain the majority of total cases. In this situation, you would select "Use specified range," then type "1" for the Lower code in the range of the ethnicity variable and "3" for the Upper code. Note that the codes for the variable would need to be consecutively ordered in the data file for this technique to work.

Table 1.4 SPSS Output Indicating Observed and Expected Values for Students by County

IEP_students			
	Observed *N*	Expected *N*	Residual
31	31	78.4	-47.4
44	44	28.3	15.7
115	115	83.3	31.7
Total	190		

SPSS Tip 4: The Expected *N* is calculated using the proportion of the student population in each county. For example, 191 out of 463 students in the population were in County 1 (proportion = .4125). If the sample proportion was equal to the population proportion, then .4125 of the total of 190 sample students (expected *N* = 78.4) in the sample would be in County 1. However, there were only 31 sample students (observed *N*) in County 1, which leads to a residual of -47.4. The actual sample proportion was .1632 (31 divided by 190), which was much smaller than the population proportion. Expected *N* and residual values for Counties 3 and 2 in Table 1.4 are calculated in the same way.

SPSS Tip 5: If you did not follow the SPSS rule to order the frequencies from lowest to highest in the data file, you will not obtain these results. The incorrect order of 31, 115, 44 (representing Counties 1, 2, and 3, respectively) will produce a chi-square result that is incorrect [χ^2 (*df* = 2) = 312.562, *p* < .001].

Observed N values show the sample frequencies of students with IEPs in County 1, 3, and 2. The next column indicates the expected values of the sample based on the population frequencies of students by county. **SPSS Tip 4

The second table of output presents the statistical results from the chi-square test. **SPSS Tip 5** Table 1.5 shows a chi-square value of 49.388 with a *p* value that is less than .001. There are two degrees of freedom for this test because three categories were examined (*df* = number of categories minus 1). The null hypothesis that the proportions in the sample are equal to the proportions in the population is rejected. Therefore, the sample proportions are significantly different from the population proportions across the three counties. In other words, the distribution of students across the three counties for the sample is not the same as the distribution in the population. This conclusion brings into question the generalizability of the results for the evaluation study.

Second Chi-Square Analysis— Standard Approach

Dr. Porter's next analysis was to examine how well the distribution of disability types for students with permission to be interviewed reflects the distribution of disability types for all sample students. The majority of parents/guardians allowed their child to be interviewed (87%). Based on the aggregated data that was available to Dr. Porter, he knew that of the 190 total students in the sample, the primary disability was documented as learning for 67% of them, mental for 19%, and emotional for the remaining 14% of students. Of the 165 students in the sample who had permission to be interviewed, percentages were somewhat similar (64% for learning, 24% for mental, and 12% for emotional disabilities). However, Dr. Porter wanted to have statistical

Table 1.5 SPSS Output Indicating the Chi-Square Test Statistic for Students by County

Test Statistics

	IEP_students
Chi-Square	49.388[a]
df	2
Asymp. Sig.	.000

[a.] 0 cells (0.0%) have expected frequencies less than 5. The minimum expected cell frequency is 28.3.

evidence to support his conclusion, so he conducted the one-sample chi-square test.

As mentioned earlier, Dr. Porter had a data file (*module1_disability_standard.sav*) containing the disability type for each student whose parent(s) agreed to participation. As described in Table 1.3, the codes of 1, 2, and 3 for *disability* represented learning, mental, and emotional disabilities. Because the file contains the same number of cases (rows) as students, he can use the standard approach when conducting the chi-square analysis. That is, he does not need to weight cases by the *disability* variable.

He begins by opening the same dialog box shown in Figure 1.4 under the **Analyze menu** as in the first analysis. The *disability* variable is moved to the **Test Variable List** box. The *county* variable is not the variable of interest in this analysis. Then, Dr. Porter selected the **Values** button in the **Expected Values** box in order to provide SPSS with the expected frequencies in each disability type across all 190 students in the sample. He typed in the value of 128 for learning disability, the first category in the *disability* variable, and clicked the **Add** button. He entered the expected values for the mental and emotional categories in the same manner (36 and 26, respectively). ****SPSS Tip 6**

Once again, two tables of output are produced. Table 1.6 indicates that the observed and expected values for each category are similar, and the residuals are small. Results from the statistical test

SPSS Tip 6: Unlike the weighted cases approach to conducting the chi-square test, the standard approach requires that the expected values match the numerical order of the categorical codes for the variable (1, 2, and 3 in this study, which represent learning, mental, and emotional disabilities). The expected values should *not* be ordered from smallest to largest frequency.

Figure 1.4 Analyze → Nonparametric Tests → Legacy Dialogs → Chi-square

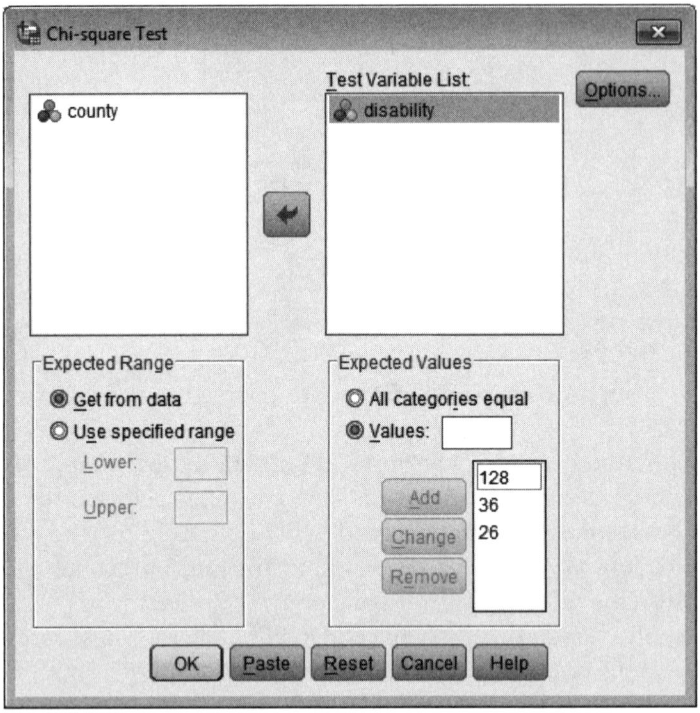

Table 1.6 SPSS Output Indicating Observed and Expected Values for Students by Disability

disability

	Observed N	Expected N	Residual
1 learning disability	105	111.2	-6.2
2 mental	40	31.3	8.7
3 emotional	20	22.6	-2.6
Total	165		

shown in Table 1.7 confirm Dr. Porter's initial thoughts about the data. The p value of .215 indicates that the null hypothesis of equality of the two sets of proportions is not rejected. Therefore, the distribution of disability type

Table 1.7   SPSS Output Indicating the Chi-Square Test Statistic for
Students by Disability

Test Statistics

	disability
Chi-square	3.077[a]
df	2
Asymp. Sig.	.215

a. 0 cells (.0%) have expected frequencies less than 5. The minimum expected cell frequency is 22.6.

for students who were permitted to participate in interviews is similar to the distribution for all students in the sample. This outcome indicates that the group of students to be interviewed generalizes well to all students in the sample with respect to the type of primary disability.

E. Reflection and Additional Decision Making   △

Dr. Porter was pleased that the group of students participating in the interview portion of the evaluation study was representative of the sample in terms of disability type. However, he was interested in further exploring data for the first chi-square analysis. He wondered if County 1 was the reason the sample distribution of students by county was not similar to the population distribution. The absolute value of its residual (observed minus expected value) was higher than the residuals for Counties 2 and 3. He decided to conduct three follow-up chi-square tests using the weighted approach, one test for each possible pair of counties, using the same procedures as described in Section D. A summary of results is presented in Table 1.8. The chi-square test results were obtained from the SPSS output. The population and sample proportions were calculated as described in SPSS Tip 4.

The first two tests included County 1 data. Results showed statistically significant chi-square values, and the sample proportions were quite different from the population proportions. Conversely, the third test of Counties

Table 1.8 Summary of Chi-Square Results for Each Unique Pair of Counties With Sample and Population Proportions

Test 1: $[\chi^2\ (df = 1) = 39.710, p < .001]$		
County	**Sample Proportions**	**Population Proportions**
1	.41	.73
3	.59	.27
Test 2: $[\chi^2\ (df = 1) = 43.388, p < .001]$		
County	**Sample Proportions**	**Population Proportions**
1	.21	.48
2	.79	.52
Test 3: $[\chi^2\ (df = 1) = .446, p = .504]$		
County	**Sample Proportions**	**Population Proportions**
3	.28	.25
2	.72	.75

2 and 3 did not produce a significant chi-square result, and the sample versus the population proportions were similar. Thus, County 1 appears to be the reason for lack of representation of the sample to the population. Only two schools were in the county. One school had a large population of students ($N = 160$), the other had a small population ($N = 31$). The large school was originally selected to be in the sample, but it declined participation in the study. The school with the small population agreed to participate. Because there was such a large difference in the number of students between the two schools in the county, regardless of which school was selected, the values would have greatly impacted the overall chi-square statistic. Unfortunately, this is one of the drawbacks of the cluster sampling method when there are only a small number of clusters/schools in each area. There is nothing Dr. Porter can do to alter his data, but at least his analysis allows him to identify the issue and acknowledge it when writing reports for his evaluation study.

△ F. Writing It Up

Dr. Porter wrote the following paragraphs to describe his sampling procedure, his approach to investigating the sample's representativeness, and the findings regarding the sample.

"A cluster sampling approach was used to randomly select approximately half of the schools in each county. The administrative office in each of the selected schools was contacted by phone and letter to request their participation in the evaluation study. Five of the seven schools agreed to participate, two schools declined. In these two cases, another school from the same county was randomly selected to be in the study. Both schools in the second round agreed to participate.

In order to determine how well the sample ($n = 190$) generalized to the population ($n = 463$) in terms of distribution of students across the three counties, a one-sample chi-square test was conducted. Results indicated that the sample proportions of students by county were significantly different from the population proportions by county (χ^2 ($df = 2$) = 49.388, $p < .001$). Overall, the sample did not represent the population. Upon further examination of the data using follow-up chi-square tests on each pair of counties, County 1 appeared to be the reason for the lack of generalization from sample to population. There were only two schools in the county. The school that participated was smaller than the school that was originally selected and declined participation (31 versus 160 students). Thus, the sample proportion in County 1 was quite different than the population proportion. The two follow-up chi-square tests that included this county produced significant results ($p < .001$). The result from the follow-up chi-square test for Counties 2 and 3 was not significant ($p = .504$). Sample proportions of students in these two counties were similar to the population proportions, indicating that the sample represented the population for Counties 2 and 3.

Of the 190 total students in the sample, 87% of the parents/guardians allowed their children to participate in the interview portion of data collection. To check whether the distribution of disability types for the 165 students to be interviewed generalized to the distribution of disability types for all students in the sample, another one-sample chi-square test was conducted. The statistical evidence indicates that the students to be interviewed are representative of all sample students in terms of disability type (χ^2 ($df = 2$) = 3.077, $p = .215$). In the full sample, the primary disability was documented to be learning for 67% of the students, mental for 19%, and emotional for 14%. Of the students to be interviewed, the percentages were 64%, 24%, and 12%, respectively."

Reflective Questions △

- Which of the two approaches to conducting a one-sample chi-square test would you use if you had a file that contained all the necessary data by individual participants? What are the processes for carrying out this approach?

- Which of the two approaches to conducting a one-sample chi-square test would you use if you had only aggregated data who represented sample and population frequencies for the variables of interest? What are the processes for carrying out this approach?

△ Extensions

- Using other research examples, discuss how well the sample generalizes to a targeted population. If possible, create the necessary data files and conduct a one-sample chi-square analysis to determine the generalizability of the sample.
- Find research articles that mention a sample's generalizability, then discuss how the authors determined if results from their sample generalized to the target population.
- Discuss the unique aspects of the cluster sampling approach in comparison to other methods for obtaining a sample. Compare the advantages and disadvantages of using this approach.

△ Note

1. Throughout the rest of this module, the use of the word "students" refers to students with IEPs that have a learning, mental, or emotional disability documented as their primary disability.

Splitting a File, Selecting Cases, and Creating Standardized Values and Ranks

❧

DATA FILES FOR THIS MODULE

module2_couns_lib.sav
module2_couns_lib_ranks.sav
module2_couns_lib_ranks_stvalues.sav
module2_couns_lib_complete.sav

❧

KEY LEARNING OBJECTIVES

The student will learn to

- create variables that represent ranks of values in an existing variable
- create standardized values for a variable
- split a file to produce output for each group of a variable
- select only a portion of the entire data file for a particular analysis

A. Description of Researcher's Study △

Dr. Baird is conducting a descriptive study of librarians and guidance counselors employed in schools. Recent reductions in federal and state funding for public education have forced schools to make cuts in their budgets.

There is a concern that some school staff positions, such as librarians and guidance counselors, are in danger of being eliminated or reduced.

However, the roles and responsibilities of these staff members have increased over the years. Guidance counselors not only support students' academic needs, but are also asked to oversee family outreach programs, develop and maintain community partnerships, and consult with outside agencies. Similarly, librarians are required to be information specialists for new resources and technologies; participants in school improvement, accreditation, and benchmarking; and partners with teachers in instruction.

Her research is exploratory in nature. At this point, Dr. Baird is interested in obtaining a broad view of the number of librarians and guidance counselors in schools across the United States. To obtain the desired information, Dr. Baird downloaded a public use data set from the National Center for Education Statistics (NCES). It contains descriptive information for all 50 states in the nation plus Washington, DC.

This module demonstrates the process Dr. Baird went through to prepare her data file and plan her descriptive analysis based on the information extracted from the national database. In order to carry out her study, she first had to create new variables containing standardized values (z) and ranks so that data across all 50 states and DC could be easily compared. Then, she needed to split the data file in order to analyze each geographic region separately. Finally, she selected only a subset of states so that a more focused analysis could be conducted for her own geographic region.

△ B. A Look at the Data

**1 Dr. Baird says: "The file I created from the CCD was in Excel format. I converted it to SPSS by selecting 'Open' and 'Data' under the 'File menu.' A new window opened up showing only my SPSS files, so in the 'Files of Type' box I clicked .xls and the Excel file was listed. After I highlighted the file and clicked 'Open,' another window opened. I checked the box beside 'Read variable names from the first row of data' and then clicked OK. This converted the data to SPSS format and I saved the file."

Dr. Baird obtained her data file from a national database called the Common Core of Data (CCD). ****Dr. Baird(1)** The CCD contains comprehensive descriptive information on public elementary and secondary education in the United States. It is a program of the U.S. Department of Education's National Center for Education Statistics (NCES), and the data are made available for public use.[2]

There are 51 cases and 17 variables in Dr. Baird's data file (*module2_couns_lib. sav*). Each case represents one of the 50 states or Washington, DC. The first two variables in the file are string variables containing the name of each state and its abbreviation. The remaining 15 variables are numeric. Three variables (*region*, *couns_sch_ratio*, and *lib_sch_ratio*) were added by Dr. Baird after she downloaded the file (her rationale for adding them is described in Section C, Planning and Decision Making). The variable *region* categorizes each state into one of four geographic regions as defined by the Census Bureau. Dr. Baird calculated the other two variables using data that already existed in her file. When dividing *counselors* by *schools*, she obtained the *couns_sch_ratio* variable. Likewise, *librarians* divided by

**2 Dr. Baird says: "The original variable names in the data file from CCD were lengthy. When creating a data file in SPSS, it is usually best to use concise variable names. Therefore, I renamed each variable. For example, the original CCD name for *teachers* was *Total Teachers (state)*. Also, because SPSS does not permit spaces in a variable name, I used the underscore, _, to separate words or abbreviations to make the name more readable."

schools led to the creation of *lib_sch_ratio*. The other numeric variables are directly from the CCD. All data in her file represent the 2009–2010 school year. Descriptions of the 17 variables are provided in Table 2.1. ****Dr. Baird(2)**

Table 2.1 Variables in the 2009–2010 Public School Data File

Variable Name	Description
state	full name of state
state_abbr	two letter abbreviation of state name
region	1 = Northeast, 2 = Midwest, 3 = South, 4 = West (from the Census Bureau)
counties	number of counties in each state
districts	number of school districts in each state
schools	number of public schools in each state
students	number of students attending public schools in each state
free_red_lunch	number of students eligible for free/reduced lunch in each state
lep_ell	number of Limited English Proficient and English Language Learner students in each state

(Continued)

Table 2.1 (Continued)

Variable Name	Description
iep	number of students with an Individual Education Plan in each state
staff	number of full time equivalent (FTE) staff in each state
teachers	number of FTE teachers in each state
st_tchr_ratio	number of students per teacher in the state
counselors	number of FTE guidance counselors in each state
librarians	number of FTE librarians in each state
couns_sch_ratio	number of guidance counselors per school in the state (calculated)
lib_sch_ratio	number of librarians per school in the state (calculated)

△ C. Planning and Decision Making

Reflecting upon the variables and data that Dr. Baird now had available to her, she finalized her exploratory questions. First, she wanted to describe and compare the number of librarians and guidance counselors across all 50 states plus DC. However, she needed to obtain values that could legitimately be compared, regardless of the number of schools and students in each state. For instance, Delaware has 141 librarians and Texas has 5,140 librarians. A comparison of these values is not accurate because they do not take into account the fact that Texas has more schools and students than Delaware. Therefore, Dr. Baird needed to create new variables to represent the number of librarians and guidance counselors per school within each state (*couns_sch_ratio* and *lib_sch_ratio*). **Dr. Baird(3)** After creating these variables, Dr. Baird finalized the following questions for the first phase of her study:

**3 Dr. Baird says: "There are other ways to create variables that allow for making comparisons across states (e.g., librarians per total number of students), but I chose to calculate the ratio of librarians per school since it provides a somewhat more meaningful number. That is, you might expect each school to have at least one or two librarians. I could also produce a variable that would factor in the size of schools as well, but for my first exploratory study of the data I decided to begin with this simple ratio."

Phase 1

1. How do the ratios of guidance counselors per school (and librarians per school) compare across all states? How do these ratios relate to other state-level variables in the file?

2. Which states have exceptionally low or high ratios of guidance counselors per school (and librarians per school)?

To answer her first question, Dr. Baird suspects that it would be useful to produce ranks for the 51 ratios in *couns_sch_ratio* and the 51 ratios in *lib_sch_ratio*. This will help her describe the relative position of one state among all others on each variable as well as compare each state's counselor ratio to its librarian ratio. An SPSS procedure can be used to create new variables containing ranks of the ratios in either ascending or descending order.

For the second question, Dr. Baird wants to determine if some ratios are considerably higher or lower compared to the entire set of ratios in the distribution. In order to do this, she will obtain standardized values, or z values, for each ratio in the SPSS file. Expressing each ratio as a standardized value will allow her to determine how far each ratio is from the mean of all ratios in terms of standard deviations. In other words, a ratio with a standardized value of 1.5 is one-and-a-half standard deviations above the mean, and a ratio with a standardized value of −2.0 is two standard deviations below the mean. If a state has a very large standardized value (e.g., above an absolute value of 3), it would be considered different from the rest of the distribution.

Phase 2

Dr. Baird's next step is to examine subsets of states. She wants to make comparisons within each of the four geographic regions defined by the Census Bureau (Northeast, Midwest, South, and West). Her second set of exploratory questions is similar to the first set in Phase 1, except that each state will be compared only to other states in the same region. For example,

1. How do ratios of guidance counselors per school (and librarians per school) compare across the nine states in the Northeast? How do these ratios relate to other state-level variables in the file within the Northeast?

2. Do any of the nine states in the Northeast have exceptionally low or high ratios of guidance counselors per school (and librarians per school)?

Similar questions are also asked of the 12 midwestern states, the 17 southern states, and the 13 western states. This will require Dr. Baird to split her data file in SPSS so that she can separately analyze each of the four regions of the United States.

Phase 3

In her final set of exploratory questions, Dr. Baird will refine her focus on a selected sample of states within one geographic region. She works and resides in the state of California, which is one of five states in the Pacific West subclassification of the western region. At this point in her study, she wants to begin incorporating student demographics, such as socioeconomic status, limited English proficiency, and students with disabilities, into the descriptive analysis. Her two exploratory questions are as follows:

1. How does California compare to the other four states in the Pacific West region (Washington, Oregon, Alaska, and Hawaii) in terms of guidance counselors per school and librarians per school?

2. How do student demographics relate to the ratios of guidance counselors and librarians per school across the five states in the Pacific West region?

To begin carrying out the analysis for these two questions, Dr. Baird will use SPSS to select only the sample of five states in which she is interested.

△ D. Using SPSS to Address Issues and Prepare Data

Phase 1: Creating Ranks

The first step in preparing the file is to obtain rank variables for *couns_sch_ratio* and *lib_sch_ratio*. Under the **Transform menu**, Dr. Baird selected **Rank Cases** and the following SPSS dialog box in Figure 2.1 appeared. She moved the two variables to the **Variable(s)** box. In the lower left corner of the dialog box there is the option of assigning a rank of 1 to the smallest value (ascending order) or assigning a rank of 1 to the largest value (descending order). Dr. Baird chose the first option (the default) so that the rankings will increase (1 to 51) as the ratios increase. Another option in the dialog box is the **By** subcommand, which will rank cases within groups of a particular variable. Dr. Baird did not use this procedure because she wanted to calculate ranks across all 51 cases.

Figure 2.1   Transform → Rank Cases

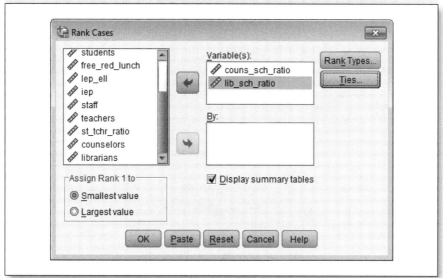

There are two buttons in the **Rank Cases** dialog box. When the **Rank Types** button is selected, another box (Figure 2.2) opens to allow for selecting a ranking method. The typical ranking method, **Rank**, is the default. For Dr. Baird's purposes, this method is sufficient. Descriptions of the other ranking methods can be found by selecting **Topics** under the **Help menu** in SPSS, then typing "ranking cases" in the **Index tab** and selecting **types**. They are also described in Huizingh (2008).

Figure 2.2   Options for Rank Types

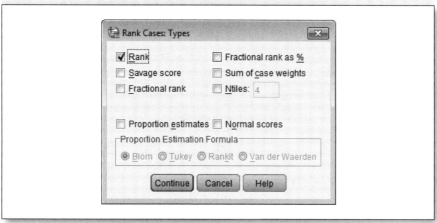

When the **Ties** button is selected, a box (Figure 2.3) opens to allow for choosing how to treat tied values in the data file. A tie occurs when more than one case has the same value within a variable. There are four methods for handling ties. The **Mean** method is the default and is the method that Dr. Baird will use. Cases with the same value are assigned the average rank. Two of the alternative methods are to assign tied cases the lowest rank

Figure 2.3 Options for Tied Ranks

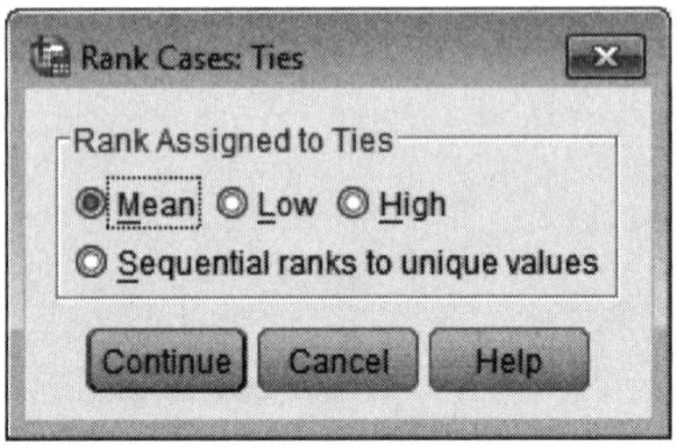

SPSS Tip 1: The names of the new rank variables can be changed if you wish. Simply go to the Variable View window in the Data Editor, highlight the original name, and type in the new name. Dr. Baird finds it helpful to keep the SPSS names so that she knows they were variables produced through the Rank procedure in SPSS.

SPSS Tip 2: Dr. Baird found it helpful to sort the cases when examining her ranking variable. Under the Data menu, choose Sort Cases. Then, place the ranked variable in the box. The default sort is by ascending order, beginning with the lowest rank of 1. You could also choose to sort by descending order, which will begin with the highest rank.

among the ties (**Low**) or the highest rank among the ties (**High**). The fourth method, called **Sequential ranks to unique values**, assigns a new sequential rank only for non-tied values of the variable. When using this method on data with many ties, the highest rank will be quite different from the total number of cases. See Green, Salkind, and Akey (2000) and Huizingh (2008) for detailed descriptions of the methods for ranking tied data, or go to **Topics** under the **Help menu** in SPSS, type "ranking cases" in the **Index tab**, and select **ties**.

After clicking the **OK** button in the initial **Rank Cases** dialog box, the procedure creates two new variables. SPSS automatically assigns names to the variables. *Rcouns_s* contains the ranks for *couns_sch_ratio*, and *Rlib_sch* contains the ranks for *lib_sch_ratio*. ****SPSS Tip 1**

As an example, Tables 2.2 and 2.3 show portions of Dr. Baird's new data file that include ratios of counselors per school and their rankings. ****SPSS Tip 2**

Table 2.2   States With the Four Lowest Ranks for Counselors per School

state	couns_sch_ratio	Rcouns_s
Minnesota	.45	1
South Dakota	.46	2
North Dakota	.56	3
Montana	.57	4

Table 2.3   States With the Four Highest Ranks for Counselors per School

state	couns_sch_ratio	Rcouns_s
Maryland	1.66	48
New Hampshire	1.75	49
Virginia	1.81	50
Hawaii	2.23	51

Notice that the highest rank is 51, which is the total number of cases in the file. Also notice that SPSS did not need to assign mean ranks because there were no tied values in *couns_sch_ratio*. ****SPSS Tip 3**

The file *module2_couns_lib_ranks* contains the two new rank variables, *Rcouns_s* and *Rlib_sch*, and is available on the website. ****SPSS Tip 4** As mentioned in the previous section, the rank variables will allow Dr. Baird to compare the relative standing of one state on both ratios. For example, California ranked 11th for the number of guidance counselors per school (meaning that only 10 other states had a lower ratio) and had a rank of 1 for the number of librarians per school (the lowest ratio among all states). She can also use the rank variables to compare two or more states with each other. For example, North Carolina had a rank of 44 and South Carolina had a rank of 45 for guidance counselors per school.

> SPSS Tip 3: Here's an example of how the mean rank method would work if there were ties. Suppose the two lowest values in a data file were unique, but the next two values were equal to each other. The first two values would be assigned ranks of 1 and 2, respectively. The following two tied values would both be assigned the mean rank of 3.5 because their positions were 3 and 4. The next highest value would have a rank of 5.

SPSS Tip 4: Ranks produced by SPSS are in decimal format (typically 3 places). For ease of viewing her data, and because she had no tied ranks, Dr. Baird changed the format to 0 decimal places in the Variable View window of the Data Editor.

Phase 1: Creating Standardized Values

To obtain standardized values for *couns_sch_ratio* and *lib_sch_ratio*, Dr. Baird selected **Descriptives Statistics** and **Descriptives** under the **Analyze menu.** The dialog box is shown in Figure 2.4. She placed the two ratio variables in the **Variables** box and clicked **Save standardized values as variables**. This will transform each variable into a standard value with a mean of 0 and a standard deviation of 1.

Figure 2.4 Analyze → Descriptive Statistics → Descriptives

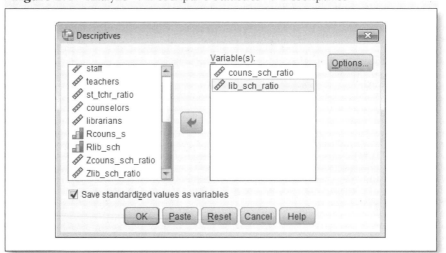

There is also an **Options** button that opens the next box, shown in Figure 2.5. Dr. Baird kept the default settings because she is primarily performing the **Descriptives** procedure in order to produce standardized values.

After clicking the **Continue** button in **Options** and the **OK** button in the main dialog box, a table of output is produced. Table 2.4 shows that the average ratio of counselors per school across all 51 cases is 1.11, which is almost twice as large as the average ratio of .57 for librarians per school.

The SPSS procedure also added two standardized variables at the end of the data file. The file *module2_couns_lib_ranks_stvalues.sav* contains the new variables and is available on the website. When naming the variables, SPSS uses the convention of adding a "Z" to the beginning of each original name (*Zcouns_sch_ratio* and *Zlib_sch_ratio*).

Figure 2.5 Options in Descriptives Process

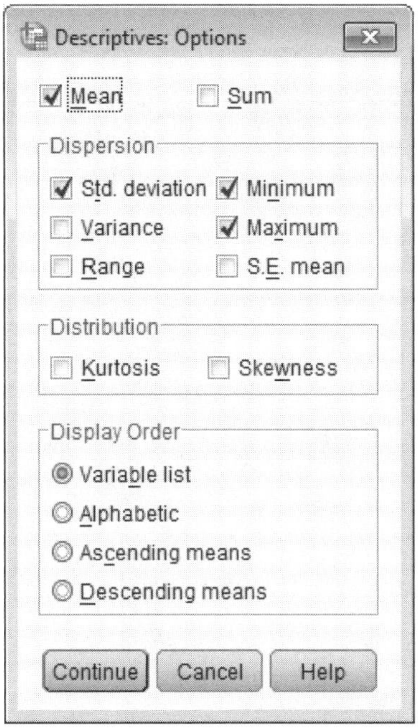

Table 2.4 SPSS Output Showing Descriptive Statistics for the Ratio Variables

	N	Minimum	Maximum	Mean	Std. Deviation
Descriptive Statistics					
couns_sch_ratio	51	.45	2.23	1.1115	.38909
lib_sch_ratio	51	.11	1.08	.5708	.23902
Valid N (listwise)	51				

Dr. Baird sorted each variable from lowest to highest standardized values to determine whether some states had particularly low or high ratios relative to the other states. For example, an examination of *Zlib_sch_ratio* showed that 33 of 51 cases (65%) were less than 1 standard deviation above or below the mean. An additional 17 cases (33%) were between 1 and 2 standard deviations above or below the mean. Only one state, Tennessee, had a standardized value above an absolute value of 2.00. Tables 2.5 and 2.6 display the lowest four and highest four standardized values of the ratios.

Table 2.5 States With the Four Lowest Standardized Values for Librarians per School

state	lib_sch_ratio	Zlib_sch_ratio
California	.11	-1.91
Idaho	.19	-1.59
South Dakota	.19	-1.59
Oregon	.25	-1.36

Table 2.6 States With the Four Highest Standardized Values for Librarians per School

state	lib_sch_ratio	Zlib_sch_ratio
Rhode Island	.93	1.48
South Carolina	.94	1.53
Georgia	.94	1.54
Tennessee	1.08	2.12

SPSS Tip 5: The only difference between the Compare groups option and the Organize output by groups option is the format of the output. "Compare groups" will produce output for all groups in one table. "Organize output by groups" produces output in a separate table for each group. Keep in mind that the values and results are the same in both options; the selection only determines how you "look" at the output.

Phase 2: Using Split File

To answer questions in the second phase of her study, Dr. Baird examined subsets of states rather than comparing all 50 states and DC with each other. She needed to prepare the file in order to make comparisons within each of four geographic regions. To do so, she selected **Split File** under the **Data menu**. Three options are provided in the dialog box shown in Figure 2.6. The first is the SPSS default, which is to **Analyze all cases, do not create groups**. The other two options will split the file according to groups identified by a variable placed in the box. Because Dr. Baird wanted each state to be compared only to other states within the same geographic region, she selected the **Compare**

Figure 2.6 Data → Split File

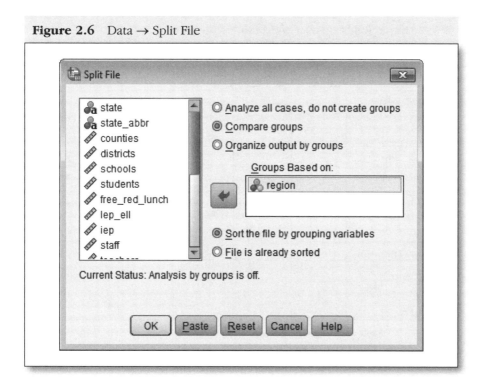

groups option and placed *region* in the **Groups Based on** box. ****SPSS Tip 5** Finally, in order for the split to work properly, the file must be sorted by the grouping variable prior to running the procedure. Dr. Baird retained the SPSS default setting, which is to **Sort the file by grouping variables**.

Unlike many other SPSS procedures, after you click the **OK** button in Split File, nothing apparent happens. That is, no output is produced. However, each SPSS procedure that is conducted after splitting the file will be run separately for each group of the specified variable. As an illustration, one of Dr. Baird's first steps in answering the questions in Phase 2 was to obtain the mean ratios and standardized values for counselors and librarians within each of the four geographic regions. She ran the same **Descriptives** procedure as she did in Phase 1.

After splitting the file, the **Descriptives** procedure created one output table with four sections. Table 2.7 shows the mean ratios and other descriptive statistics for each geographic region. The 17 southern states have the highest mean for both ratios (1.34 counselors per school and .79 librarians per school). The 12 midwestern states, on average, have the lowest counselor per school mean (.75), and the 13 western states, on average, have the lowest librarian per school mean (.38).

Table 2.7 SPSS Output for Counselor and Librarian Ratios by Geographic Region

Descriptive Statistics

region		N	Minimum	Maximum	Mean	Std. Deviation
1 northeast	couns_sch_ratio	9	.93	1.75	1.3248	.27457
	lib_sch_ratio	9	.37	.93	.6428	.15664
	Valid N (listwise)	9				
2 midwest	couns_sch_ratio	12	.45	1.07	.7542	.20276
	lib_sch_ratio	12	.19	.63	.4109	.13151
	Valid N (listwise)	12				
3 south	couns_sch_ratio	17	.96	1.81	1.3391	.25507
	lib_sch_ratio	17	.47	1.08	.7883	.17151
	Valid N (listwise)	17				
4 west	couns_sch_ratio	13	.57	2.23	.9962	.45449
	lib_sch_ratio	13	.11	.78	.3840	.17968
	Valid N (listwise)	13				

SPSS Tip 6: One final word about the Split File procedure is that when you are done running all analyses for the subsets of cases in your file, you must go back to the Split File dialog box and turn off or cancel the split. In other words, you need to select the "Analyze all cases" option.

The procedure also added two variables to the data file. They contain the standardized values for counselor and librarian ratios in each region, and the default SPSS names are *Zsco01* and *Zsco02*, respectively. Now there are two sets of standardized variables in Dr. Baird's data file. In order to distinguish between them, she added a phrase to SPSS's default variable label in **Variable View** in the **Data Editor** to indicate that the first set of standardized variables was calculated across all states. Likewise, she added a phrase to indicate that the second set was calculated within region. She also changed SPSS's default of five decimal places for standardized values to two decimal places. The data file *module2_couns_lib_complete.sav* includes these two new variables as well as the four previous variables Dr. Baird added. ****SPSS Tip 6**

Phase 3: Using Select If

The final phase involves a further refinement of the sample. Dr. Baird lives and works in California and wanted to compare her state to the 12 other states in the West region and then, more specifically, to the four other states in the Pacific West subclassification.

To do so, she chose **Select Cases** under the **Data menu.** In the dialog box (Figure 2.7), she selected **If condition is satisfied**. For the output, she kept the SPSS default as **Filter out unselected cases**, which means that cases not selected will be filtered out (that is, not included) in the subsequent analyses she conducts, but they will remain in her data file. The two other options are to create a new data file that includes only the selected cases (**Copy selected cases to a new dataset**) or to delete the cases from the data file that were not selected (**Delete unselected cases**). ****SPSS Tip 7**

SPSS Tip 7: The most common option is the default, which is to Filter out unselected cases. This option does not change the original data file. Typically, researchers do not want to permanently delete data from their file, nor do they want to create many additional data files because it may cause confusion down the road.

After clicking the **OK** button, another window appears (Figure 2.8). This is the place to create the **If statement**. First, Dr. Baird wanted to

Figure 2.7 Data → Select Cases

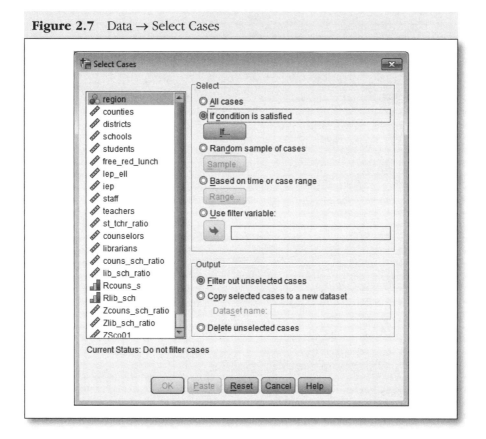

Figure 2.8   Defining the Region to be Selected

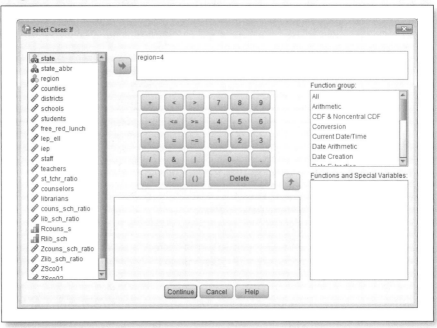

SPSS Tip 8: After you finish conducting analyses of the selected cases, it is imperative that you remember to return to "All cases" in the dialog box. This is even more critical in the Select If procedure than it was in the Split File procedure. The output from a split file is obvious (i.e., you notice immediately that the analysis was conducted separately for groups). However, output from a selected set of cases is not as immediately apparent. The only indication that the analysis was conducted on the full data file versus the selected data is the total *n* provided in the output. This can easily be overlooked, and incorrect results may be reported.

examine all states in the western region. The logical expression shown in the box below (region = 4) tells SPSS to select cases only when *region* equals the value of 4, which is the group number for the West region. All analyses she conducted after this point had only a total of 13 states. All other states remained in the data file, but had a slash through their case number, indicating they are not included in the analyses. The **Select Cases** procedure also created a new variable called *filter_$* which has a value of 1 for all selected cases and a value of 0 for nonselected cases.

After Dr. Baird answered her exploratory questions for states in the West region, her last step was to conduct analyses only on states in the Pacific

West. Her logical expression for selecting the five states is shown below in the **If statement** of the **Select Cases** procedure. She chose to use *state_abbr* so that she would not need to type in the full name for each state. Because it is a string variable, quotes must be placed around each state's abbreviation, and then each equality is connected by "or." Now, Dr. Baird is ready to examine only this subset of states in order to complete the final phase of her study. ****SPSS Tip 8**

Figure 2.9 Defining the States to be Selected

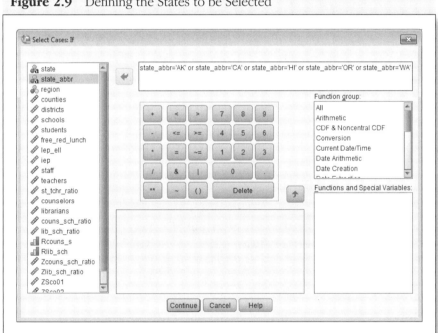

E. Reflection and Additional Decision Making △

Dr. Baird's data file is now ready for running analysis to answer her questions regarding the number of guidance counselors and librarians across the United States. This study is the beginning of a research agenda that will eventually have a more refined focus on these two school staff positions in her own state of California.

One of her immediate follow-up steps will be to return to the NCES database and download previous years of data. One reason she's interested in looking at past data is that California had the lowest ratio of librarians per school (rank of 1) and a relatively low ratio of guidance counselors per school (rank of 11). It would be useful to know if the ratios have increased, decreased, or stayed the same.

She also wants to obtain additional variables from the NCES database, such as student ethnicity and the number of library media support staff. Regarding the latter variable, these personnel are not librarians per se, but rather other staff members who provide library or media services to teachers. Possibly, states with low ratios of librarians per school have higher numbers of library support staff.

Finally, based on the findings in her study, Dr. Baird will obtain information from the state department of education in California on other factors that may correlate with the number of librarians and guidance counselors in schools. Some of these additional variables include school level (elementary, middle, junior high, senior high); school size; location (urban, suburban, rural); and other student characteristics.

△ F. Writing It Up

The steps in preparing the data file presented in this module would not typically be described in a research paper or technical report. However, methodology sections do include a description of the data, how the data were collected or gathered, and the variables. Dr. Baird's description follows:

"Data for this exploratory study were obtained from a national database called the Common Core of Data (CCD) which is a program of the National Center for Education Statistics (NCES) in the U.S. Department of Education. The CCD contains annual, descriptive information on public elementary and secondary education across all 50 states and Washington, DC. It is a comprehensive database with a wide variety of variables for states and also schools within states. The data are made available for public use through the NCES website.

The school year selected for analysis in this study was 2009–10, and data obtained were at the state level. In other words, each case in the data file represented a state, and the values for each variable represented totals across the entire state. Fourteen variables relevant to this study were downloaded. They included the name and abbreviation of the state; the number of counties, districts, schools, and students in each state; the number of students eligible for free/reduced lunch; the number of Limited English Proficient students; the number of students with an Individualized Education Plan; the number of staff, teachers, guidance counselors, and librarians in each state; and the student/teacher ratio. To prepare the data for analyzing the exploratory research questions, the researcher added a geographic region variable and created several new variables from the existing ones. These included the ratios of guidance counselors and librarians per school, ranking variables, and standardized values.

Reflective Questions △

- What are the procedures for creating a variable that contains ranks for an existing variable?
- What are the procedures for creating a variable that contains standardized values for an existing variable?
- Why do researchers sometimes need to split a file in SPSS? What are the procedures for doing so?
- Why do researchers sometimes need to select a subset of their data file for analysis? What are the procedures for doing so?

Extensions △

- Answer the exploratory questions in the three phases of Dr. Baird's study and discuss them.
- Create two additional ratio variables (librarians and counselors per total number of students in the state) and compare the data to Dr. Baird's ratios of librarians and counselors per total number of schools in the state.
- Display the distributions for Dr. Baird's variables that contain standardized values. What shape do they have?
- Practice creating ranks and standardized values for other data files, then use the new variables to make comparisons across cases.
- Practice splitting a file and selecting subsets of cases in other data files, then conduct a statistical analysis.
- Obtain data files in other formats (e.g., Excel or Microsoft Access), practice converting them to SPSS format, and check to ensure that all data were converted and are accurate. Because each file has its own unique aspects, it may be necessary to make some adjustments to variable attributes.

Note △

2. National Center for Education Statistics (NCES). Common Core of Data. U.S. Department of Education (http://nces.ed.gov/ccd/).

△ Additional Resources for Section 1: The Sample

Bryman, A., & Cramer, D. (2009). *Quantitative data analysis with SPSS 14, 15, & 16: A guide for social scientists*. New York: Routledge. (See Chapter 3 for numerous examples of relational operators and logical expressions used in selecting cases)

Gay, L. R., Mills, G. E., & Airasian, P. W. (2012). *Educational research: Competencies for analysis and applications* (10th ed.). Boston: Pearson. (See Chapter 5 on samples)

Green, S. B., Salkind, N. J., & Akey, T. M. (2000). *Using SPSS for Windows: Analyzing and understanding data* (2nd ed.). Upper Saddle River, NJ: Prentice Hall. (See Lesson 13 on ranking data, Lesson 14 on splitting files, and Lesson 39 on one-sample chi-square tests)

Holcomb, Z. C. (2009). *SPSS basics: Techniques for a first course in statistics* (2nd ed.). Glendale, CA: Pyrczak. (See Chapter 8 for a full discussion of standardized values (z) and their interpretations)

Huizingh, E. (2008). *Applied statistics with SPSS*. Thousand Oaks, CA: Sage. (See Section 9.4 on ranking methods, Section 10.1 on splitting files, and Section 10.2 on conditional selections of cases)

IBM. (2011). *SPSS Statistics 20 core systems user's guide*. Author. (A pdf version can be obtained from http://www.ibm.com)

Kinnear, P. R., & Gray, C. D. (2009). *SPSS 16 made simple*. Sussex, UK: Psychology Press.

Kulas, J. T. (2009). *SPSS essentials: Managing and analyzing social sciences data*. San Francisco: Jossey-Bass.

INTRODUCTION TO SECTION 2

The Nature and Distribution of Variables

The set of three modules in this section describes how researchers recode variables to alter their nature, compute new variables, and examine a variable's distribution of values from categorical variables with nominal scales of measurement to continuous variables with ratio scales of measurement. It should be noted that the focus of these modules is on the nature of the variables, their distributions, and how to classify them in terms of the scale of measurement. The following section, Section 3, focuses more specifically on evaluating model assumptions, including the assumption of normal distributions.

Module 3: Recoding, Counting, △ and Computing Variables

The research in this module involves a study of the social behavior of twin preschool-age children. Variables in the file consist of data from a parent questionnaire and observational data collected during a 15-minute play session. The researcher, Dr. Greenlee, needed to recode several variables for different reasons. One variable was recoded from string to numeric format. Another recode involved changing the number of months into the number of years. A set of variables was recoded to reverse the scale for Likert options on certain questionnaire items. She also needed to compute several new variables in order to represent means for sets of questionnaire items as well as counts of frequencies across observational variables.

△ Module 4: Determining the Scale of a Variable

Data preparation in this module also involves some recoding of variables, but it differs from Module 3 in that the variable modifications were guided by an examination of data distributions for each variable. In this scenario, Dr. Mendoza is working with a company to improve upon employees' level of job satisfaction through participation in a job enrichment program. He examined the distributions of four variables in his initial data file. Determining the correct scale of measurement is extremely important because it guides the decision as to which statistical analyses are appropriate for answering the research questions. The module demonstrates how the researcher used frequency distributions and crosstabs to make decisions about the appropriate number of groups to retain in nominal and ordinal variables given his sample sizes. He also examined two continuous variables using histograms to determine if the distributions were truly interval or ratio variables.

△ Module 5: Identifying and Addressing Outliers

This module continues the research scenario in Module 4. Here, Dr. Mendoza investigated two continuous variables that contained participants' scores on a motivation instrument and a job satisfaction instrument administered prior to the beginning of the study. He used the Explore procedure to obtain skewness and kurtosis values as well as stem-and-leaf plots and boxplots to identify possible outliers in the data. To help him decide how to handle the outliers, he conducted two *t*-tests, one with outliers and one without outliers, to determine whether the outlying data points impacted the results from a comparison of mean differences for the group who participated in the program and the group who did not.

MODULE 3

Recoding, Counting, and Computing Variables

DATA FILES FOR THIS MODULE

module3_twins.sav
module3_twins_recode.sav
module3_twins_recode_count.sav
module3_twins_recode_count_compute.sav

KEY LEARNING OBJECTIVES

The student will learn to

- recode variables in several ways, such as converting string to numeric, using a range of values, and reversing response options
- compute new variables that contain counts of values across a set of existing variables
- compute new variables that represent mean composite scores for a set of existing variables.

A. Description of Researcher's Study △

One of Dr. Greenlee's research interests is the social behavior of twin children. In her current study, she recruited a sample of 65 sets of twin preschool children ages three to five. Some twins are the only children in their families, whereas other twins have younger or older siblings. Dr. Greenlee has both identical and fraternal twins in her sample. Identical twins are monozygotic, meaning they share the same DNA set. Fraternal twins, dizygotic, share about the same portion of their DNA with each other as nontwin

▶ 41

siblings having the same mother and father. One reason twin studies are conducted is to examine if certain traits or behaviors are more likely due to genetic similarity or environmental factors.

Dr. Greenlee collected a variety of data, both quantitative and qualitative, from parents and their twin children. Two forms of data are used in this module. One is a 10-item parent questionnaire. Items asked parents to indicate their level of agreement or disagreement with statements about the twins' social behavior within the family and while playing with other children. Observational data were also collected during a 15-minute play session in which small groups of twin children had the opportunity to play at six activity stations throughout the room. Observers rated several aspects of their play. Two aspects are included in the data file for this module: the type of activity station each twin visited during his or her session and the number of times he or she visited it.

This module describes how Dr. Greenlee prepared her data to answer two research questions in her study.

1. How do the parental reports of social behavior in the family and social behavior with other children vary by age, by zygosity, and within sets of twins?

2. How do the type of activity station visited during the play session and the number of times it was visited vary by age, by zygosity, and within sets of twins?

Her preparation involved recoding string variables into numeric variables, reverse coding questionnaire items, and recoding ranges of continuous values into discrete values for a descriptive variable. Dr. Greenlee also computed mean variables for sets of questionnaire items and counted frequencies across observational variables.

△   B. A Look at the Data

Dr. Greenlee's file (*module3_twins.sav*) contains 65 cases and 38 variables. All data were entered by her assistant. Each case represents one set of twins. The first six variables are descriptive. Two of these, *gender* and *zygosity*, are string variables. All other variables are numeric.

Even though there are only 65 cases, the file includes questionnaire and observational data for each of the 130 children. Ten variables contain questionnaire results regarding the twins' social behavior within the family. Parents were asked to indicate the extent to which they agreed with a set of five statements for each twin. In other words, the parent responded twice to each statement. For example, *family1_1* contains data for Item 1, Twin 1 and

family1_2 contains data for Item 1, Twin 2.
**Dr. Greenlee(1)

Similarly, the next 10 variables represent parent responses to the five items regarding social behavior in play situations with other children. For instance, data for Item 1, Twin 1 is in *play1_1* and data for Item 1, Twin 2 is in *play1_2*.

The final set of variables represents the observational data. These 12 variables indicate how many times each twin was observed playing at the six activity stations (blocks, dolls, vehicles, store, puzzles, and tent). There is a variable for each twin. For instance, *blocks_1* represents the number of times Twin 1 visited the blocks station, and *blocks_2* represents the number of times Twin 2 visited the blocks station. Table 3.1 lists the name and description of all variables.

**1 Dr. Greenlee says: "I wanted to create consistency in variable names for the questionnaire items, so I decided to begin each name with *family* or *play* to distinguish items that were about behavior in the family versus behavior when playing with other children. Next, I followed each word with the specific item number from the questionnaire (1 through 5). Finally, the next number (separated by an underscore) indicated whether the response was for Twin 1 or Twin 2. This convention produced simple and concise names which helped me to quickly identify specific variables when I needed them."

Table 3.1 Variables in the Twins Study Data File

Variable Name	Description
id	numerical identifier for each set of twins (1 to 65)
age	age in months (range = 36 to 71 months)
gender	gender of each twin (BB = two boys, GG = two girls, BG = one boy and one girl)
zygosity	1 = monozygotic (identical twins); 2 = dizygotic (fraternal twins)
siblings	total number of brothers and sisters in the twins' family (0 = none, 1 = one brother or sister, 2 = two brothers or sisters, and so on)
order	order of the twins' birth in the family (0 = no siblings, 1 = younger than siblings, 2 = between siblings, 3 = older than siblings)
family1_1 family1_2 . . . to . . . family5_1 family5_2	parent responses to five statements about social behavior in the family for each twin (the first number refers to the item, the second number refers to Twin 1 or Twin 2). Item options are 1 = *strongly disagree*, 2 = *somewhat disagree*, 3 = *neutral*, 4 = *somewhat agree*, 5 = *strongly agree*

(Continued)

Table 3.1 (Continued)

Variable Name	Description
play1_1 play1_2 . . . to . . . play5_1 play5_2	parent responses to five statements about social behavior in play situations with other children (the first number refers to the item, the second number refers to Twin 1 or Twin 2). Item options are 1 = *strongly disagree,* 2 = *somewhat disagree,* 3 = *neutral,* 4 = *somewhat agree,* 5 = *strongly agree*
blocks_1 blocks_2 dolls_1 dolls_2 vehicles_1 vehicles_2 store_1 store_2 puzzles_1 puzzles_2 tent_1 tent_2	number of times Twin 1 and Twin 2 were observed visiting each of the six activity stations (blocks, dolls, vehicles, store, puzzles, tent) 0 = never visited, 1 = visited 1 time, 2 = visited 2 times

△ C. Planning and Decision Making

2 Dr. Greenlee says: "Although some SPSS procedures can be conducted on string variables (e.g., frequencies and comparisons of group means), correlational analysis and inferential tests such as *t*-tests and analysis of variance require that all variables are numeric, even when used as grouping or categorical variables in the analysis. Typically, researchers who conduct quantitative analysis find it desirable for all variables to be numeric with a few exceptions, such as names or dates."

After an assistant entered all data, Dr. Greenlee looked carefully at her file to determine if the nature of the variables had to be modified in any way. First, she wanted all variables to be numeric. Two were entered as string variables (*gender* and *zygosity*), so she needs to convert them. Value labels will also be added when necessary so that everyone using the data file will know what each numerical identifier represents. **Dr. Greenlee(2)**

Next, Dr. Greenlee would like to have *age* represented in two ways. Currently, it contains the age in months for each set of twins. This is a useful variable to answer questions in one portion of her study. But she also wants a variable that represents age in years, so she will recode *age*. ****Dr. Greenlee(3)**

With regard to the parent questionnaire, she needs to recode two items. Options for each item are on a scale from *strongly disagree* (1) to *strongly agree* (5). Most of the item statements are worded positively, so that when a parent selects one of the "agree" options, he or she is indicating positive social behavior for the twin child (e.g., child comforts her twin when she is sad). Two item statements, however, have a negative connotation, meaning that when an "agree" option is selected, it indicates negative social behavior (child has difficulty sharing toys with her twin). ****Dr. Greenlee(4)** In order to combine item data to answer her research questions, the response options from 1 to 5 for each variable must convey the same meaning. The simplest solution is to reverse the numerical codes for the two negatively worded items. Dr. Greenlee will recode a total of four variables because there are two variables per item, one representing each twin. The variables she will reverse code are *family2_1, family2_2, play4_1,* and *play4_2.*

After the recodes are performed, Dr. Greenlee will then be able to create composite variables for sets of questionnaire items. Previous research on her family social behavior items indicated they are unidimensional; thus, data for the five items can be combined to form one overall

**3 Dr. Greenlee says: "When you recode a variable in SPSS, the researcher has a choice between replacing data in the original variable or creating a new variable while retaining the original. I almost never rewrite over the original variable because I like to check my recodes to ensure the procedure worked as I intended. Then, depending upon how I will use the variable, I will either remove the original or keep it in the data file. After I prepare all my data for this study, I will probably delete the two original string variables, since I don't foresee using them again. But I will keep both *age* variables since there will be times when I want to refer to age in years versus age in months."

**4 Dr. Greenlee says: "I use the words 'positive' and 'negative' only to describe the direction of the wording for the social behavior statements on the questionnaire. The social behavior of preschool age children is just beginning to develop, so it would not be expected that all twins in this study would be able to share all their toys or recognize when their twin is feeling sad."

composite score. Likewise, the five play social behavior items are unidimensional. Using the Transform procedure in SPSS, she will compute a set of four new variables, one for each twin on the two types of social behavior.

**5 Dr. Greenlee says: "There is no right or wrong decision. It's just a matter of choosing the type of composite score that's most easily interpreted for your study. For example, when the data consist of options on a Likert scale, as in my study, it's helpful to compute the mean. For example, a composite score of 2.1 would indicate that on average, a parent's responses indicated somewhat negative social behavior, whereas a score of 4.8 would indicate that, on average, a parent's responses indicated somewhat positive social behavior. In studies involving test scores, a more meaningful composite score might be the total score. If there were 30 dichotomous items on a test, the total composite score would represent the number of items each person answered correctly."

First, however, she needs to make a decision regarding the type of composite score. The two most common are the mean, which represents the average of all values across items, and the total, which represents the sum of all values across items. She decided to compute the mean composite score. **Dr. Greenlee(5)**

Another aspect of Dr. Greenlee's data preparation will involve a summary of the observational data. Twelve variables represent the frequency of visits to the six activity stations in the play area. In addition to analyzing the stations individually, Dr. Greenlee would like to know the total number of stations each twin visited at least one time so she can determine, for example, how many twins visited only one station versus how many twins visited five of the six stations during the 15-minute play session. The Count procedure in the Transform procedure will allow Dr. Greenlee to easily create this variable.

△ D. Using SPSS to Address Issues and Prepare Data

SPSS Tip 1: Instead of using the Recode procedure, you may be tempted to change the type of variable from String to Numeric in the Variable View tab within the Data Editor. This will work for numeric strings (as in *zygosity*). However, if your strings are non-numeric (as in *gender*) changing from String to Numeric in Variable View will wipe out all data in the cells of your variable, and you can't get them back. Therefore, you must start the recoding process using the Transform → Recode procedure.

Recoding Variables

Dr. Greenlee performed four different types of recodes. She began each of them by selecting **Recode into Different Variables** under the **Transform menu. **SPSS Tip 1** This choice keeps the original variable in the file and places the recodes into a new variable. The first recode changes *gender* from a string variable to a numeric variable. In the dialog box shown in Figure 3.1, she placed *gender* in the variable box, and typed *gender_r* for the new variable's name in the **Output Variable** box.

Dr. Greenlee(6) Before moving further ahead, she clicked the **Change button to confirm the new variable's name. ****SPSS Tip 2**

The next step is to tell SPSS how to recode the variable. Dr. Greenlee clicked the **Old and New Values** button to obtain the following window (Figure 3.2). She typed BB, GG, and BG into the **Old Value** box one at a time and placed the values of 1, 2, and 3, respectively, into the **New Value** box. The **Old → New** box on the right side shows that she already added the first two recodes. She clicked the **Add** button one last time to add the third and final recode. After she clicked **Continue** and **OK**, SPSS replaced each string code with its corresponding numeric value and *gender_r* was added to the end of the data file. The new variable will automatically be a numeric variable.

**6 Dr. Greenlee says: "I use a standard naming convention for all my newly recoded variables. I add "r" at the end of the original variable's name. This makes it easy for me to identify which variables have been recoded. I can always go back and change the name later if I need to be more specific."

SPSS Tip 2: There is also an If statement in the Recode dialog box. Dr. Greenlee did not need this option for her study, but it is available when a researcher wants to recode only a subset of cases rather than all cases in the file.

Figure 3.1 Transform → Recode into Different Variables

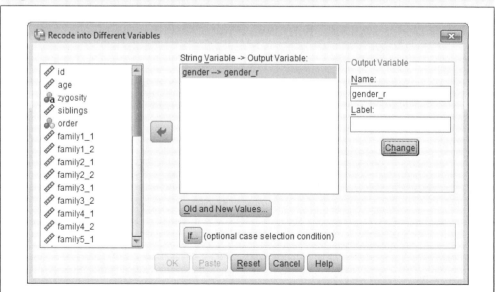

Figure 3.2   Old and New Values

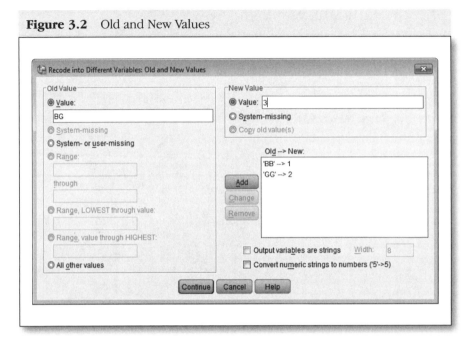

To ensure that the recode went as planned, Dr. Greenlee produced frequencies for *gender* and *gender_r* by selecting **Descriptive Statistics** and **Frequencies** under the **Analyze menu**. This check also allowed her to identify any potential data entry errors. Suppose the assistant accidentally typed BF instead of BG for one set of twins. The frequency output would alert her to the error so that it could be corrected, and she would then run the recode procedure again. In this case, however, the assistant was careful when entering data and there were no errors. The frequencies for BB, GG, and BG in the string variable were 18, 17, and 30, respectively. The same results were produced for values 1, 2, and 3 in the numeric variable.

Dr. Greenlee's final step for *gender_r* was to add value labels so that she (and others using her data file) will remember which gender combinations of the twins are associated with each number. In the **Data Editor**, she chose the **Variable View** tab and highlighted the cell under the **Values** column for *gender_r*. It opened the **Value Labels** window shown in Figure 3.3. She placed each numeric value in the **Value** box and typed its description in the **Label** box. The first two labels have been added, so now she will click the **Add** button to add the third label to her list. After **OK** is clicked, value labels are added to the variable and can be displayed in SPSS output in addition to, or instead of, the numeric values.

Figure 3.3 Variable View

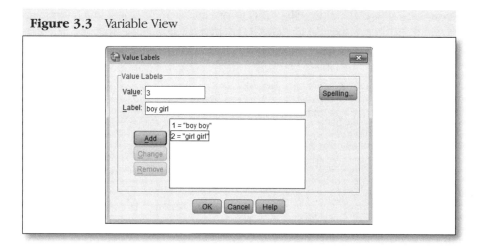

Dr. Greenlee's second recode was to change *zygosity* from a string to a numeric variable. Currently, the values are numeric strings; that is, they appear as numbers, but the variable is not numeric. As she did for the *gender* recode, she identified *zygosity* as the variable to recode in the **Recode into Different Variables** dialog box and created the new variable *zygosity_r*. ** **SPSS Tip 3** In the **Old and New Values** box shown in Figure 3.4, she simply typed the numeric string values (1, 2) in the **Old Value** box and, respectively, the numbers 1 and 2 in the

SPSS Tip 3: In order to remove the recoding instructions for *gender*, Dr. Greenlee clicked the Reset button in the Recode window. It removed the previous variable names and their old and new values so that she could conduct her next recode.

Figure 3.4 Old and New Values

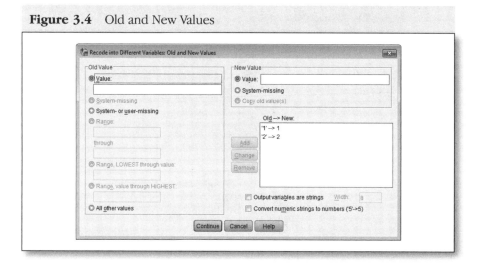

New Value box. As before, SPSS will automatically make the conversion from string to numeric variable. Dr. Greenlee added value labels for *zygosity_r* so that 1 = monozygotic and 2 = dizygotic. She also double-checked the recode procedure. Both variables, *zygosity* and *zygosity_r,* contained the same frequencies (19 monozygotic and 46 dizygotic twins).

> SPSS Tip 4: If you are unsure of the minimum or maximum values of a variable, you can use the other Range buttons (LOWEST through value or value through HIGHEST), which ask you to identify only one value as a cut point. SPSS will recode all values either lower or higher than that value.

The third recode was to transform *age* from months to years. This required Dr. Greenlee to specify a range of values for each new code. After selecting *age* as the variable to be recoded and typing *age_r* as the new variable's name, she clicked the **Range** button under **Old Value** in the window shown in Figure 3.5. She entered the lowest and highest months in the range for 3-year-olds (36 and 47, respectively), and then, under **New Value,** she entered the number 3 and clicked the **Add** button. Dr. Greenlee repeated these steps for 4-year-olds (48 through 59 months) and 5-year olds (60 through 71 months). After clicking **Continue** and **OK**, every month in *age* will be recoded to the appropriate year in *age_r*. ****SPSS Tip 4**

Once again, Dr. Greenlee checked whether the variable recoded properly. Frequency results for *age* showed that there were 35 twins between the ages of 36 and 47 months, 20 twins between 48 and 59 months, and 10 twins between the ages of 60 and 71 months. The recoded *age_r* variable showed

Figure 3.5 Old and New Values

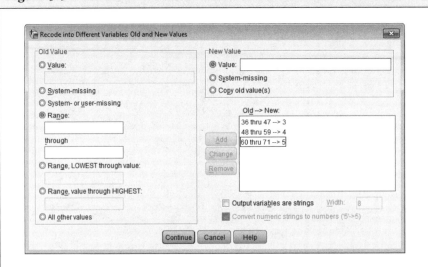

the same results: 35 three-year-old twins, 20 four-year-old twins, and 10 five-year-old twins.

The last recode involved a set of variables. Dr. Greenlee needed to reverse the values for two questionnaire variables (Item 2 for family social behavior and Item 4 for play social behavior) so that the values would have a consistent meaning across all questionnaire items. Higher values are associated with more positive social behavior. Because there are two variables for each item (for Twin 1 and Twin 2), she recoded a total of four variables. All recodes were performed in one SPSS run because the recoding was identical for each variable. Figure 3.6 shows the four original and the four new variables.

Figure 3.6   Transform → Recode into Different Variables

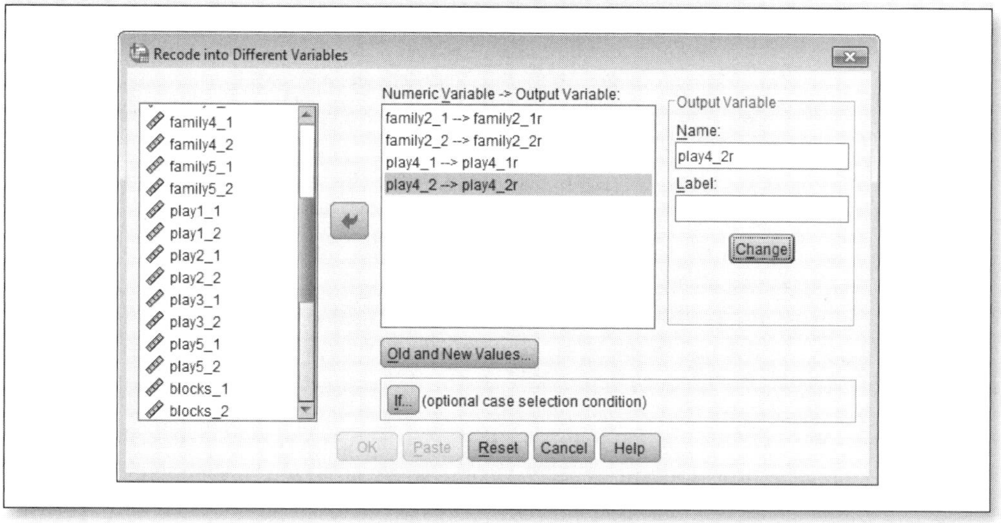

As you can see in the following **Old and New Values** box (Figure 3.7), the original values of 1, 2, 3, 4, and 5 were recoded as 5, 4, 3, 2, and 1, respectively. ****SPSS Tip 5** These four reverse recoded variables, as well as the other recoded variables in this section, are available in the file *module3_twins_recode.sav*.

Counting Values Across Variables

After all necessary recodes were performed, Dr. Greenlee turned her attention

SPSS Tip 5: If one or more values remain unchanged in the new variable (such as the value of 3 in this set of variables), another option for recoding is to click the All other values button under Old Value and the Copy old value(s) button under New Value. After clicking Add, you will see ELSE → Copy in the list of Old and New values, which indicates that all other values not specifically recoded will retain their original values.

Figure 3.7 Old and New Values

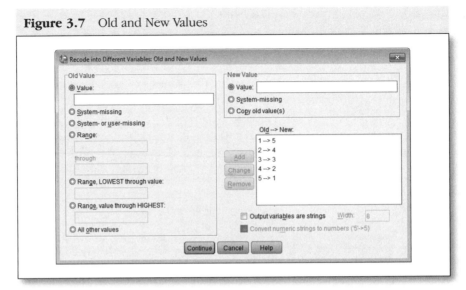

to creating a variable that would indicate the number of activity stations each twin visited during the 15-minute observational play session. She selected **Count Values Within Cases** under the **Transform menu** and typed a new variable name, *count_1* into the **Target Variable** box (see Figure 3.8). Then, she selected the six variables to be counted (*blocks_1, dolls_1, vehicles_1, store_1, puzzles_1,* and *tent_1*) and placed them in the **Numeric Variables** box. This procedure counts the values for Twin 1.

Figure 3.8 Transform → Count Values Within Cases

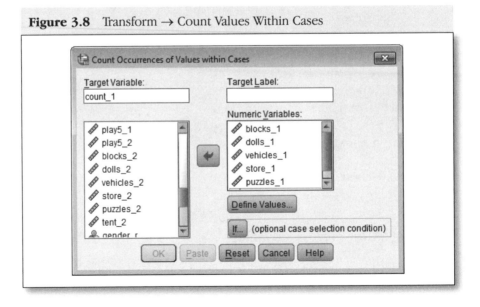

After selecting the **Define Values** button, another window opened and the values to be counted were identified (see Figure 3.9). Dr. Greenlee was interested in knowing how many activities each twin visited at least one time, so she clicked the **Range, value through HIGHEST** button under **Value**, typed the number 1, then clicked **Add.**

Figure 3.9 Values to Count

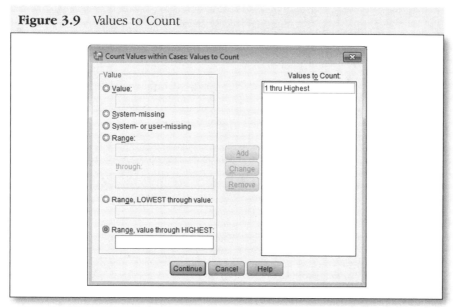

After clicking **Continue**, *count_1* was added to the file. Dr. Greenlee visually checked a few cases to determine whether the procedure worked as intended, then conducted a frequency analysis as before. The output in Table 3.2 shows

Table 3.2 SPSS Output for the Total Number of Activity Stations Visited by Twin 1 Children

		Frequency	Percent	Valid Percent	Cumulative Percent
Valid	1	1	1.5	1.5	1.5
	2	1	1.5	1.5	3.1
	3	18	27.7	27.7	30.8
	4	28	43.1	43.1	73.8
	5	16	24.6	24.6	98.5
	6	1	1.5	1.5	100.0
	Total	65	100.0	100.0	

SPSS Tip 6: There were no missing data in this file. If there were, the MEAN function allows you to control how it will be treated. Suppose there are 10 variables and a researcher wants to compute mean values for cases with at least 80% non-missing data. The function MEAN.8 would be used to indicate that a case must have a non-missing value for at least eight of the 10 variables in order for a mean to be calculated. If a case had 3 missing values, the mean would not be computed since only 70% of the data were non-missing. Researchers use different criteria for determining how much missing data they are willing to tolerate. It often depends upon the number of variables used to calculate the mean or the total number of cases.

**7 Dr. Greenlee says: "A common mistake is forgetting to use your reverse recoded variables for questionnaire items. Item 2 on the family social behavior scale was reverse coded, so I had to be sure to use the correct variable (*family2_1r*) in the mean function. Because I prefer to keep both variables in my data file, I did not delete the original. One way I decrease the likelihood of using the wrong variable is to place the recoded variable next to its original in the data file. When I can see both variables together, it helps me remember to use the new variable. If the new variable is at the end of the file, I may be likely to forget it. To move a variable's placement in the data file, go to the Variable View tab within the Data Editor, highlight the row that contains its information, and move the row to the desired position in the variable list."

that the values in *count_1* ranged from 1 to 6. Only one Twin 1 child stayed at one station the entire time. Likewise, only one Twin 1 child visited all six stations. The highest percentage of children visited four of the six stations (43.1%).

Dr. Greenlee needed to perform the same **Count** procedure once again to obtain the data for Twin 2. She named the variable *count_2*. Both new count variables are available in the *module3_twins_recode_count.sav* file.

Computing New Variables

The final additions to Dr. Greenlee's data file were mean composite scores for the five parent questionnaire items related to social behavior within the family and the five items related to social behavior at play. Altogether, she computed four new variables representing mean scores for Twin 1 and Twin 2 for each type of social behavior: *family_1mean, family_2mean, play_1mean,* and *play_2mean*. Each mean was created individually using the **Compute Variable** procedure under the **Transform menu**.

In Figure 3.10, Dr. Greenlee typed the name of the first new variable under **Target Variable**. In the **Numeric Expression** box, she used one of the common functions available in SPSS. This function [**MEAN(?,?)**] is listed in the **Functions and Special Variables** box under **Function group: Statistical**. For each case, it will produce the mean value across all variables inserted within the parentheses and separated by commas. ****SPSS Tip 6**

Figure 3.10   Transform → Compute Variable

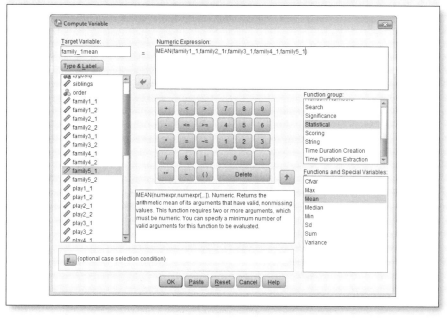

Here, the mean of five family social variables (*family1_1, family2_1r, family3_1, family4_1,* and *family5_1*) were created for each Twin 1 and placed in a new variable called *family_1mean*. ****Dr. Greenlee(7)**

As always, Dr. Greenlee checked her new mean variable. The case with *id = 1* in the file had values of 4, 2, 4, 3, and 4 for the five family social behavior variables. The mean for this Twin 1 child calculated by SPSS in *family_1mean* was 3.40, which is correct. Then, Dr. Greenlee performed the same procedures to produce the three additional mean composite variables needed for her study: *family_2mean, play_1mean,* and *play_2mean*. ****SPSS Tip 7** The file *module3_twins_recode_count_compute.sav* contains all new variables created in this module (recodes, counts, and means).

SPSS Tip 7: Another option for finding the mean is to type the arithmetic equation for mean in the Numeric Expression box:

(*family1_1* + *family2_1r* + *family3_1* + *family4_1* + *family5_1*)/5

Both procedures (using the MEAN function or the arithmetic equation) will produce the same mean value if there are no missing data in any of the variables. When data are missing, however, the two procedures can produce different results. Unlike the MEAN function, there is no control over how missing data are treated when using the arithmetic equation. If a case has at least one missing value across the variables, it will have a missing value for the mean. This is problematic when there are a large number of variables producing the mean composite score.

△ E. Reflection and Additional Decision Making

As part of her larger study, Dr. Greenlee collected a great deal of information observing twin behavior in the activity stations. She and her assistant are now determining the best way to code the observational data and represent them all in one data file. Most likely, some of the procedures she used here to prepare and create new variables will be utilized again. Given the nature of her data, she will probably use the **Count** and **Compute** procedures under the **Transform menu** in order to condense the large number of specific data coded by observers during the play session.

For some of Dr. Greenlee's research questions, data analysis may require that the twin data be in two separate columns/variables (as it is in her current data file). However, it might be beneficial in some circumstances to have one variable that captures the difference between Twin 1 and Twin 2's questionnaire responses or visits to activity stations. She can create "difference" variables by using the **Compute** procedure. For example, subtracting *count_1* from *count_2*, or vice versa, would produce a variable that allows for determining how many of the twin sets visited the same number of activity stations during the play session. To remove the direction of the difference (the positive and negative signs), she can take the absolute value of the difference (by using **Compute** or by recoding values). For example, if Twin 1 visited 3 activity stations and Twin 2 visited 5 activity stations, the twins' data differs by 2, regardless of whether the difference was calculated by subtracting Twin 2 from Twin 1 data or vice versa.

△ F. Writing It Up

Typically, most raw data files require some recoding of variables. Detailed accounts of these procedures are not usually considered necessary to include in research articles or technical reports. However, it is desirable to include descriptions of variables in the study. Dr. Greenlee did not feel the need to mention the conversion of string variables to numeric variables, but she did want to briefly describe her other recoded and computed variables. She wrote the following paragraph for inclusion in the Variables subheading of her Methodology section.

"Originally, age was coded in months, but in order to perform some analysis, months was converted to years to form a new variable. For the parent questionnaire, two items had to be reverse coded (item 2 for family and item 4 for play) so that high values on the scale from 1 to 5 were consistently associated with positive social behavior for all items. In addition, mean composite scores, one for each twin, across the five family social behavior items were computed. Similarly, mean composite scores were computed across the five items relating to social behavior in play with other children. Lastly, two new variables were created to represent the total number of activity stations each twin visited over the course of 15 minutes."

Reflective Questions △

- For what purpose might a researcher need to recode variables? What are the processes for recoding values of a variable?
- For what purpose might a researcher need to compute a new variable that counts values across a set of variables? What are the processes for computing a count variable?
- For what purpose might a researcher need to compute a new variable that contains the mean composite value across a set of variables? What are the processes for computing a mean variable?

Extensions △

- Create a new difference variable, as described in Dr. Greenlee's reflection, in order to represent the difference between Twin 1 and Twin 2 in terms of the total number of different activity stations visited. Then, perform descriptive statistics to examine the data. Remember to find the absolute value of the difference (hint: either by using the absolute value function or by recoding values after obtaining the difference).
- Create a new variable that would allow for determining whether Twin 1 and Twin 2 children visited the same types of activity stations (e.g., blocks, store, etc.) during the play session.
- What other new variables can be created from the observation data? How would they be created?
- For an existing data file, determine if there might be reasons why a researcher might want to recode certain variables, then conduct the recoding. Be sure to check that the recoding produced the intended results.
- Find an existing data file in which it would be useful to compute a mean composite score for a set of variables. Decide whether to compute the mean or the total of the values. Then create the composite variables in two ways: by using the appropriate function (MEAN or SUM), and by creating an arithmetic expression. Compare the results for the two methods and check to ensure that the new variables contain accurate values.

Determining the Scale of a Variable

༄✿

DATA FILES FOR THIS MODULE

module4_jobsatis.sav
module4_jobsatis_final.sav

༄✿

KEY LEARNING OBJECTIVES

The student will learn to

- create and interpret tables and graphs that display information about a variable's distribution, specifically
- use Crosstabs to examine frequencies and percentages in each subgroup of two nominal variables to determine if sample sizes are adequate
- use frequency distributions to examine frequencies and percentages in groups of an ordinal variable to determine if sample sizes are adequate
- examine the distributions of continuous variables using histograms to determine if their scales are truly continuous in nature.

A. Description of Researcher's Study △

Dr. Mendoza, a social science researcher, has been working with a large company that wants to improve upon the level of job satisfaction among its employees. Management within the company decided to provide employees with the opportunity to participate in a 3-month job enrichment program. As a starting point, participation in the program was offered to all employees in each sector of the business. Employees who agreed to participate in the study were randomly assigned to a group that receives the program or to a control group that does not. Employees in the control group will be given the opportunity to participate in the program upon completion of the study.

All participants, regardless of whether they were in the program or not, were given three instruments to complete prior to the beginning of the study. One instrument was an assessment of their knowledge and aptitude. The other two instruments measured their level of motivation and job satisfaction. Upon completion of the study, the three instruments will be administered again. Throughout the course of the study, several other forms of data will be collected, such as interviews with participants and supervisors, assessment of job productivity, and an evaluation of job skills and knowledge.

The overarching goal of this experimental research is to determine whether the job enrichment program is useful in improving job satisfaction. Some of the specific questions investigated are the following: Did participants in the program have a higher average score on the job satisfaction survey than employees in the control group, after controlling for their level of satisfaction prior to the study? Were there differences in how well the program worked, or did not work, across the geographic locations of the business? What factors were related to the difference between pre and post job satisfaction scores (i.e., demographic characteristics of employees, prior knowledge and aptitude, prior motivation, change in level of job productivity, interaction among employees during the study, and so on)?

Currently, the data file for this research consists of a few descriptive variables for the participants as well as their scores on the aptitude, motivation, and job satisfaction surveys prior to the beginning of the study. During implementation of the job-enrichment program, Dr. Mendoza wants to look at the data he has now in order to determine the proper measurement scale for each variable. From his past experiences, he knows that the number of groups in nominal or ordinal variables must sometimes be reduced because of small sample sizes in certain categories. Likewise, continuous variables, which are considered to be either interval or ratio, may end up being converted to ordinal or nominal variables depending on how the values are distributed across the scale. Finally, some continuous variables may have outliers that need to be identified and addressed.

Dr. Mendoza's data file preparation is described over two modules. In this module, he examines variables for geographic location, years of experience, reprimands received, and the aptitude instrument. Module 5 describes how he examined distributions of prescores on the motivation and job satisfaction surveys for outliers.

B. A Look at the Data △

There are nine variables and 265 cases in Dr. Mendoza's current data file (*module4_jobsatis.sav*). Each case represents one employee who agreed to be a participant in the study. Employees are in one of seven geographic locations of the company. A total of 127 participants are receiving the job enrichment program, and the remaining 138 participants are in the control group. Table 4.1 displays each variable name and its description.

Table 4.1 Variables in the Job Satisfaction Data File

Variable Name	Description
id	numerical identifier for each participant from 1 to 265
location	geographic location of the company in which the participant is employed, coded 1 to 7
program	0 = no (participant is not receiving the program, he or she is in the control group); 1 = yes (participant is receiving the program)
size	total number of employees in each geographic location of the company across all its sectors. This variable is a constant value for participants within the same location.
yrs_exper	total number of years of experience within the company for each participant. Codes for the categories are 2 = 0 to 2 years of experience, 4 = 3 to 4 years of experience, 6 = 5 to 6 years of experience, 8 = 7 to 8 years of experience, 10 = 9 to 10 years of experience, and so on until the final code of 32 = 31 years of experience or more.
reprimand	total number of reprimands received by each employee during his or her total years of experience with the company
aptitude	score on an aptitude instrument prior to implementing the study
motivation	score on a motivation survey prior to implementing the study
job_satis	score on a job satisfaction survey prior to implementing the study

△ C. Planning and Decision Making

While Dr. Mendoza is waiting for the study to be completed, he will use this time to identify the measurement scale of some of the variables that are currently in his file. All variables can be classified into one of four hierarchical scales (nominal, ordinal, interval, or ratio). It is important to identify the scale for each variable because it determines the type of statistical procedures that can be used to analyze the data.

A nominal variable is a grouping variable in which cases are categorized according to a particular attribute, such as gender or ethnicity. Numbers may be assigned to represent the categories, but the numbers have no meaning other than to make the groups distinct from each other. Variables in the next scale of the hierarchy, ordinal, make use of the ordering property of numbers. Data in ordinal variables represent different degrees or amounts of an attribute (e.g., academic class ranks in high school). Interval variables contain values that are ordered but also have equal intervals, thus addition and subtraction of the values becomes meaningful. For example, means and standard deviations can be obtained for scores on an assessment. Finally, ratio variables have the same properties as interval variables, but, in addition, they have a meaningful and absolute zero point. Some examples are height and weight.

Dr. Mendoza plans to obtain frequency distributions and other visual displays of data to examine the scale of measurement for his variables. First, he will focus on *location* and *program*, two important independent variables in the study. Both variables are nominal, meaning that each case is placed into one group of the variable according to a specific characteristic or attribute. For *location*, there are seven groups, coded 1 to 7, that represent the geographic location of the company in which the participant is employed. There is no order to the groups. If there were, the variable would be considered ordinal. For *program*, there are two groups, coded 0 and 1, that indicate if the participant is in the control group or the group that receives the job enrichment program. It is a nominal variable, but may also be called a dichotomous variable because there are only two groups.

Dr. Mendoza can choose from several different summary displays of data for *location* and *program,* such as frequency distributions, bar charts, and customized tables. One aspect of the data in which he is interested is whether participants are distributed somewhat equally between the control and program groups within each location. Therefore, he decides to create a table that shows frequencies for *location* by *program*. In SPSS, this type of table is called a Crosstabs. He knows that another useful feature of the Crosstabs procedure is that percentages as well as frequencies can be obtained within *location* and within *program*. This will help him find out whether the sample size of participants in each location is adequate for analyzing the research questions. If not, he may need to eliminate a location, or possibly combine locations. **** Dr. Mendoza (1)**

The total number of years participants worked for the company is found in *yrs_exper*. This variable is ordinal. Like *location* and *program*, it is a categorical variable, but the categories express different amounts of the characteristic and are ordered sequentially from lowest to highest. Lower codes represent fewer years of experience, higher codes represent more years of experience. With the exception of the first and last code, each code encompasses a 2-year span. For example, a code of 4 identifies employees who worked for the company 3 to 4 years. **** Dr. Mendoza (2)** To examine this distribution, Dr. Mendoza will use a frequency distribution to provide frequencies and percentages of participants in each category. This summary view of the data will allow him to determine if frequencies are large enough for conducting analysis for all categories. If sample sizes are too small, categories can be collapsed.

The next variable, *reprimand*, is a continuous variable and, more specifically, a ratio variable. The numeric values represent equally spaced intervals. The difference between one and two reprimands is one, the difference between

**1 Dr. Mendoza says: "Eliminating people from the study is not usually desirable unless there is a particularly good reason for doing so. Hopefully, if one or two locations have small numbers of participants, I will be able to find a way to combine locations based on a similar characteristic so that I don't have to delete participants from the data analysis."

**2 Dr. Mendoza says: "Although most codes represent a span of 2 years, the first and last codes do not. The first code (2) spans 3 years, from 0 to 2 years. The last code (32) encompasses employees who worked more than 30 years with the company. If it weren't for these two codes, the variable may be considered interval since the other groups represent equal intervals of the characteristic."

**3 Dr. Mendoza says: "When choosing an appropriate statistical procedure, typically the distinction between interval and ratio variables is not critical. Rather, one of the most important characteristics guiding the selection of data analysis is whether the variable is categorical (nominal or ordinal) or continuous (either interval or ratio). Dependent variables must be continuous in order to use inferential tests that involve means and standard deviations

(Continued)

(Continued)

[i.e., parametric tests such as *t*-tests and analysis of variance (ANOVA)] and to use multiple regression analysis. Another important consideration when choosing a statistical test is the number of groups in an independent, categorical variable. Two groups (dichotomous) versus more than two groups guides the decision to use a *t*-test or an ANOVA and also guides how a categorical predictor will be used in multiple regression analysis. Nonparametric tests, such as chi-square analysis, are appropriate for research questions involving only categorical variables."

**4 Dr. Mendoza says: "Although it is possible for a participant to receive a score of 0 for *aptitude*, scores on assessments are not usually considered ratio variables. A score of 0 does not indicate complete absence of knowledge; rather, it only indicates that the participant was not able to correctly answer any of the items on that particular assessment."

two and three reprimands is one, and so on. This attribute makes the variable at least an interval variable. However, it is more correctly classified as a ratio variable because the value of 0 denotes the absence of any reprimands. **Dr. Mendoza (3)** Dr. Mendoza will examine its distribution to determine if the data values are truly continuous. He suspects that only a few employees will have large numbers of reprimands, so it is possible that *reprimand* may be converted to an ordinal variable. He will begin by producing a histogram of the values to determine whether it is positively skewed, as he is predicting it might be. If so, then he will recode the variable into ordered groups, using the data values to determine the appropriate number of groups.

Finally, he will examine *aptitude*, an interval variable containing scores on an instrument that assesses job knowledge and skills. **Dr. Mendoza (4)** Similar to *reprimand*, he will check whether the values can truly be considered continuous. If so, he will leave the variable as is. If not, values will be recoded to transform it into a categorical variable.

△ D. Using SPSS to Address Issues and Prepare Data

Location and Program

SPSS Tip 1: The results will be the same regardless of which variables are in rows or columns. The way in which the researcher wants to view the results is what should guide the decision.

To obtain a Crosstabs table for *location* and *program*, Dr. Mendoza went to the **Analyze menu** and selected **Descriptive Statistics** and **Crosstabs**. In the dialog box shown in Figure 4.1, he chose to have results for *program* in rows and results for *location* in columns. **SPSS Tip 1**

Figure 4.1 Analyze → Descriptive Statistics → Crosstabs

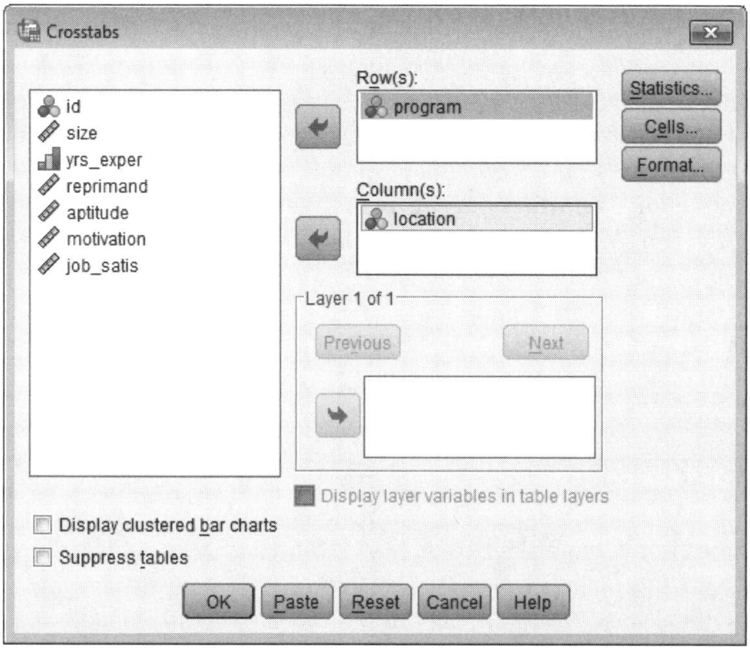

After he clicked **OK**, the output in Table 4.2 displayed the count (i.e., number of cases) in each cell of *program* by *location*. Three locations (2, 4, and 5) have small numbers of participants in the "no" and "yes" groups for *program* compared to the other locations.

Table 4.2 SPSS Output Showing Frequencies of Participants in Each Location by Program

program * location Crosstabulation

Count

		location							Total
		1	2	3	4	5	6	7	
program	no	23	9	27	6	5	36	32	138
	yes	21	8	25	4	5	36	28	127
Total		44	17	52	10	10	72	60	265

Locations 2, 4, and 5 serve similar demographic areas. They are also relatively small in terms of total number of employees as indicated according to the *size* variable in the data file (90, 134, and 70 total employees, respectively) compared to the other locations 1, 3, 6, and 7 (259, 231, 380, and 450 total employees, respectively). Because of these similar characteristics, Dr. Mendoza felt comfortable combining locations 2, 4, and 5 together. So as not alter the original codes for *location*, he created a new code of 9 for the combined group and kept codes for the other locations (1, 3, 6, and 7) unchanged. Under the **Transform menu**, he selected **Recode into Different Variables** and named the newly recoded variable *location_r*. In the dialog box shown in Figure 4.2, the **Old Values** of 2, 4, and 5 are recoded into **New Values** of 9. All other location values remain the same (**Else** → **Copy**). (See Module 3 for a scenario that describes in detail how to recode a variable.)

Figure 4.2   Transform → Recode into Different Variables

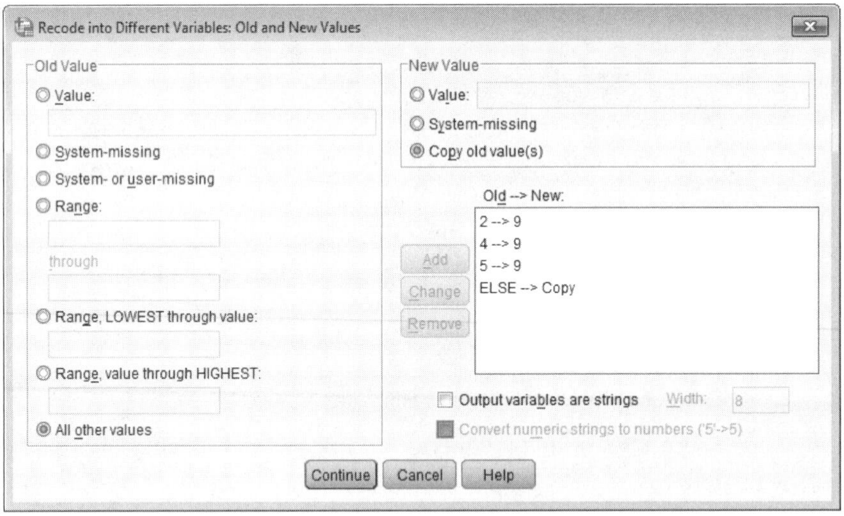

Now that locations have been combined, Dr. Mendoza wanted to produce another Crosstabs. But this time, he wanted to view percentages as well as frequencies. The **Cells** button in the **Crosstabs** dialog box in Figure 4.3 allows for requesting several types of percentages. He wanted to look at row, column, and total percentages, so he checked those boxes in addition to the observed counts.

Figure 4.3 Information to Display in Cells

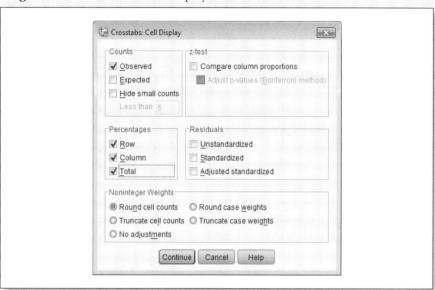

The new Crosstabs for *program* by *location_r* shown in Table 4.3 may look a bit overwhelming upon first glance, but identifying which percentages represent rows, columns, and totals will help. First, Dr. Mendoza noticed that the frequencies for Location 9 are now adequate and somewhat similar to the frequencies in the other locations.

Values highlighted in light gray are the row percentages. The first row represents percentages of participants in each location that are not receiving the program ("no" for *program*). For example, 23 of the 138 total employees not receiving the program are in Location 1 (16.7%). Likewise, the second light gray row contains percentages of participants in each location that are receiving the program ("yes" for *program*). For example, 36 of the 127 total employees who are receiving the program are in Location 6 (28.3%). ****SPSS Tip 2**

Values highlighted in dark gray are the column percentages. The first column represents the percentages of all participants in Location 1 in each of the *program* categories. For example, 23 out of 44 participants in Location 1 (52.3%) are not receiving the program. The remaining 21 of the 44 participants in Location 1 (47.7%) are receiving the program.

SPSS Tip 2: Note that in the column labeled Total, the light gray row percentages sum to 100%. This is another indication that these rows represent the distribution of participants across locations within each program group.

Table 4.3 SPSS Output Showing Frequencies and Percentages of Participants by Program for the New Location Variable

program * location_r Crosstabulation

			location_r					Total
			1	3	6	7	9	
program	no	Count	23	27	36	32	20	138
		% within program	16.7%	19.6%	26.1%	23.2%	14.5%	100.0%
		% within location_r	52.3%	51.9%	50.0%	53.3%	54.1%	52.1%
		% of Total	8.7%	10.2%	13.6%	12.1%	7.5%	52.1%
	yes	Count	21	25	36	28	17	127
		% within program	16.5%	19.7%	28.3%	22.0%	13.4%	100.0%
		% within location_r	47.7%	48.1%	50.0%	46.7%	45.9%	47.9%
		% of Total	7.9%	9.4%	13.6%	10.6%	6.4%	47.9%
Total		Count	44	52	72	60	37	265
		% within program	16.6%	19.6%	27.2%	22.6%	14.0%	100.0%
		% within location_r	100.0%	100.0%	100.0%	100.0%	100.0%	100.0%
		% of Total	16.6%	19.6%	27.2%	22.6%	14.0%	100.0%

SPSS Tip 3: Note that each set of column percentages sums to 100% in the row labeled Total % within location_r at the bottom of the table. This is another indication that these columns represent the distribution of participants across the categories of program within each location.

Recall that Dr. Mendoza wanted to know if the percentages receiving the program were similar across all locations, and they appear to be. They range from 45.9% in Location 9 to 50.0% in Location 6. The percentages who will not receive the program are also similar across locations, ranging from 50.0% in Location 6 to 54.1% in Location 9. **SPSS Tip 3

Other percentages of interest are the two circled. They represent the percentages for the "no" versus "yes" groups in *program* across all locations. For example, 47.9% of all participants will receive the program (127 out of 265).

Finally, the values highlighted in black represent percentages for each location across both program categories. They are somewhat similar across locations, ranging from 14.0% (37 out of 265) in Location 9 to 27.2% (72 out of 265) in Location 6. If *location* had not been recoded, the percentages would have been markedly smaller in the original locations of 2, 4, and 5.

Figure 4.4 Analyze → Descriptive Statistics → Frequencies

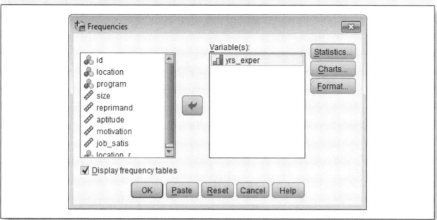

Years of Experience

For this variable, Dr. Mendoza created a frequency table. Under the **Analyze menu**, he selected **Descriptive Statistics** and **Frequencies**, which produces the dialog box shown in Figure 4.4. He moved *yrs_exper* into the **Variable(s)** box, then clicked **OK. **SPSS Tip 4**

The output is shown in Table 4.4. Results in the frequency column indicate that the large majority of participants worked for the company for 10 years or less. Only a few participants had more than 10 years of experience. ****SPSS Tip 5** The percentage column shows that each of the upper categories represented only 1.5% or less of the total sample. ****SPSS Tip 6**

Because of the small sample size in the higher end of the distribution, Dr. Mendoza decided to combine all categories above 10 into one category that represents all participants with more than 10 years of experience. As before, he used the **Recode into Different Variables** procedure to create a new

SPSS Tip 4: For Dr. Mendoza's purposes, the default selections for Frequencies were adequate. However, under the Charts button in the Frequency dialog box, you can request bar charts, pie charts, or histograms of the data. The Format button provides options for ordering the frequency results. They can be displayed by ascending values of the variable (the default) or as ascending/ descending counts/frequencies, which could be helpful if you had a nominal variable with many categories. For continuous variables, options under the Statistics button include percentiles, measures of central tendency, and measures of variability.

SPSS Tip 5: Notice that some of the variable's categories are missing from the table, such as Category 12. The frequency procedure excludes categories with zero cases.

variable called *yrs_exper_r*. Using the **Range button**, he created a **New Value** of 30 to represent all participants in the original catego-ries of 12 through 30. All other categories (2 through 10) remained unchanged. He checked the recoding by conducting another frequency analysis. The output in Table 4.5 shows that the first five cat-egories have the same frequencies as the original variable. The final new category of 30 includes 17 participants that have more than 10 years of experience. (See Module 3 for a scenario that describes how to recode ranges of data.)

SPSS Tip 6: For these data, the Valid Percent column has the same values as the Percent column. If there were miss-ing values for the variable, results in the two columns would differ. The denominator for Percent is the total number of cases, whereas the denomi-nator for Valid Percent is the number of non-missing cases.

Table 4.4 SPSS Frequency Distribution Output for the Years of Experience Variable

yrs_exper

		Frequency	Percent	Valid Percent	Cumulative Percent
Valid	2	77	29.1	29.1	29.1
	4	60	22.6	22.6	51.7
	6	50	18.9	18.9	70.6
	8	32	12.1	12.1	82.6
	10	29	10.9	10.9	93.6
	14	2	.8	.8	94.3
	16	2	.8	.8	95.1
	18	1	.4	.4	95.5
	20	4	1.5	1.5	97.0
	24	3	1.1	1.1	98.1
	26	4	1.5	1.5	99.6
	28	1	.4	.4	100.0
	Total	265	100.0	100.0	

Table 4.5 SPSS Frequency Distribution Output for the Recoded Years of Experience Variable

yrs_exper_r		Frequency	Percent	Valid Percent	Cumulative Percent
Valid	2	77	29.1	29.1	29.1
	4	60	22.6	22.6	51.7
	6	50	18.9	18.9	70.6
	8	32	12.1	12.1	82.6
	10	29	10.9	10.9	93.6
	30	17	6.4	6.4	100.0
	Total	265	100.0	100.0	

Reprimand

To examine the number of reprimands employees received, Dr. Mendoza produced a histogram. This is an appropriate visual display of the distribution because the variable is continuous. ****SPSS Tip 7**

Histograms are options in the **Explore** and **Frequencies** procedures. However, the most straightforward way to obtain one is in the **Graphs menu**. Dr. Mendoza selected **Legacy Dialogs**, then **Histogram** (see Figure 4.5). This procedure will produce only the histogram.

SPSS Tip 7: Bar charts and histograms both produce bars whose length represent the number or percentage of cases for each value. It is important, however, to select the appropriate one for your variable. Bar charts are appropriate for categorical variables, either nominal or ordinal. The bars do not touch. Histograms should only be used to display data in interval or ratio variables. The bars in these graphs do touch, implying that the distribution is continuous and the intervals are equal.

After he placed *reprimand* in the dialog box and clicked **OK**, the graph shown in Figure 4.6 appeared. Notice that it contains summary descriptive statistics off to the side.

Labels and increments for the *x*- and *y*-axes are automatically chosen by SPSS. Also, the default is not to display frequencies or percentages on the bars. This may be fine for some purposes, but it is possible to make

Figure 4.5 Graphs → Legacy Dialogs → Histogram

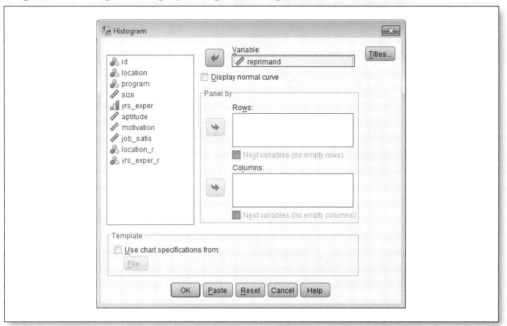

Figure 4.6 SPSS Histogram for the Number of Reprimands Employees Received

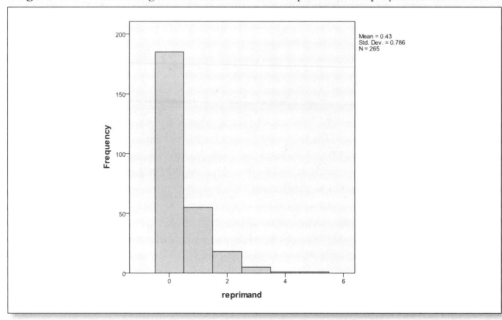

modifications by double-clicking the graph in the output. A new window called the **Chart Editor** will open (see Figure 4.7). Here, many aspects of the histogram can be altered. Notice the menu options at the top of the **Chart Editor. **SPSS Tip 8**

The major alteration Dr. Mendoza made was to add frequencies for each bar. Under the **Elements menu** of the **Chart Editor**, he selected **Show data labels**. Frequencies (or counts, as SPSS calls them) will appear in the middle of the bars, and

SPSS Tip 8: Although Dr. Mendoza used the menu options, it is also possible to click or double-click various aspects of the chart and a window will pop up letting you make those specific changes. So go ahead and play around with the Chart Editor to become familiar with all it can do. Don't worry about making changes you don't want because you can always delete the histogram, quickly make a new one, and start over.

Figure 4.7 Chart Editor

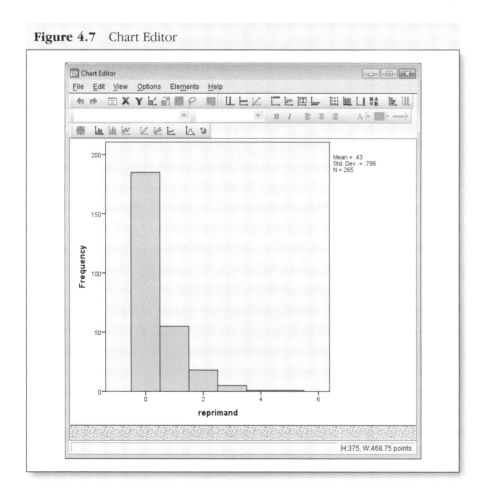

SPSS Tip 9: It's possible that the Show data labels tab will be grayed out, meaning that it cannot be selected. This may happen if a particular aspect of the graph was highlighted (other than the bars). If this is the case, then click on one of the bars in the graph, and the tab can then be selected.

as shown in Figure 4.8, a **Properties** window with the **Data Value Labels** tab will also open. ****SPSS Tip 9**

Because some of the bars are very low, he wanted to put the data label at the top of each bar, so he selected the **Custom Label Position** and clicked the first choice. After clicking the **Apply button**, the counts are moved to the top of each bar. One final change Dr. Mendoza made was to increase the font size for the counts so they can be seen more easily. He selected the **Text Style tab** and changed the font size from 7 to 11. After clicking the **Apply button** to check his alteration, he

Figure 4.8   Chart Editor → Elements → Show Data Labels

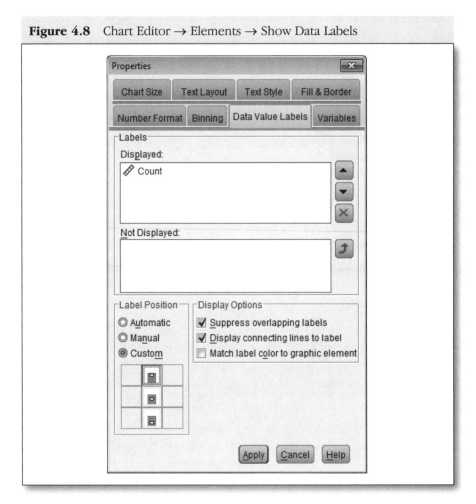

clicked **Close**. Figure 4.9 is his altered histogram. ****SPSS Tip 10**

The distribution is very skewed to the right, which is what Dr. Mendoza suspected. In order to have a variable that is more useful in analysis, he decided to convert this continuous variable into an ordinal variable with only three categories: 0 reprimands, 1 reprimand, and 2 or more reprimands. The

> SPSS Tip 10: The Apply button will let you see your changes on the graph. If you don't like them and want to change again, make the changes and click Apply. When you are satisfied with the modifications, click Close.

recode procedure is the same as the one he used for *yrs_exper*, except with different values. After recoding, he changed the variable's scale of measurement from "scale" (which is SPSS's designation for interval or ratio variables) to "ordinal" in the **Variable View** window of the **Data Editor.**

Because *reprimand_r* is no longer continuous, he does not produce a histogram. A simple frequency table allows him to view the final counts and percentages in each category. Output from the frequency procedure (see Table 4.6) showed that 69.8% of employees had no reprimands, 20.8% had one reprimand, and only 9.4% had two or more reprimands.

Figure 4.9 SPSS Output Showing a Modified Histogram for the Reprimand Variable

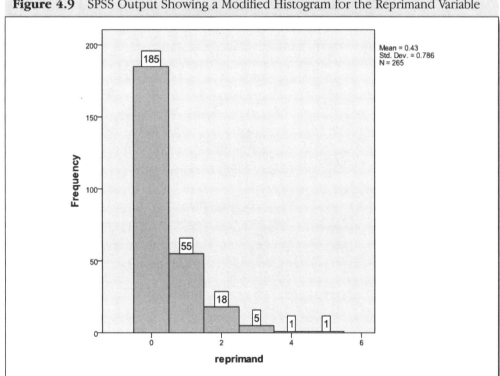

Table 4.6 SPSS Output Showing Frequencies for the Newly Recoded Reprimand Variable

reprimand_r

		Frequency	Percent	Valid Percent	Cumulative Percent
Valid	0	185	69.8	69.8	69.8
	1	55	20.8	20.8	90.6
	2	25	9.4	9.4	100.0
	Total	265	100.0	100.0	

Aptitude

The final distribution to examine is *aptitude*. Using the same procedure as he did for *reprimand*, Dr. Mendoza created a histogram. Because this variable consists of scores on an assessment and will likely have many bars on the histogram, he wanted to overlay the normal curve on top of the graph. To do so, he clicked **Display normal curve** in the **Histogram** dialog box shown in Figure 4.10.

Figure 4.10 Graphs → Legacy Dialogs → Histogram

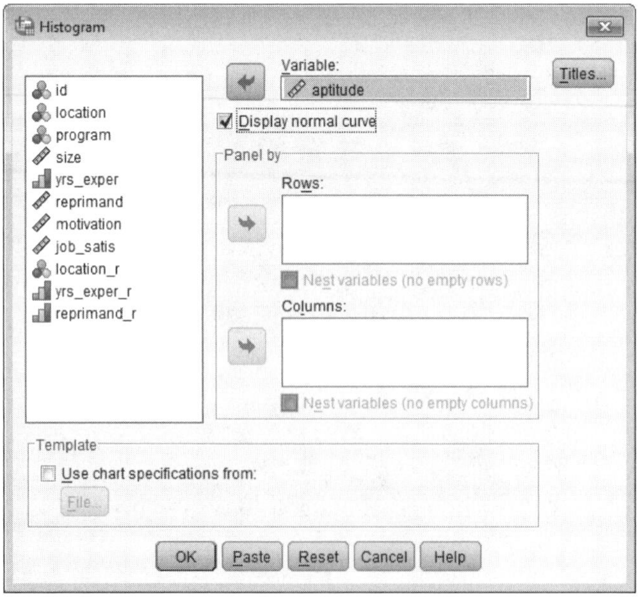

When looking at the histogram in Figure 4.11, Dr. Mendoza concluded that the variable is continuous and thus it will be appropriate to obtain descriptive statistics such as the mean and standard deviation. Also, the overlaid normal curve shows that the values approximately represent a normal distribution. Therefore, Dr. Mendoza will not modify *aptitude* for his study. (See Section 3 for more specific information on how to determine whether a distribution is normal.) The file *module4_jobsatis_final.sav* contains the three recoded variables in this module.

Figure 4.11 SPSS Histogram for the Aptitude Variable

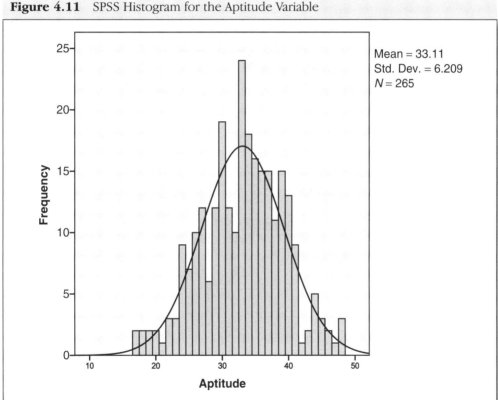

E. Reflection and Additional Decision Making △

Dr. Mendoza is satisfied with the work he has done so far in identifying the appropriate measurement scale for *location*, *yrs_exper*, *reprimand*, and *aptitude*. He is also pleased with the new categories he created for some of these variables. At some point, he will be presenting results from his study to the company. With this in mind, several of the visual displays he created to examine the variables' distribution will come in handy for his presentation. He can use the Crosstabs table to show frequencies and percentages of participants by *location* and *program*. The frequency tables for *yrs_exper* and its recoded variable will be useful for demonstrating that most employees in the study worked for the company 10 years or less. Also, the histogram for *aptitude* will allow the company to visualize the score distribution for the assessment of knowledge and skills.

However, Dr. Mendoza would like to make a few additional alterations to the *x*- and *y*-axes of the histogram for *reprimand*. He believes it is a good visual display that shows how the frequencies decrease quite dramatically after one reprimand. Under the **Edit menu** in the **Chart Editor** he chooses **Select x-axis**. It opens a **Properties** window with the **Scale** tab displayed. Here, he can alter how the values for *reprimand* are displayed on the *x*-axis. The values for Minimum, Maximum, Major Increment, and Origin are chosen automatically by SPSS given the range of data for the variable. He does not want Minimum to be –1 because it is a meaningless value for this variable, so he changed it to 0. He also changed Maximum to 5 and Major Increment to 1 rather than 2, so that each bar in the histogram has the associated value. He did not make any changes to the *y*-axis. He kept the default increment of 50 because the exact frequencies were displayed on each bar.

Dr. Mendoza can now continue examining the remaining two variables in the data file, *motivation* and *aptitude* (see Module 5).

△ F. Writing It Up

After the study is completed, Dr. Mendoza will give the company a full report of its outcomes. To begin, he wrote the following descriptions of *location*, *yrs_exper*, *reprimand*, and *aptitude* as well as the modifications he made to three of these variables. He also plans to insert the visual displays of data that he created.

"A total of 265 employees across all seven locations of the company chose to participate in the study. Currently, 48% of the participants are receiving the job enrichment program, and 52% are not. Three locations (coded as 2, 4, and 5) had relatively small samples of participants compared to the other four locations. These locations encompassed demographically similar regions and were also smaller in overall size, meaning that the total number of employees in each of these locations was less than the total employees in each of the other four locations. For locations 2, 4, and 5, the total sizes were 90, 134, and 70, respectively. For locations 1, 3, 6, and 7, the total sizes were 259, 231, 380, and 450, respectively. For purposes of statistical analysis, the three small locations were collapsed into one location coded as a 9. Percentages of participants in each location of the newly recoded variable are 17%, 20%, 27%, 23%, and 14% (1, 3, 6, 7, and 9, respectively)."

"A frequency distribution for years of experience showed that the large majority of participants were employed in the company for 10 years or less (94%). Thus, all the remaining original categories for this variable were combined into one broad category that represented participants employed for 11 years or more (6%)."

"Reprimand was initially a continuous variable representing the total number of reprimands each participant received during his or her employment with the company. When examining a histogram of the data, it showed a distribution that was skewed in the positive direction; that is, the majority of participants had 0 or 1 reprimand. Only a small number of participants had 2, 3, 4, or 5 reprimands. A decision was made to change the scale of the variable from continuous to ordinal. The newly recoded variable contains only three categories: 0 reprimands, 1 reprimand, and 2 or more reprimands. The percentage of participants in each category are 70%, 21%, and 9%."

"The final variable examined was aptitude. It is a continuous variable that represents participants' prescores on an assessment of knowledge and aptitude. A histogram of the data showed that the distribution appeared to be approximately normal. Scores ranged from 17 to 48, the majority were in the middle of the scale, and the size of each tail was about the same. No modifications were made to the variable at this time."

Reflective Questions △

- How can visual displays of data help determine the scale of measurement for a variable?
- What visual displays are useful for examining values of a nominal or ordinal variable? How are they created and interpreted?
- What visual displays are useful for examining values of a continuous variable? How are they created and interpreted?

△ Extensions

- Make the modifications to the reprimand histogram that Dr. Mendoza described in the "Reflection and Additional Decision Making" section.
- Obtain a data file that contains nominal, ordinal, and continuous variables. Create the appropriate visual displays to examine the distributions, and, if necessary, recode the variables.
- Create a histogram for a continuous variable and practice making a variety of modifications using the Chart Editor in SPSS (e.g., adding labels to bars, changing number and text formats, altering the scale and increments on the axes).
- Find and discuss journal articles that describe the variables' scales of measurement. Also, discuss the types of statistical tests used to analyze data for categorical versus continuous variables.

Identifying and Addressing Outliers

⤜⤛

DATA FILES FOR THIS MODULE

module5_jobsatis.sav
module5_jobsatis_final.sav

⤜⤛

KEY LEARNING OBJECTIVES

The student will learn to

- use summary descriptive statistics (e.g., skewness and kurtosis) to help determine the shape of a continuous variable's distribution
- create and interpret stem-and-leaf plots and boxplots to help determine the shape of a distribution and identify outliers
- create, interpret, and compare a set of boxplots for a continuous variable by groups of a categorical variable
- conduct and compare *t*-tests on data with outliers and data without outliers to determine whether the outliers have an impact on results.

A. Description of Researcher's Study △

This module is a continuation of Dr. Mendoza's collaboration with a company that is conducting experimental research to improve the level of job satisfaction among its employees. In Module 4, he examined the distributions for descriptive variables in his current data file as well as scores on an assessment of knowledge and aptitude. Using frequency tables, crosstabs, and histograms to display information about the distributions, he made modifications to condense the number of groups for the nominal and ordinal variables and to change the measurement scale of one variable from ratio (continuous) to ordinal (categorical).

Here, Dr. Mendoza will examine the final two continuous variables in the data file, which contain scores on two instruments designed to measure motivation and job satisfaction prior to the beginning of the 3-month study. This module demonstrates how he used boxplots to look at the shape of the distributions, identify potential outliers, and decide how outliers will be handled when analyzing the data. Upon completion of the study, the instruments will be administered again to measure potential change in the constructs for employees who received the job enrichment program and to compare results to those who did not receive the program.

△ B. A Look at the Data

The data file used in this module (*module5_jobsatis.sav*) contains all nine original variables in Dr. Mendoza's initial file plus the newly modified variables he created in Module 4. There are 265 cases (participants) and a total of 12 variables. As before, each case represents one employee who agreed to be in the study. Employees are in one of seven geographic locations of the company. A total of 127 participants are receiving the job enrichment program, and the remaining 138 participants are in the control group. Table 5.1 lists each variable and its description.

Table 5.1 Variables in the Job Satisfaction Data File

Variable Name	Description
id	numerical identifier for each participant 1 to 265
location	geographic location of the company in which the participant is employed, coded 1 to 7
program	0 = no (participant is not receiving the program, he or she is in the control group); 1 = yes (participant is receiving the program)
size	total number of employees in each geographic location of the company across all its sectors. This variable is a constant value for participants within the same location.
yrs_exper	total number of years of experience within the company for each participant. Codes for the categories are 2 = 0 to 2 years of experience, 4 = 3 to 4 years of experience, 6 = 5 to 6 years of experience, 8 = 7 to 8 years of experience, 10 = 9 to 10 years of experience, and so on until the final code of 32 = 31 years of experience or more.

Variable Name	Description
reprimand	total number of reprimands received by each employee during his or her total years of experience with the company
aptitude	score on an aptitude instrument prior to implementing the study
motivation	score on a motivation survey prior to implementing the study
job_satis	score on a job satisfaction survey prior to implementing the study
location_r	revised variable with only five codes (1, 3, 6, 7, and 9). Due to the small number of participants in locations 2, 4, and 5, these locations were combined and assigned a new code of 9.
yrs_exper_r	revised variable with only six codes (2, 4, 6, 8, 10, and 30). The first original five codes remained unchanged. Due to small sample sizes in the remaining codes, they were combined into a new code of 30 that represents participants with 11 or more years of experience.
reprimand_r	revised variable is now an ordinal variable with three levels: 0 reprimands, 1 reprimand, and 2 or more reprimands. Original values of 2, 3, and beyond were collapsed into one level due to small sample sizes.

C. Planning and Decision Making △

To examine prescores on the two constructs of motivation and job satisfaction, Dr. Mendoza decided to create boxplots in SPSS. There are several beneficial features of this type of graphic display. First, it allows you to view aspects of the distribution in a way that histograms do not. The length of the "box" spans the middle 50% of the values, that is, from the 1st quartile (25th percentile) to the 3rd quartile (75th percentile), and the median appears as a solid line in the box. In a distribution with no outliers, the length of the two "whiskers" represent the bottom 25% of values and the top 25% of values. When a distribution is approximately normal, the median will be in the center of the "box" and the two "whiskers" will be equal in length. The extent to which this does not occur indicates potential positive or negative skewness or kurtosis.

A second beneficial feature of the boxplot over the histogram is that it can identify potential outliers. Outliers are values at the lower or

**1 Dr. Mendoza says: "There is not a hard and fast rule for identifying outliers in a distribution. SPSS uses one particular method, but others exist. For example, standardized values can be used with a general guideline that absolute *z* values larger than 3 are considered to be outliers. However, for large samples, some statisticians use a cutoff *z* value of 4 or greater, and for small sample sizes, a cutoff of 2.5" (Stevens, 2009).

upper end that lie apart from the distribution. These values are identified on the box plot as cases below or above the end of each "whisker." More specifically, SPSS identifies outliers as cases that fall more than 1.5 box lengths from the lower or upper hinge of the box. The box length is sometimes called the "hspread" and is defined as the distance from one hinge of the box to the other hinge. It is also called the interquartile range. SPSS further distinguishes "extreme" outliers by identifying values more than 3 box lengths from either hinge. ****Dr. Mendoza (1)**

Statistical inferential tests can be quite sensitive to outliers, often because the calculations rely on squared deviations from the mean. One or two values that are far from the mean can alter the results considerably. Therefore, if outliers are identified, Dr. Mendoza must decide how to handle them. First, he will go back to the data collection instrumentation to determine whether the outlier was due to a data entry error or an instrumentation error. The former can be corrected, and the latter probably should be deleted. However, if the outlier was not due to one of these reasons and was an actual value obtained from the participant, then he has a few options. The most undesirable option is to delete the case from further analysis. This is not the best solution because the value is a legitimate case in the data file, and with large samples, it can be expected that a few outliers may occur and probably will not greatly impact results. Another option is to conduct data analysis with and without the outlier(s) and compare the two outcomes. If results are the same, then the outlier(s) did not have a great influence in the distribution of the variable. If results are not the same, both outcomes can be reported. A third option is to transform the variable and hopefully reduce the influence of the outlier(s). Finally, outliers could be recoded into the lowest (or highest) value that is not determined to be an outlier by SPSS (or any other method that is used).

Dr. Mendoza will obtain the boxplots for *motivation* and *job_satis* using the **Explore procedure**. Although there are a few other ways to get boxplots in SPSS, he chose this procedure because it produces descriptive statistics such as skewness and kurtosis as well as a stem-and-leaf plot, which is another type of visual display of data.

D. Using SPSS to Address Issues and Prepare Data △

Motivation

A visual scroll through the data file is sometimes the first indication a researcher has that potential outliers may exist. For *motivation*, Dr. Mendoza noticed that a few low scores seemed to stand apart from the rest of the distribution. To help him determine whether these low values are actually outliers, he obtained a boxplot under the **Analyze menu**. Selecting **Descriptive Statistics** and **Explore** produced the dialog box shown in Figure 5.1. He placed *motivation* in the **Dependent List box.**

Figure 5.1 Analyze → Descriptive Statistics → Explore

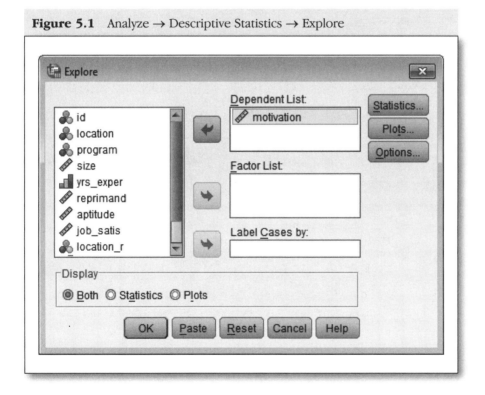

Dr. Mendoza kept the default settings under the **Statistics** and **Plots buttons** as is. The **Options** button offers different ways to treat missing values, but he has none in his study, so he does not need the options. As shown in Figure 5.2, the default for **Statistics** is **Descriptives**. This will produce a variety of descriptive summary statistics for *motivation*, including the skewness and kurtosis values.

Figure 5.2 Statistics in Explore

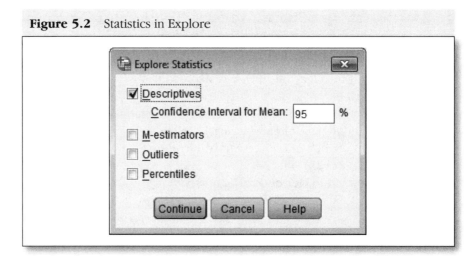

For **Plots**, the default is to produce a boxplot and a stem-and-leaf plot, as shown in Figure 5.3.

Figure 5.3 Plots in Explore

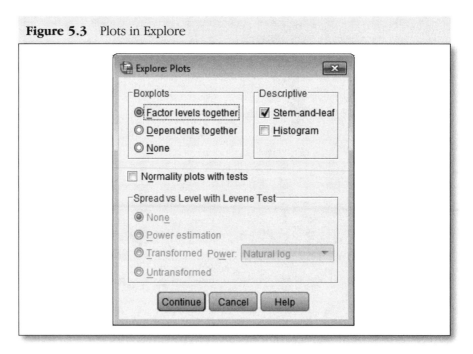

After he clicked **OK** in the **Explore** dialog box, Dr. Mendoza obtained output that includes a table of values, a stem-and-leaf plot, and a boxplot. Table 5.2 displays the summary descriptive statistics. He noticed that the mean, median, and trimmed mean are nearly identical. This is one indication that the distribution is not skewed in one direction or another. To examine skewness and kurtosis, Dr. Mendoza used the standard errors provided for each value in order to obtain standardized values for each statistic. Dividing skewness by the standard error (–.602 divided by .150) yields a standardized value of –4.01, which does indicate a somewhat negatively skewed distribution. In a similar fashion, he divided kurtosis by its standard error (1.891 divided by .298) to obtain a standardized value of 6.35, which indicates a peaked, or slender and narrow, distribution. **SPSS Tip 1** Dr. Mendoza kept these values in mind as he looked at the next section of output from the **Explore procedure.**

> SPSS Tip 1: A distribution with a considerably high positive kurtosis value is called leptokurtic, meaning that it is slender and narrow. A distribution with a considerably high negative kurtosis value is called platykurtic, meaning flat or broad. Low absolute values close to 0 for kurtosis are said to be mesokurtic or intermediate.

Table 5.2   First Portion of SPSS Explore Output: Summary Statistics for Motivation

Descriptives			Statistic	Std. Error
Motivation	Mean		20.02	.221
	95% Confidence Interval for Mean	Lower Bound	19.58	
		Upper Bound	20.45	
	5% Trimmed Mean		20.11	
	Median		20.00	
	Variance		12.932	
	Std. Deviation		3.596	
	Minimum		4	
	Maximum		30	
	Range		26	
	Interquartile Range		4	
	Skewness		-.602	.150
	Kurtosis		1.891	.298

Figure 5.4 displays the stem-and-leaf plot. The stems represent the two-digit data values for *motivation*. Each leaf represents a case with that particular data value. The frequency column represents the total number of cases

Figure 5.4 Second Portion of SPSS Output From Explore: Stem-and-Leaf
Plot for Motivation

```
motivation Stem-and-Leaf Plot

 Frequency Stem & Leaf

 5.00 Extremes  (=<9.0)
 1.00  12 . 0
 4.00  13 . 0000
 5.00  14 . 00000
 8.00  15 . 00000000
11.00  16 . 00000000000
25.00  17 . 0000000000000000000000000
18.00  18 . 000000000000000000
30.00  19 . 000000000000000000000000000000
39.00  20 . 000000000000000000000000000000000000000
27.00  21 . 000000000000000000000000000
36.00  22 . 000000000000000000000000000000000000
20.00  23 . 00000000000000000000
13.00  24 . 0000000000000
 7.00  25 . 0000000
 7.00  26 . 0000000
 6.00  27 . 000000
 2.00  28 . 00
 1.00 Extremes  (>=30.0)

Stem width: 1
Each leaf: 1 case(s)
```

SPSS Tip 2: Because the leaves represent the number of cases for each data value, a stem-and-leaf plot provides a visual display of the variable's distribution (similar to a histogram) when turned 90 degrees on its side.

for each data value shown in the stem and leaf. **SPSS Tip 2** This plot also indicates whether outliers are present in the data. Here, it shows five "extreme" values at the lower end of the distribution that are less than or equal to 9, and one "extreme" value at the upper end of the distribution that is greater than or equal to 30.

Finally, the boxplot in Figure 5.5 is produced. Dr. Mendoza saw the five outliers at the lower end of the motivation scale and the one outlier at the upper end. The values next to each represent the case numbers. ****SPSS Tip 3** Five of the six values are denoted by a circle. Recall earlier (from Section C in this module) that SPSS makes a distinction between outliers that are more than 1.5 box lengths from one hinge of the box (using a circle) and outliers that are more than 3 box lengths from a hinge (using an asterisk).

The lowest value came from case/id number 19. It had a value of 4. Four additional values were also identified as outliers: case/id numbers 25, 13, 91, and 12.

SPSS Tip 3: Prior to running the Explore procedure, Dr. Mendoza's file had been sorted by id in ascending order, which is a sequential match with the case numbers in SPSS from 1 to 265. If the file was sorted in a different way, then the SPSS case number shown on the boxplot would not coincide with the id variable in the data file. This is not a problem, but when going back to the data file to examine outlying cases, care must be taken to ensure that you are looking at the correct case and not mistaking the value in the id variable for the actual SPSS case number.

Figure 5.5   Third Portion of SPSS Explore Output: Boxplot for Motivation

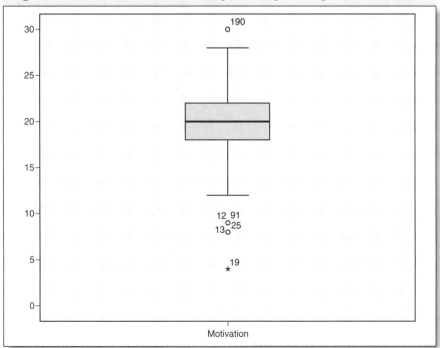

Their values for *motivation* were 8, 9, 9, and 9, respectively. Although it was not initially apparent to Dr. Mendoza when he visually scrolled through his data file, the highest value of 30 for case number 190 was also identified as an outlier.

To decide how to handle the outliers, Dr. Mendoza's first step was to go back to the data collection materials and ensure that there were no data entry or instrument errors. There were not, so this indicates that the values are legitimate. He would rather not delete the cases because the sample is somewhat large, and it is to be expected that a few values will appear in the far lower and upper ends of the distribution. Although these cases were identified as outliers according to SPSS specifications, he wanted to check their standardized values. Under the **Analyze menu**, he selected **Descriptive Statistics** and **Descriptives**, put *motivation* in the **Variable(s)** box, and clicked the **Save standardized values as variables** box. This created a new variable, *Zmotivation,* that contains the corresponding z values for all values in *motivation*. Using a cutoff value of 4, only one of the cases was identified as an outlier. Case number 19 had a score of 4 for *motivation* and a z value of –4.45 for *Zmotivation*. (For a more detailed description of this SPSS procedure, refer to Module 2 in Section 1.)

Dr. Mendoza was still interested in conducting an analysis with and without the outliers that SPSS identified. If results are the same (that is, produce similar statistical decisions), then the outliers are not influential in that particular analysis. If results differ, then he will report both sets of results. Even though he does not have the full set of data because the study is not yet complete, he decided to conduct an independent *t*-test to determine if the prescores on *motivation* are statistically similar for the two groups of *program*. His hypothesis is that there is no difference between the average motivation prescores for participants in the program versus participants not in the program.

In order to conduct the *t*-test without outliers, Dr. Mendoza selected only those cases that are nonoutliers. To do so, he used the **Select Cases procedure** under the **Data menu**. (Refer to Module 2 in Section 1 for a detailed description and example of the use of the Select Cases procedure.) After he clicked the **If condition is satisfied** button, he created the logical expression in the dialog box shown in Figure 5.6 to tell SPSS that he did not want cases with id values equal to 190, 12, 91, 13, 25, and 19 to be included in the analysis. After he clicked **OK**, a variable called *filter_$* (the default name) was

SPSS Tip 4: If he didn't create this variable, Dr. Mendoza would need to recreate the logical expression and rerun Select Cases each time he wanted to conduct analysis with and without outliers. This is time-consuming and can lead to errors if any part of the expression is retyped incorrectly.

Figure 5.6 Data → Select Cases

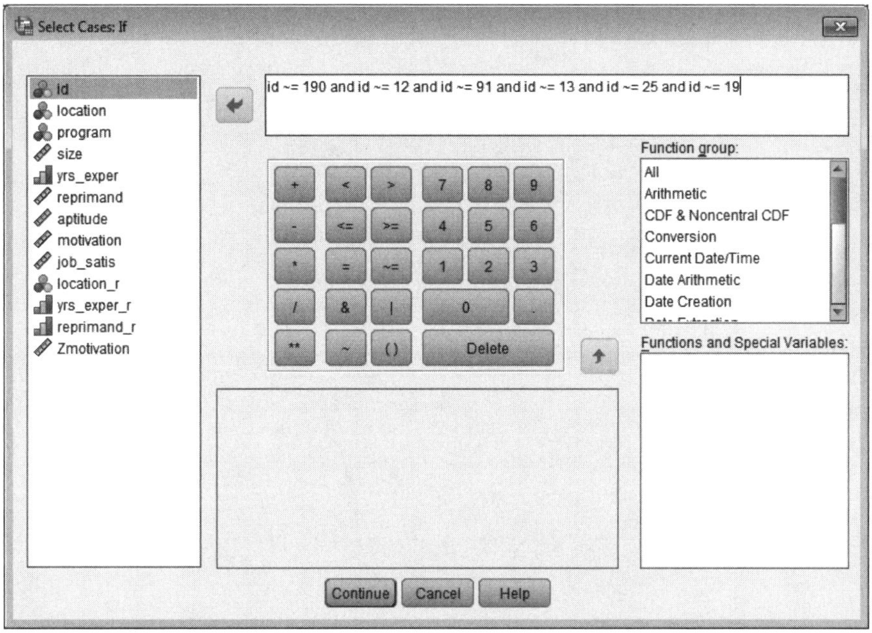

added to the file. It contains values of 0 and 1. Dr. Mendoza renamed this variable *motivation_nonoutliers* in case he decides to use it again in future analysis. This new variable as well as *Zmotivation* are included in the file *module5_jobsatis_final.sav*. **SPSS Tip 4**

Dr. Mendoza was curious about the nature of the distribution without the outliers ($n = 259$), so prior to running the *t*-test, he decided to run the **Explore procedure** again. He found that it was no longer negatively skewed or peaked. Standardized values for skewness and kurtosis were .013 and −.391, respectively. Also, the box plot in Figure 5.7 indicates no outliers, and the distribution looks approximately normal.

Now Dr. Mendoza performed the *t*-test by choosing **Compare Means** and **Independent-Samples T Test** under the **Analyze menu**. The dependent variable (**Test Variable,** as SPSS calls it) is *motivation*, and the independent variable (**Grouping Variable,** as SPSS calls it) is *program* (see Figure 5.8). **SPSS Tip 5**

SPSS Tip 5: Do not make the mistake of using *motivation_nonoutliers* as the dependent variable in this *t*-test. If you do, no results will be produced because the values for this variable are constant (all 1). The *motivation_nonoutliers* variable is only used in this context to select cases that are not outliers.

Figure 5.7 SPSS Boxplot for the Distribution of Motivation After Outliers Were Removed

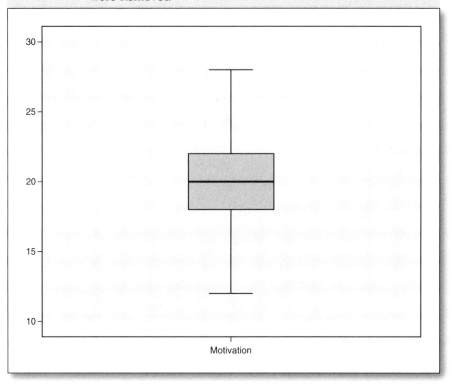

Figure 5.8 Analyze → Compare Means → Independent-Samples T Test

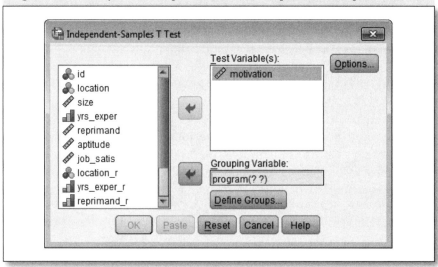

Codes for *program* must be defined. He clicked **Define Groups**, and it opened the box shown in Figure 5.9. He entered the two codes (0, 1) he used for *program*.

Figure 5.9 Define Groups in *T*-Test

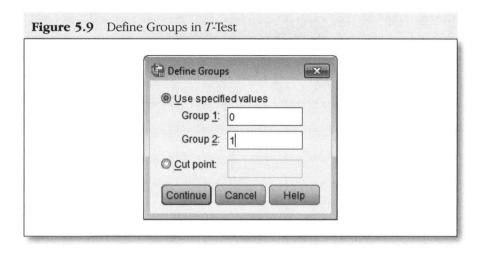

The first table of output produced by the *t*-test is shown in Table 5.3. As a double-check that the *t*-test was conducted only on the nonoutliers, Dr. Mendoza made sure that the total *N* for both groups sums to 259, and it does. He noticed that the group means are quite similar to each other, approximately 20, which likely indicates no significant difference between the two means.

Table 5.3 SPSS Output for Descriptive Statistics of the *t*-Test on Motivation Without Outliers

	Group Statistics				
	Program	N	Mean	Std. Deviation	Std. Error Mean
Motivation	0 no	135	20.26	3.357	.289
	1 yes	124	20.16	2.892	.260

The second set of output from the *t*-test is not reprinted here. The *t* statistic and *p* value indicate that the difference between the average motivation score for participants who are not receiving the job enrichment program compared to participants who are receiving the program was not statistically significant [$t(257) = .251, p = .802$].

Dr. Mendoza's final step for *motivation* was to conduct another *t*-test using the full sample with outliers. Before doing so, however, he went to the **Data menu**, chose **Select Cases**, and clicked the box next to **All cases** to tell SPSS to run the analysis on all 265 cases. Then he conducted the *t*-test, and the statistical results led to the same conclusion. There is no significant difference between motivation scores for employees who are not receiving the program and those who are [$t(263) = -.173, p = .862$]. The means for the two groups (19.98 and 20.06, respectively) were nearly identical to the means produced without the outliers. The overall conclusion is that the outliers are not affecting the outcomes of the *t*-test.

Job Satisfaction

The final variable Dr. Mendoza examined in this module was *job_satis*. Results after running the **Explore procedure** (in the same way he did for *motivation*) are in Table 5.4 and Figures 5.10 and 5.11. The descriptive statistics indicate a negatively skewed distribution, but no kurtosis. Using the values in Table 5.4 for each statistic and its standard error, he calculated the standardized values to be –6.707 for skewness and 2.218 for kurtosis.

Table 5.4 First Portion of SPSS Explore Output: Summary Statistics for Job Satisfaction

Descriptives

			Statistic	Std. Error
job_satis	Mean		16.59	.266
	95% Confidence Interval for Mean	Lower Bound	16.07	
		Upper Bound	17.11	
	5% Trimmed Mean		16.90	
	Median		18.00	
	Variance		18.713	
	Std. Deviation		4.326	
	Minimum		2	
	Maximum		23	
	Range		21	
	Interquartile Range		6	
	Skewness		-1.006	.150
	Kurtosis		.661	.298

The stem-and-leaf plot in Figure 5.10 indicates five outliers that are less than or equal to 4. The distribution of the leaves in the plot shows some negative skewness because there are larger clusters of values in the upper portion of the scale and fewer values in the lower portion.

Figure 5.10   Second Portion of SPSS Explore Output: Stem-and-Leaf Plot for Job Satisfaction

```
job_satis Stem-and-Leaf Plot

 Frequency Stem & Leaf

   5.00 Extremes  (=<4.0)
   2.00  5 . 00
   2.00  6 . 00
   2.00  7 . 00
   1.00  8 . 0
   6.00  9 . 000000
   6.00 10 . 000000
  15.00 11 . 000000000000000
  11.00 12 . 00000000000
   8.00 13 . 00000000
  15.00 14 . 000000000000000
  16.00 15 . 0000000000000000
  15.00 16 . 000000000000000
  26.00 17 . 00000000000000000000000000
  24.00 18 . 000000000000000000000000
  28.00 19 . 0000000000000000000000000000
  38.00 20 . 00000000000000000000000000000000000000
  28.00 21 . 0000000000000000000000000000
  14.00 22 . 00000000000000
   3.00 23 . 000

 Stem width: 1
 Each leaf: 1 case(s)
```

The boxplot in Figure 5.11 shows a somewhat negatively skewed distribution. The upper 50% of the distribution (from the median line to the end of the top whisker) is a narrower portion of the *job_satis* scale compared to the lower 50% of the distribution (from the median

Figure 5.11   Third Portion of SPSS Explore Output: Boxplot for Job Satisfaction

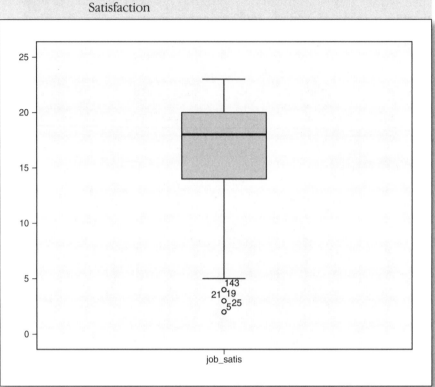

line to the end of the bottom whisker). The plot also shows the case numbers of the five outliers. As before, Dr. Mendoza had the file sorted by *id* in ascending order so that the case numbers coincide with the *id* values for participants. He checked cases 143, 25, 21, 19, and 5 in his data file and found they had values for *job_satis* of 4, 4, 3, 3, and 2, respectively.

He also noticed that four of the five outliers were from Location 1, the other was from Location 6. This result made Dr. Mendoza curious about the shape of each individual *job_satis* distribution across *location*. Therefore, he decided to run the **Explore procedure** again in order to obtain a boxplot for each location. To do so, he placed the revised location variable, *location_r*, in the **Factor List** box in the **Explore** dialog box shown in Figure 5.12.

The five boxplots appear in Figure 5.13. When looking at these distributions for *job_satis* by *location_r*, Dr. Mendoza noticed additional

Figure 5.12 Analyze → Desctiptive Statistics → Explore

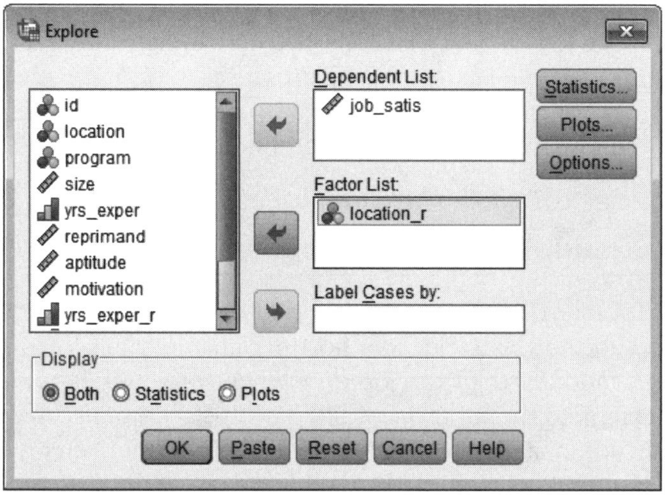

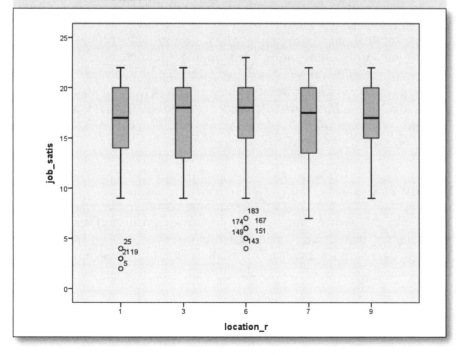

Figure 5.13 SPSS Boxplots Displaying Distributions for Job Satisfaction by Location

outliers. Within Location 6, there are six outliers (cases 183, 174, 167, 151, 149, and 143), and only one of them was previously identified as an outlier on the entire set of data. These outliers had values of 7, 6, 6, 5, 5, and 4, respectively. Three locations had no outliers. Dr. Mendoza has identified an important aspect of the prescores for *job_satis*. When post-data at the end of the study become available, he will need to ensure that analysis is conducted with and without the outliers.

△ E. Reflection and Additional Decision Making

Dr. Mendoza made some interesting discoveries about the prescores for *motivation* and *job_satis*. He will go through the same steps described here in this module when the job enrichment program ends and all participants complete the motivation and job satisfaction instruments again. Recall that additional data are being collected during and after the study in the form of interviews with participants and supervisors, assessment of job productivity, and an evaluation of job skills and knowledge. Based on the information he obtained in the preliminary steps described in this module, especially for *job_satis*, he believes that results across locations are likely to be quite interesting.

In this module, he examined univariate outliers, which are outliers on one variable. If some of his research questions require a multiple regression analysis to determine which factors impact job satisfaction, he will need to examine multivariate outliers (defined as outliers on two or more variables). Procedures are available to identify cases that have unusual combinations of values on multiple variables as well as cases that are influential data points. (See Section 3, Module 7, for another research scenario that demonstrates how to examine these types of cases.)

△ F. Writing It Up

Dr. Mendoza's written summary of the outlier portion of his investigation on the distribution of variables is provided below. He will also include the boxplots in Figure 5.13 in his report to the company because they show a great deal of information about the five *job_satis* distributions by location.

"Skewness and kurtosis values as well as boxplots were obtained to examine the distributions for two variables that examined motivation and job satisfaction prior to beginning the job enrichment program. Motivation contained five outliers at the lower end of the scale with values of 9 or less and one outlier at the upper end with a value of 30. Based on the standardized values for skewness (−4.01) and kurtosis (6.35) the distribution was somewhat negatively skewed and peaked. After the cases identified as outliers were removed from the sample, the distribution for motivation was examined again. No outliers were identified and the distribution appeared to be approximately normal which was supported by low skewness and kurtosis standardized values (.013 and −.391, respectively).

"To determine whether the outliers influenced results for a *t*-test on motivation, this inferential statistical test was conducted twice, with outliers (i.e., the entire sample) and without outliers. Results were nearly identical. Both analyses concluded there was no significant difference between average motivation prescores for participants who experience the job enrichment program and participants who do not. Both p-values were above a significance level of .05 (p = .802 without outliers and p = .862 with outliers).

"For job satisfaction, the boxplot showed a skewed distribution in the negative direction with a standardized skewness value of −6.707. Scores were clustered at the upper end of the scale, and there were five outliers less than or equal to 4. All but one of these outliers came from location 1. Therefore, another analysis of the job satisfaction distribution was conducted by location. An individual boxplot was produced for each location and two locations (1 and 6) showed a cluster of outliers at the bottom of the scale. This indicates that prior to the beginning of the study, there was a very low level of job satisfaction for a small subset of employees at these two locations. As additional data become available upon conclusion of the study, analyses will determine whether these outlying cases, as well as other outliers that may occur on post scores of motivation and job satisfaction, will have an impact on the study's outcomes."

Reflective Questions △

- How can skewness and kurtosis values be used to describe the shape of a continuous variable's distribution?
- What is the process for creating stem-and-leaf plots and boxplots? What information do these visual displays provide about a variable's distribution?

- Why is it important to identify outliers?
- After identifying outliers, how are they handled in future data analysis?

△ Extensions

- Dr. Mendoza created a variable to identify outliers and nonoutliers for motivation. Create a variable to identify outliers and nonoutliers for job satisfaction.
- Discuss standardized z values. Do you think Dr. Mendoza should be concerned about outliers for job satisfaction? Find the z scores for this variable. How many are above 3, above 4? Can high standardized values occur in a normal distribution? Look through research and statistics books to find out what researchers and statisticians say about outliers and how to handle them.
- Dr. Mendoza conducted t-tests on motivation to compare results with and without outliers. Conduct t-tests to determine if means for job satisfaction prescores differ for employees who are participating in the program versus employees who are not. Compare the results from the two t-tests (one with outliers and one without outliers). Do the outliers have an impact on the results?
- Examine descriptive statistics (e.g., mean, median, mode, skewness, kurtosis) for continuous variables in other research studies and discuss the information they provide about the distribution. For instance, what can differences in the values for mean, median, and mode tell you about the shape of a distribution?

△ Additional Resources for Section 2: The Nature and Distribution of Variables

Abu-Bader, S. H. (2010). *Advanced and multivariate statistical methods for social science research with a complete SPSS guide*. Chicago: Lyceum. (For Module 5, see Section 2 on outliers.)

Glass, G. V, & Hopkins, K. D. (1996). *Statistical methods in education and psychology* (3rd ed.). Needham Heights, MA: Allyn & Bacon. (For Module 4, see Chapters 2 and 3 on variables, their scales and measurements, and visual display of data.)

Gravetter, F. J., & Wallnau, L. B. (2013). *Statistics for the behavioral sciences* (9th ed.). Wadsworth. (See Chapter 1 for more information on scales of measurement.)

Holcomb, Z. C. (2009). *SPSS basics: Techniques for a first course in statistics* (2nd ed.). Glendale, CA: Pyrczak.

Huizingh, E. (2008). *Applied statistics with SPSS*. Thousand Oaks, CA: Sage. (For Module 3, see Section 9 on computation and classification of variables, which contains details about each SPSS function that computes new variables, what it does, and the information necessary to supply.)

IBM. (2011). *SPSS Statistics 20 core systems user's guide*. Author. (A pdf version can be obtained from http://www.ibm.com)

Kinnear, P. R., & Gray, C. D. (2009). *SPSS 16 made simple*. Sussex, UK: Psychology Press.

Kulas, J. T. (2009). SPSS *essentials: Managing and analyzing social sciences data*. San Francisco: Jossey-Bass.

Mertler, C. A., & Vannatta, R. A. (2005). *Advanced and multivariate statistical methods: Practical application and interpretation* (3rd ed.). Los Angeles: Pyrczak. (For Module 5, see Chapter 3, which gives information on identifying and handling outliers.)

INTRODUCTION TO SECTION 3

Model Assumptions

T his section describes the preliminary data analysis that Dr. Novak, a social sciences researcher, conducted in her study of life domain constructs on a sample of college students. The scales and inventories she administered measure ego identity status, masculine and feminine gender roles, locus of control, motivation, hyperfemininity, depression, and aggression, to name a few. Because of the wealth of information that now resides in her data file, she has several sets of analyses planned to investigate a variety of questions in this field of research. The first aspect of her study is to simply describe and compare scores on each instrument in terms of student characteristics such as gender and identity status. To this end, she will compare group means using *t*-tests and analysis of variance. After obtaining this overall view of data, one portion of her research focuses on studying the nature of relationships among the life domains. One of the research questions uses a multiple regression to determine the amount of variance in depression scores explained by several measures of the life domain constructs.

As a well-trained and experienced researcher, Dr. Novak knows the importance of evaluating the assumptions of statistical tests before making inferences and conclusions about the data. If assumptions are not met, then the probability statements attached to the results may be invalid. She also knows there is a unique set of assumptions associated with each type of statistical model. Module 6 describes how she evaluated the model assumptions for testing mean differences. Module 7 describes her evaluation of model assumptions for multiple regression analysis.

Module 6: Evaluating Model Assumptions △ for Testing Mean Differences

Dr. Novak used her sample of 1,088 college students when comparing mean score differences on the constructs by student characteristics. This module describes how she evaluated the model assumptions of independence, normality, and equal variances for this aspect of her analysis. Specifically, it shows how she tested assumptions for a set of four *t*-tests on motivation, a one-factor analysis of variance on hyperfemininity, and a two-factor analysis of variance on locus of control. When assumptions were violated, the module describes how Dr. Novak used alternative procedures to further examine the validity of results, including modifications of the test statistic, use of nonparametric tests, and a data transformation.

△ Module 7: Evaluating Model Assumptions for Multiple Regression Analysis

The multiple regression used in this module examines a subset of the full sample. The subset consists of 283 female students who were administered a hyperfemininity scale in addition to the other instruments. Dr. Novak evaluated the assumptions of linearity among variables, independence of residuals, normality of residuals, and homoscedasticity of residuals. She also examined other important aspects of multiple regression, such as multicollinearity and the identification of outliers and influential data points.

Evaluating Model Assumptions for Testing Mean Differences

❧❦
DATA FILES FOR THIS MODULE

module6_lifedomains.sav
module6_lifedomains_final.sav

❧❦

KEY LEARNING OBJECTIVES

The student will learn to

- examine model assumptions for *t*-tests and analyses of variance (independence, normality, and homogeneity of variance)
- conduct and interpret results from nonparametric tests (Mann-Whitney and Kruskal-Wallis)
- produce modifications of the *F*-test statistic (Welch and Brown-Forsythe)
- transform a continuous variable using the square root transformation
- compare the alternate analyses above to results from the original *t*- or *F*-test and make a conclusion about the validity of its results.

A. Description of Researcher's Study △

Dr. Novak is currently investigating a series of life domain constructs on a large sample of college students, the majority of whom are young adults. To measure the constructs, she collected data through a series of inventories and scales on ego identity status, masculine and feminine gender roles, locus of control, motivation, hyperfemininity, depression, and aggression, to name a few. The first aspect of her study is broad in nature. She wants to determine whether average scores on the instruments differ significantly across participant characteristics such as gender and identity status. Therefore, her statistical analysis involves the use of *t*-tests and analysis of variance (ANOVA). These inferential tests examine differences between mean scores on a continuous dependent variable across groups of categorical independent variables.

Prior to making any conclusions about the sample means and *p* values produced by the statistical tests, she must determine whether certain assumptions about the model are satisfied. This is a very important beginning step when using inferential statistics. If assumptions are not tenable (i.e., not met), then the probability results obtained from the test may not be valid. Assumptions for *t*-tests and ANOVAs state that participant observations are independent from each other (independence), scores on the dependent variable are normally distributed (normality), and variances for each group of the independent variable are equal (homogeneity of variance).

This module describes how she evaluated and addressed potential violations of the assumptions for a portion of the statistical tests she conducted. First, she tested assumptions for a set of four *t*-tests that examine gender differences on motivation subscales from an inventory of learning processes. Second, she tested assumptions for a one-factor ANOVA to determine whether mean scores on a hyperfemininity instrument differed across four ideology identity status groups. Finally, the third analysis demonstrates testing assumptions for a two-factor ANOVA in which mean scores on the locus of control instrument were examined for the main effects of gender, ideology identity status, and the interaction of the two independent variables. For some analyses, the assumptions were met. In other analyses, when the assumptions were violated, Dr. Novak used alternative procedures to further examine the validity of results, such as modifications of the test statistic, the use of nonparametric procedures, and transformation of the dependent variable. To reach a conclusion about the validity of the *t*-test and ANOVA, she compared results of all analyses.

Some of the procedures described here are similar to those in Section 2, such as obtaining skewness and kurtosis values and creating histograms. However, the reasons for using them differ. For example, in Module 4 of Section 2, the purpose for looking at the data distributions was to determine each variable's measurement scale so that appropriate statistical tests could be selected in future analyses. Here, in Modules 6 and 7, the purpose for examining data distributions is to ensure that the assumptions of a particular statistical model are met.

B. A Look at the Data △

A portion of Dr. Novak's complete data file is used to demonstrate the analyses in this module. The data file (*module6_lifedomains.sav*) contains 1,088 cases and 10 variables. As shown in Table 6.1, seven variables represent data from the life domain instruments, including locus of control, hyperfemininity, motivation, and ego identity status. Six of these variables are continuous and one is categorical. The other three variables indicate the participant number, gender, and whether the participant was administered the hyperfemininity scale.

Table 6.1 Variables in the Life Domains Study Data File

Variable Name	Description
partno	participant number is a numerical identifier for each study participant
gender	gender (1 = female, 2 = male)
hypfem_taken	this variable indicates whether the participant received the Hyperfemininity Scale (0 = participant did not receive the instrument, 1 = participant received the instrument and has a total score on it). Only a subsample of female students was administered this instrument.
locsum	total score on items from a locus of control survey. There were 29 items on the survey, 6 of which were filler items with responses not included in the sum. Each item on the survey had two options, 0 and 1; thus, the possible range for *locsum* is 0 to 23.
hypfem	total score on items from the Hyperfemininity Scale. There were 26 items on the survey. Each item had three options, 0, 1, and 2; thus, the possible range for *hypfem* is 0 to 52.
imai	total score for the Motivation Academic Interest subscale on the Inventory of Learning Processes instrument. The subscale contains five items, each with two options, 0 and 1. The possible range for *imai* is 0 to 5.
impr	total score for the Motivation Personal Responsibility subscale on the Inventory of Learning Processes instrument. The subscale contains five items, each with two options, 0 and 1. The possible range for *impr* is 0 to 5.

(Continued)

Table 6.1 (Continued)

Variable Name	Description
ime	total score for the Motivation Effort subscale on the Inventory of Learning Processes instrument. The subscale contains five items, each with two options, 0 and 1. The possible range for *ime* is 0 to 5.
iom	sum of the three motivation subscale scores (*imai*, *impr*, *ime*) on the Inventory of Learning Processes instrument. These total scores represent Overall Motivation. The possible range for *iom* is 0 to 15.
idstatus	represents the final/dominant identity status for ideology on the Objective Measure of Ego-Identity Status. There are four categories: 1 = diffusion, 2 = foreclosure, 3 = moratorium, 4 = achievement.

△ C. Planning and Decision Making

The Assumptions

For each of her statistical tests involving mean differences (*t*-tests and ANOVAs), Dr. Novak knows there are three model assumptions she must evaluate: independence, normality, and homogeneity of variance.

The assumption of independence states that observations are independent of each other. One participant's score on a variable is not influenced by (or related to) another participant's score. The normality assumption states that the continuous scores in each population group of a categorical variable are normally distributed around the mean for that group. **Dr. Novak(1)** The third assumption of homogeneity of variance indicates that the variances of scores in each population group of a categorical variable are equal to each other.

> ****1 Dr. Novak says:** "A common misconception when testing this assumption is to examine the distribution for all data rather than separately for each group of the independent variable. In order to conclude that the assumption is satisfied, the data for each sample group must be examined for normality."

What Dr. Novak Knows About the Assumptions and Their Impact on Validity

To begin planning her approach, Dr. Novak reflected on what she knows about these assumptions and their impact on the validity of *t*-tests and ANOVAs when violated. First, the independence assumption can be examined by considering the study's design. For example, if data are collected from participants who are involved in pair or group work, then scores obtained from people in the same group may be dependent on each other. Also, scores that are collected from participants on a variable at more than one time point are related. Given her research design, Dr. Novak does not suspect that dependency is a problem. **Dr. Novak(2)**

With regard to normality, Dr. Novak is aware that the t-test and analysis of variance procedures are quite robust to violations of this assumption, especially with large sample sizes as in her study. **Dr. Novak(3)** She should not be too concerned if there is only a slight or moderate departure from normality, although more severe non-normality can produce incorrect results for tests of the homogeneity of variance assumption described later. There are several ways to evaluate normality. One is to calculate standardized skewness and kurtosis values. These descriptive statistics are helpful indicators of how the distribution may deviate from normality. Plots and graphs of data, such as histograms and normal Q-Q plots, also help to visualize the distribution. **Dr. Novak(4)** Finally, statistical tests can be used to determine whether or not the data are normal. Kolmogorov-Smirnov and Shapiro-Wilk are two available tests to evaluate the null hypothesis of normal data. If the p values from these normality tests are not significant (e.g., above .05), then the distribution is considered to be approximately normal. If the p values are

**2 Dr. Novak says: "If my research design was one in which dependency might exist, there is a way to quantify it. The intraclass correlation coefficient is a measure of dependence among observations. Once obtained, the calculated coefficient can be compared to a table of actual Type I error rates for correlated observations. For example, moderate dependence (e.g., an intraclass correlation coefficient of .30) among a sample 30 subjects in each of two groups has an actual alpha of .5928 (Scariano & Davenport, 1987; Stevens, 2009)."

**3 Dr. Novak says: "Saying that a test is 'robust' indicates that even if an assumption is violated, it does not disrupt the validity of the probability statements. In other words, results from the tests are accurate, and valid conclusions can be made. Statistically speaking, when a test is robust, the actual alpha differs very little or not at all from the nominal significance level you set for your test (e.g., .05)."

**4 Dr. Novak says: "The normal Q-Q plot displays the actual quantiles of your distribution against the quantiles that would be obtained with a normal distribution. If the points in the graph fall close to a diagonal line from bottom left to top right, then the distribution is approximately normal. The extent to which points stray from the line is an indication of possible non-normality."

significant, then the distribution is statistically different from a normal distribution.

Although non-normality may not have a great impact on the validity of *t*-tests and ANOVA, a violation of the homogeneity of variance assumption does have a more serious impact for an unbalanced design. A design that is said to be unbalanced has unequal sample sizes across groups. Some statisticians say that if the largest group is one-and-a-half times the size of the smallest group, then the groups are considered unequal (Stevens, 2009). If this is the case, then the *t*- and *F*- test results will yield either conservative results or liberal results with respect to the probability statements. If the large sample has the largest variance, then results will be conservative (the actual alpha will be less than the nominal alpha). In this case, the power of the test will be reduced. If the null hypothesis from the *t*- or *F*- test was not rejected, maybe it should have been. On the other hand, if the large sample has the smallest variance, then results will be liberal. Type I error is an issue (the actual alpha will be greater than the nominal alpha). In this case, there is a higher risk of falsely rejecting the null hypothesis. If the null hypothesis for the *t*- or *F*- test was rejected, maybe it should not have been.

To evaluate homogeneity of variance, a statistical test can be conducted. Levene's test is quite common; others include Cochran's C test and Bartlett's chi-square test. A fourth test, Hartley's F max, can be calculated easily by hand; however, it was developed based on groups with equal sample sizes, so it is not useful for evaluating this assumption. As with the normality tests, the null hypothesis for each homogeneity of variance test states that the variances are equal. Therefore, the assumption is satisfied if the results from these tests are not significant.

How Dr. Novak Plans to Evaluate the Assumptions

Dr. Novak now focuses her attention on exactly how she will evaluate normality and homogeneity of variance for the specific *t*-tests and ANOVA included in this module. Although the *t*- and *F*- statistics are robust to some level of non-normality, she still needs to examine this assumption because of the negative impact deviations from normal may have on the results of homogeneity of variance tests.

For each of her four *t*-tests in which *gender* is the independent variable and one of four motivation subscales (*imai, impr, ime, iom*) is the dependent variable, she will obtain skewness and kurtosis values for males and females using the Descriptive command in SPSS. To obtain histograms, normal Q-Q plots, and tests of normality for males and females, she will use the Explore procedure. **Dr. Novak(5)**

Dr. Novak will run the same procedures for her one-factor ANOVA that examines mean differences in the hyperfemininity dependent variable (*hyperfem*) across the four groups of ideology identity status (*idstatus*) as well as for her two-factor ANOVA that examines mean differences in the locus of control dependent variable (*locsum*) across the groups of *gender* and *idstatus*.

Because her sample sizes are unequal, she needs to be concerned about the homogeneity of variance assumptions. The ratio of females to males is two to one, and the ratio of the largest and smallest *idstatus* group is three to one. She will use Levene's test, which is available in SPSS, to evaluate this assumption. Many of the tests that determine whether groups' variances are equal are sensitive to non-normality. Levene's test is somewhat more robust for slight violations of normality, but can be compromised if there is considerable skewness.

What Dr. Novak Plans to Do If Assumptions Are Violated

For the *t*-tests, if Levene's test is significant and the distributions are considerably non-normal, then Dr. Novak will compare two *p* values produced by the *t*-tests in SPSS (one for equal variances assumed, the other for equal variances not assumed). The latter is actually an unpooled version of the *t*-test that uses the variances for each group to calculate the *t*-statistic rather than using the pooled variance. For extremely skewed distributions that are also platykurtic or leptokurtic, she will conduct a nonparametric

**5 Dr. Novak says: "It is important to use all the information together when making conclusions about the assumption and determining whether or not there is cause for concern. The significance tests should not be relied upon alone. For large sample sizes, significant results for Kolmogorov-Smirnov and Shapiro-Wilks tests are not uncommon even when the distribution is fairly close to normal."

**6 Dr. Novak says: "The Mann-Whitney test is a nonparametric alternative to the independent *t*-test. It ranks all scores from highest to lowest, then examines whether the ranks are similar for the two groups. If I were using a paired (or dependent) *t*-test, then the nonparametric alternative would be the Wilcoxon signed rank test for paired groups."

**7 Dr. Novak says: "These two procedures involve adjusting the degrees of freedom for the F statistic in an ANOVA to account for the unequal variances across groups. Statisticians have found that they produce valid results when populations are relatively normal, but when the data is substantially non-normal, it may be useful to use a transformation (Howell, 2002; Tomarken & Serlin, 1986)."

**8 Dr. Novak says: "There is some debate among statisticians as to whether it is beneficial or desirable to transform data when assumptions are violated and validity results are in question (Tabachnick & Fidell, 2007). Some say that we should not be afraid of transformations, that they are mere reexpressions of data that measure a construct. A transformation performed to make variances equal may also end up making the data more closely approximate normality (e.g., Howell, 2002). Others say that transformations don't always work. They may fix problems in one or two groups, but create problems in other groups of the variable. Another reported downside is that conclusions from transformed data may not be aligned with the original means for the variable (e.g., Grissom, 2000)."

Mann-Whitney test. Instead of evaluating a null hypothesis about the difference between two group means, it evaluates whether or not two distributions have the same shape. There are no assumptions made about the population data; that is, the data do not have to be normal, nor must the groups have equal variances. **Dr. Novak(6)**

If assumptions are violated for the one-factor and two-factor ANOVAs and it appears that the validity of the F statistics may be compromised, Dr. Novak will request the Welch and Brown-Forsythe modifications of ANOVA that are available in SPSS. **Dr. Novak(7)** Depending on the way in which data deviate from a normal distribution, she may also apply a transformation of the data, check the assumptions again, and rerun the ANOVA. **Dr. Novak(8)** A third option is to use the Kruskal-Wallis nonparametric test, which does not require normality or equal variances.

△ D. Using SPSS to Address Issues and Prepare Data

Evaluating Assumptions for *t*-Tests on Four Motivation Subscales

Dr. Novak evaluated the assumptions for each of the four *t*-tests that examine differences in *gender* mean scores on the *imai*, *impr*, *ime*, and *iom* subscales. Because she needed to evaluate normality for each group of the independent variable, her first step was to split the file by gender so that skewness and kurtosis values, histograms, and results from normality tests would be provided separately for males and females. This step made the process more efficient than using other alternatives. **SPSS Tip 1** Under the **Data menu**, she selected **Split File** and the dialog box shown in Figure 6.1 appeared. She clicked **Compare**

SPSS Tip 1: One alternative is to use the Select Cases procedure under the Data menu in order to select only females and obtain their skewness and kurtosis values. However, the procedure would need to be conducted again in order to obtain the values for males.

Figure 6.1 Data → Split File

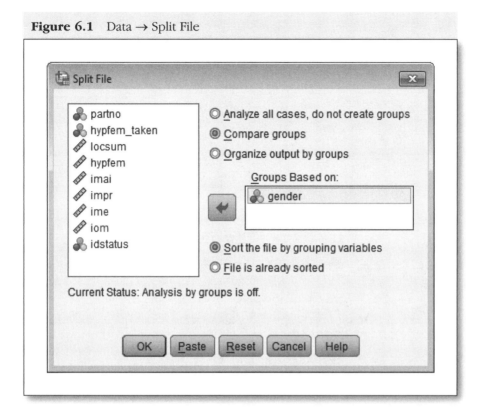

groups and moved *gender* into the **Groups Based on** box. (For more details on the **Split File procedure,** see Section 1, Module 2.)

She then requested skewness and kurtosis values under the **Analyze menu** by selecting **Descriptive Statistics** and **Descriptives**. ****SPSS Tip 2** She placed all four dependent variables (*imai*, *impr*, *ime*, and *iom*) in the **Variable(s)** box (see Figure 6.2), and clicked the **Options** button.

SPSS Tip 2: There are other ways to obtain skewness and kurtosis values, such as using the Explore procedure. However, Dr. Novak is not interested in all the other descriptive statistics provided in Explore output. She prefers the succinct table of results that the Descriptives procedure provides for all four motivation variables.

Default selections in the **Options** window are the mean, standard deviation, minimum, and maximum. Dr. Novak deselected these options and selected **Kurtosis** and **Skewness** (see Figure 6.3).

After she clicked **Continue** and **OK**, all the values she needed were clearly and succinctly provided in one table of output. In order to evaluate

Figure 6.2   Analyze → Descriptive Statistics → Descriptives

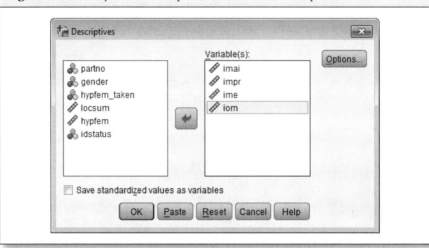

Figure 6.3   Options for Descriptive Statistics

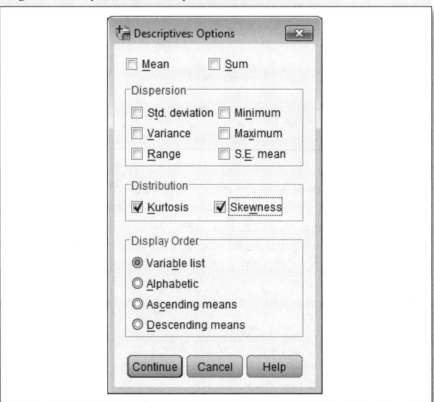

the skewness and kurtosis values in Table 6.2, she divided each statistic by its associated standard error to produce standardized values.

As an example, gender 1 (female) has a skewness statistic of –.099 and a standard error of .091 for *imai*, so the standardized skewness value for *imai* is –1.088 (–.099 divided by .091). All standardized skewness values for the female and male groups on each motivation scale are presented in Table 6.3. Dr. Novak used an absolute standardized value of 3.000 as the cutoff to identify groups for which skewness and kurtosis may be of concern.

Table 6.2 SPSS Output for Skewness and Kurtosis by Gender for Four Motivation Scales

Descriptive Statistics		N	Skewness		Kurtosis	
gender		Statistic	Statistic	Std. Error	Statistic	Std. Error
1 female	imai	719	-.099	.091	-1.096	.182
	impr	719	-1.328	.091	1.761	.182
	ime	721	-2.382	.091	5.698	.182
	iom	717	-.598	.091	.271	.182
	Valid N (listwise)	717				
2 male	imai	359	.014	.129	-1.079	.257
	impr	359	-.881	.129	-.049	.257
	ime	359	-1.494	.129	1.478	.257
	iom	358	-.167	.129	-.682	.257
	Valid N (listwise)	358				

Table 6.3 Standardized Skewness and Kurtosis Values for Motivation Subscales

	Skewness	**Kurtosis**	**Summary**
Female			
imai	–1.088	–6.022	neg kurt
impr	–14.593	9.676	neg skew, pos kurt
ime	–26.176	31.308	neg skew, pos kurt
iom	–6.571	1.489	neg skew
Male			
imai	0.109	–4.198	neg kurt
impr	–6.829	–0.191	neg skew
ime	–11.581	5.751	neg skew, pos kurt
iom	–1.295	–2.654	normal

SPSS Tip 3: A distribution with a kurtosis value near 0 is called mesokurtic. A normal distribution has a value of 0. Distributions with considerable skewness in one direction or the other are often leptokurtic because they have more scores far from the mean compared to a normal distribution.

She noticed that when skewness existed within a group, it was always negative. This means that scores are clustered together at the upper end of the scale, and the tail is longer in the lower end. For kurtosis, some groups had positive values and others had negative values. Distributions with negative kurtosis are called platykurtic. There are fewer values in the tails and the distribution is broad and flat. Distributions with positive kurtosis are called leptokurtic. Values in the tails are far from the mean and the distribution is slender, narrow, or peaked. **SPSS Tip 3 Only the distribution for males on *iom* is considered to be normal.

Next, Dr. Novak obtained histograms and tests of normality for each group on each dependent variable. Under the **Analyze menu**, she selected **Descriptive Statistics** and **Explore**. She placed all four motivation subscales in the **Dependent List**. Under **Display** at the bottom of the dialog box, she selected only **Plots**. The default is **Both** (meaning **Statistics** and **Plots**) (see Figure 6.4).

After she clicked the **Plots button**, the window shown in Figure 6.5 opened. Dr. Novak clicked on **None** under **Boxplots**, checked the box for **Normality plots with tests**, and under **Descriptive** deselected **Stem-and-leaf** and selected **Histogram**.

Figure 6.4 Analyze → Descriptive Statistics → Explore

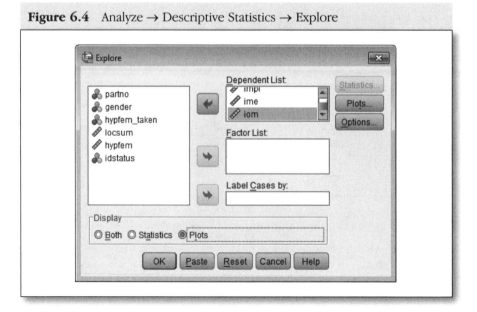

Figure 6.5 Plots in Explore

All these actions produced normality tests and histograms for each dependent variable and gender group. As shown in Table 6.4, all Kolmogorov-Smirnov tests are significant. The *p* values are less than .001, which indicates rejection of the null hypothesis that the distribution is normal. Dr. Novak was not surprised with these results for two reasons: because of the magnitude of the previous skewness and kurtosis values, and because her sample is large. Both statistical tests are prone to rejection of the null hypothesis when the sample size is large.

Table 6.4 SPSS Output for Tests of Normality on Motivation Scales by Gender

Tests of Normality

gender		Kolmogorov-Smirnov[a]			Shapiro-Wilk		
		Statistic	df	Sig.	Statistic	df	Sig.
1 female	imai	.145	717	.000	.920	717	.000
	impr	.258	717	.000	.782	717	.000
	ime	.447	717	.000	.539	717	.000
	iom	.124	717	.000	.946	717	.000
2 male	imai	.149	358	.000	.926	358	.000
	impr	.248	358	.000	.822	358	.000
	ime	.358	358	.000	.698	358	.000
	iom	.096	358	.000	.967	358	.000

[a] Lilliefors Significance Correction

Next, she turned her attention to the visual displays. Recall that for *imai*, there was negative kurtosis for males and females. The distributions in Figures 6.6 and 6.7 coincide with this outcome because they are flat and broad, a characteristic of platykurtic distributions. Skewness was not an issue for either males or females on this variable.

Figure 6.6 SPSS Output of the Distribution for Female Scores on imai

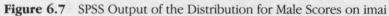

Figure 6.7 SPSS Output of the Distribution for Male Scores on imai

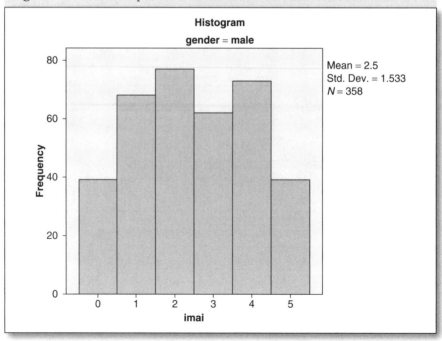

For *impr*, distributions were negatively skewed for males and females. Both histograms in Figures 6.8 and 6.9 clearly show this type of skewness. Results from Table 6.3 also showed positive kurtosis for females, but not males, indicating that the distribution is more peaked and slender than a normal distribution.

Skewness and kurtosis results were the same for both genders on *ime*. Figures 6.10 and 6.11 both show negative skewness because the scores are clustering at the upper end of the scale. The positive kurtosis also indicates leptokurtic distributions that are narrow and peaked. Essentially, the majority of scores for females and males were 5. This variable deviated the most from normality.

Dr. Novak also examined the normal Q-Q plots along with the histograms. Figures 6.12 and 6.13 show these plots for *ime*. The actual quantile values in the sample distributions do not fall along the diagonal line that represents the quantile values for a normal distribution. This is especially true for the female group, which was shown to have higher standardized skewness and kurtosis than the male group.

Figure 6.8 SPSS Output of the Distribution for Female Scores on impr

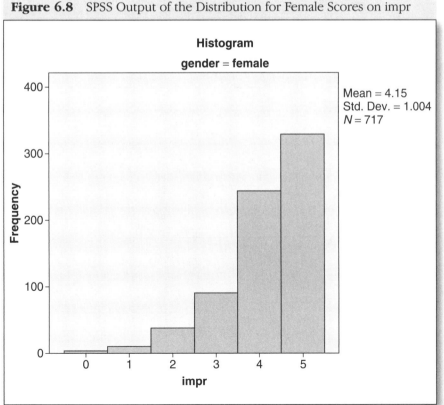

Figure 6.9 SPSS Output of the Distribution for Male Scores on impr

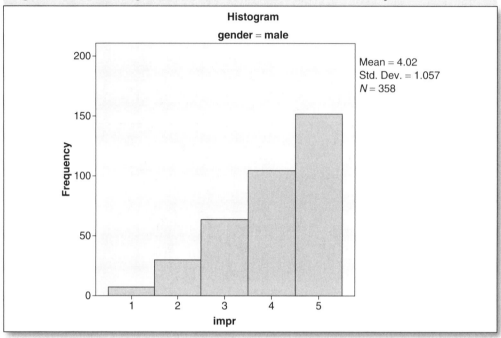

Figure 6.10 SPSS Output of the Distribution for Female Scores on ime

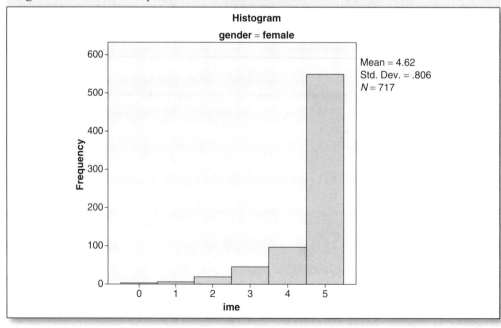

Figure 6.11 SPSS Output of the Distribution for Male Scores on ime

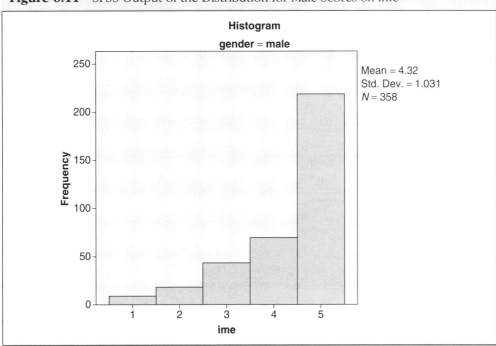

Figure 6.12 SPSS Output of the Normal Quantile Plot for Female Scores on ime

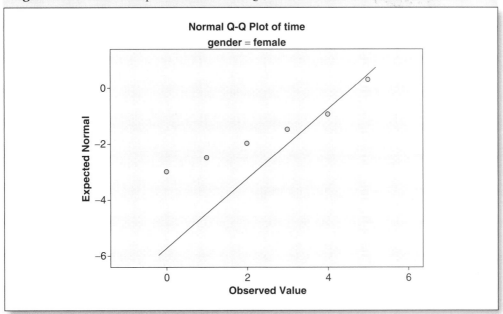

Figure 6.13 SPSS Output of the Normal Quantile Plot for Male Scores on ime

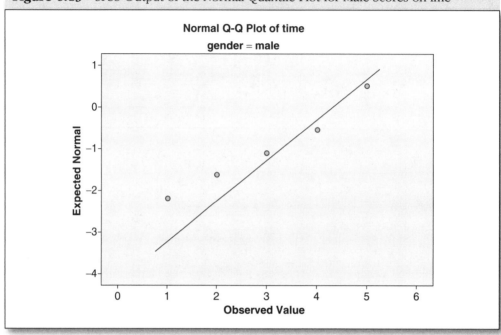

For *iom*, the overall motivation subscale, the female distribution had negative skewness, which is somewhat evident in Figure 6.14. The male distribution was considered normal according to standardized skewness and kurtosis values in Table 6.3, and the distribution in Figure 6.15 appears to approximate normality.

Dr. Novak also noticed that the quantile plot for males in Figure 6.16 showed approximate normality. Actual quantiles fall close to the diagonal line that represents the normal quantile values.

Dr. Novak's evaluation of the normality assumption is now complete. Most distributions showed some deviations from normal. Next, she turned her attention to examining the homogeneity of variance assumption by conducting four *t*-tests. She remembered that her file was split to display output for males and females separately, so her first step was to undo the split. She selected the **Analyze all cases, do not create groups** button in the **Split File** dialog box under the **Data menu**. ****SPSS Tip 4**

SPSS Tip 4: If Dr. Novak forgot to remove the gender split, the *t*-test would not be conducted. Instead, a warning would appear in the output saying that the gender variable is specified both as a grouping variable and as a split variable.

Figure 6.14 SPSS Output of the Distribution for Female Scores on iom

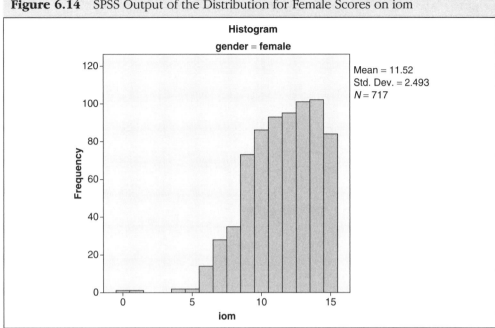

Figure 6.15 SPSS Output of the Distribution for Male Scores on iom

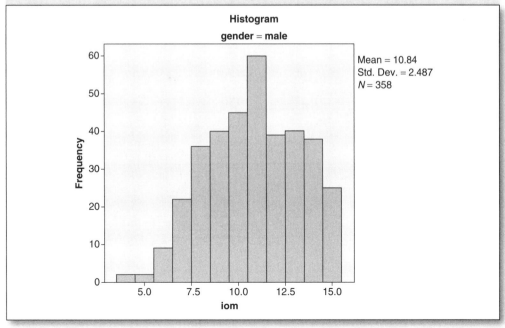

Figure 6.16 SPSS Output of the Normal Quantile Plot for Male Scores on iom

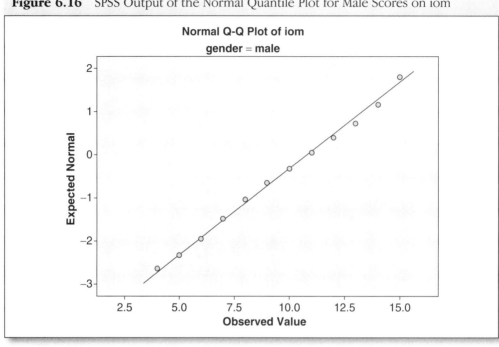

To obtain the *t*-tests, she selected **Compare Means** under the **Analyze menu**, then selected **Independent-Samples T Test**. As shown in Figure 6.17, she placed all four dependent variables, *imai*, *impr*, *ime*, and *iom*, in the **Test Variable(s)** box and *gender* in the **Grouping Variable** box.

Figure 6.17 Analyze → Compare Means → Independent-Samples T Test

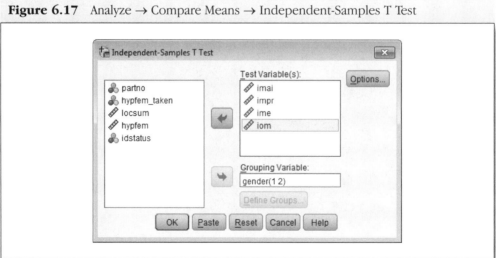

Before running the test, Dr. Novak specified the values assigned to each group for *gender*. She clicked the **Define Groups** button, and it opened up the window shown in Figure 6.18 in which she typed her numerical codes for the two genders.

Figure 6.18 Codes for Grouping Variable

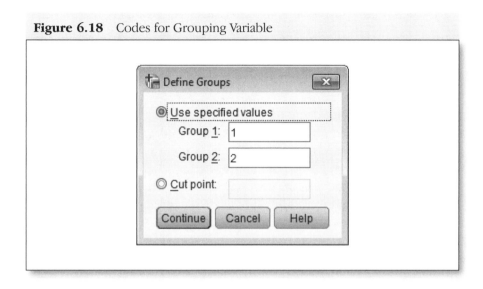

After she clicked **Continue** and **OK**, two tables of output were created. Table 6.5 provides the means, standard deviations, and standard errors for males and females on each variable.

Table 6.5 Descriptive Statistics for Four Motivation Subscales

Group Statistics

	gender	N	Mean	Std. Deviation	Std. Error Mean
imai	1 female	719	2.74	1.571	.059
	2 male	359	2.50	1.532	.081
impr	1 female	719	4.15	1.003	.037
	2 male	359	4.01	1.067	.056
ime	1 female	721	4.61	.818	.030
	2 male	359	4.31	1.029	.054
iom	1 female	717	11.52	2.493	.093
	2 male	358	10.84	2.487	.131

Tables 6.6 and 6.7 provide results of *t*-tests for each dependent variable as well as the results for the homogeneity of variance assumption. In SPSS, the output is produced in one long table and also includes confidence intervals around the means, but because Dr. Novak does not need them at this point, they are not shown here. The *p* values for Levene's test shown in Table 6.6 indicate that the assumption is satisfied for three of the four subscales. For *ime*, Levene's *p* value is < .001, which indicates rejection of the null hypothesis that variances in *ime* are equal for the two groups of males and females.

Looking back at the standard deviations for *ime* in Table 6.5, Dr. Novak saw that the group with the largest sample size (females) has a smaller variance (i.e., standard deviation squared). This scenario leads to *t*-test results that are liberal. Type I error may be an issue if the null hypothesis for the *t*-test is rejected. SPSS produces two *p* values for each *t*-test, one when equal variances are assumed and another when they are not. As shown in Table 6.7, the *p* values in both cases are < .001. Therefore, even though the assumption was not satisfied, the *t*-test result, which indicates a

Table 6.6   First Portion of SPSS Output for *t*-Tests on Four Motivation Subscales

Independent Samples Test

		Levene's Test for Equality of Variances		t-test for Equality of Means	
		F	Sig.	t	df
imai	Equal variances assumed	.169	.681	2.411	1076
	Equal variances not assumed			2.431	732.167
impr	Equal variances assumed	2.305	.129	2.120	1076
	Equal variances not assumed			2.077	677.596
ime	Equal variances assumed	42.408	.000	5.119	1078
	Equal variances not assumed			4.744	589.354
iom	Equal variances assumed	.042	.837	4.250	1073
	Equal variances not assumed			4.254	715.357

Table 6.7 Second Portion of SPSS Output for *t*-Tests on Four Motivation Subscales

Independent Samples Test

| | | *t*-test for Equality of Means | | |
		Sig. (2-tailed)	Mean Difference	Std. Error Difference
imai	Equal variances assumed	.016	.243	.101
	Equal variances not assumed	.015	.243	.100
impr	Equal variances assumed	.034	.140	.066
	Equal variances not assumed	.038	.140	.068
ime	Equal variances assumed	.000	.296	.058
	Equal variances not assumed	.000	.296	.062
iom	Equal variances assumed	.000	.685	.161
	Equal variances not assumed	.000	.685	.161

significant difference between the *ime* means for males and females, is valid. ****SPSS Tip 5**

Dr. Novak ran one final analysis to examine the validity of the *t*-test results. She was still somewhat concerned about the considerable non-normality, especially for the *ime* subscale, so she conducted a nonparametric test called the Mann-Whitney U. Under the **Analyze menu**, she selected **Nonparametric Tests**, **Legacy Dialogs**, and **2 Independent Samples**. In the dialog box shown in Figure 6.19, she placed *ime* in the **Test Variable List** box and *gender* in the **Grouping Variable** box. She defined gender as having codes of 1 and 2, similar to the *t*-test procedure.

SPSS Tip 5: When Levene's test indicates that the homogeneity of variance assumption is not satisfied, it is useful to look at both *p* values for the *t*-test. Suppose that the "equal variances assumed" *p* value rejected the null hypothesis for the *t*-test, but the *p* value for "equal variances not assumed" did not reject. In a situation where the largest sample had the smallest variance, then the researcher would know that the unequal variances were having a detrimental effect on Type I error, and he or she would report that the null hypothesis for the *t*-test was not rejected.

Figure 6.19 Analyze → Nonparametric Tests → Legacy Dialogs →
2 Independent Samples

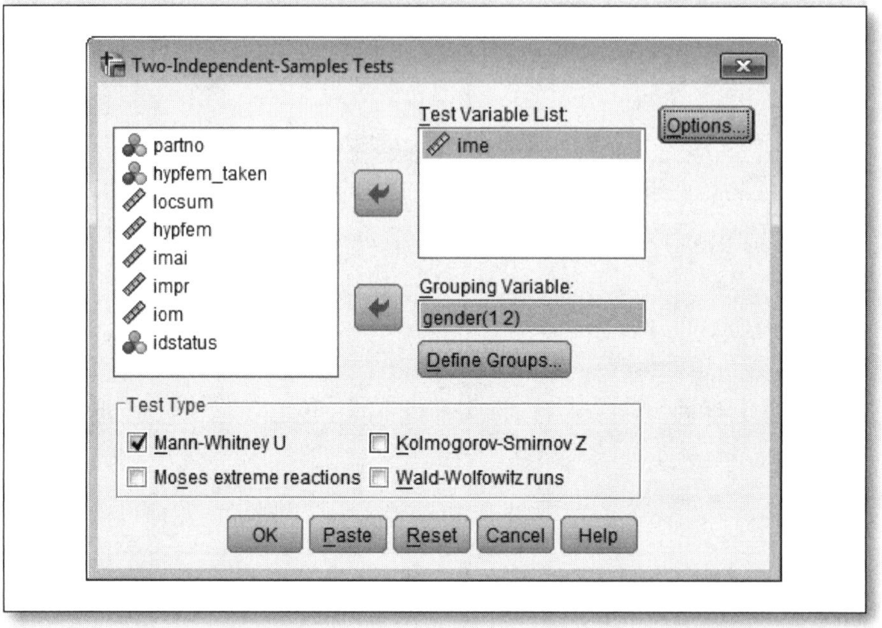

There are several types of nonparametric tests to choose from under **Test
Type**, but the default is **Mann-Whitney U**.

After she clicked **OK**, two tables of output were produced. Table 6.8
contains the descriptive statistics, which include the average ranks of *ime*
scores for females and males. The *p* value in Table 6.9 for the Mann-Whitney
U test statistic indicates rejection of the null hypothesis that the distributions for females and males are the same. This result provides further support for the validity of the parametric *t*-test result.

Table 6.8 Descriptive Statistics From SPSS Output for the Mann-Whitney
Test

Ranks

	gender	N	Mean Rank	Sum of Ranks
ime	1 female	721	569.11	410327.00
	2 male	359	483.04	173413.00
	Total	1080		

Table 6.9 Inferential Statistics From SPSS Output for the Mann-Whitney Test

Test Statistics[a]

	ime
Mann-Whitney U	108793.000
Wilcoxon W	173413.000
Z	-5.362
Asymp. Sig. (2-tailed)	.000

[a.] Grouping Variable: gender

To be complete, Dr. Novak decided to also conduct the Mann-Whitney test for the other motivation subscales. Because Levene's statistic is somewhat sensitive to violations of the normality assumption, she wanted to ensure that the non-normality was not compromising results from the homogeneity of variance tests and, in turn, the *t*-tests. The Mann-Whitney *p* values for *imai*, *impr*, and *iom* were .017, .046, and < .001, respectively. The *p* values from the *t*-tests in Table 6.7 were .016, .034, and < .001. She was pleased to see that they were quite similar and led to the same conclusion about the mean differences by gender.

Evaluating Assumptions for a One-Factor ANOVA on Hyperfemininity

Dr. Novak's next evaluation of assumptions is for the one-factor ANOVA model that she will conduct to examine the effect of *idstatus* on *hypfem*. The hyperfemininity scale was administered only to a subset of the female college students in her sample. Therefore, before proceeding, she needed to **Select Cases** under the **Data menu** to include only those cases with *hypfem_taken* equal to 1, as shown in Figure 6.20. This procedure filters out all but 285 cases. (See Module 2 in Section 1 for a detailed description of using the **Select Cases procedure**).

Figure 6.20 Data → Select Cases

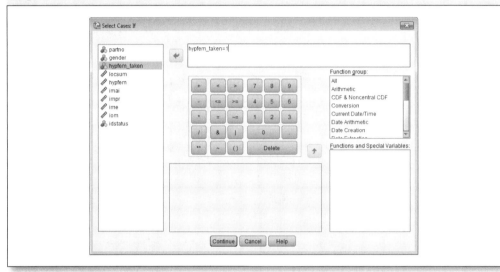

The steps she took to evaluate the ANOVA assumptions were similar to those she performed for *t*-tests on the motivation subscales. Not all the SPSS screen shots are included here because they are the same as those previously used, except with different variables. First, she split the file by the independent variable *idstatus*, then she conducted **Descriptives** to obtain skewness and kurtosis values for *hypfem*. The values are shown in Table 6.10 for each of the four *idstatus* groups.

Table 6.10 SPSS Output for Skewness and Kurtosis Values by idstatus for hypfem

Descriptive Statistics						
idstatus		N	Skewness		Kurtosis	
		Statistic	Statistic	Std. Error	Statistic	Std. Error
diffusion	hypfem	71	-.046	.285	-.252	.563
	Valid N (listwise)	71				
foreclosure	hypfem	45	.871	.354	.221	.695
	Valid N (listwise)	45				
moratorium	hypfem	133	.502	.210	.532	.417
	Valid N (listwise)	133				
achievement	hypfem	36	1.132	.393	2.615	.768
	Valid N (listwise)	36				

Skewness does not appear to be a problem for the *idstatus* groups based on the standardized values of –.161, 2.460, 2.390, and 2.880 for diffusion, foreclosure, moratorium, and achievement, respectively. Standardized kurtosis values are –.448, .318, 1.276, and 3.405, respectively. The last group (achievement) is somewhat leptokurtic, a peaked and slender distribution.

After running the **Explore procedure**, the tests of normality in Table 6.11 showed significance at the .01 or .05 alpha level for some groups but not others. Notice that the two tests are not in agreement for the achievement group. Recall that significant results from these tests are not uncommon with large sample sizes even if the distribution approximates normality.

Table 6.11 SPSS Output for Tests of Normality on hypfem by idstatus

Tests of Normality

idstatus		Kolmogorov-Smirnov[a]			Shapiro-Wilk		
		Statistic	df	Sig.	Statistic	df	Sig.
diffusion	hypfem	.077	71	.200[*]	.988	71	.732
foreclosure	hypfem	.183	45	.001	.927	45	.008
moratorium	hypfem	.102	133	.002	.963	133	.001
achievement	hypfem	.108	36	.200[*]	.919	36	.012

[a.] Lilliefors Significance Correction

[*] This is a lower bound of the true significance.

The **Explore procedure** also produced histograms, which are not shown here due to space considerations. For the most part, the distributions appeared to be somewhat non-normal but not as severely skewed, broad, or peaked as the previously examined motivation subscales.

Next, Dr. Novak turned her attention to examining homogeneity of variance, which is likely to be the most critical assumption in this analysis because of the unequal sample sizes across the four groups. The largest sample size is 133 and the smallest is 36, a ratio of almost four to one. She remembered to remove the **Split File** on *idstatus* before conducting the ANOVA to obtain Levene's test statistic and *p* value. Then, under the **Analyze menu**, she selected **Compare Means** and **One-Way ANOVA**. After placing *hypfem* in the **Dependent List** and *idstatus* in the **Factor** box, she clicked the **Options button** (see Figure 6.21).

She selected **Descriptive** and **Homogeneity of variance test** (see Figure 6.22), then clicked **Continue** and **OK**.

Figure 6.21 Analyze → Compare Means → One-Way ANOVA

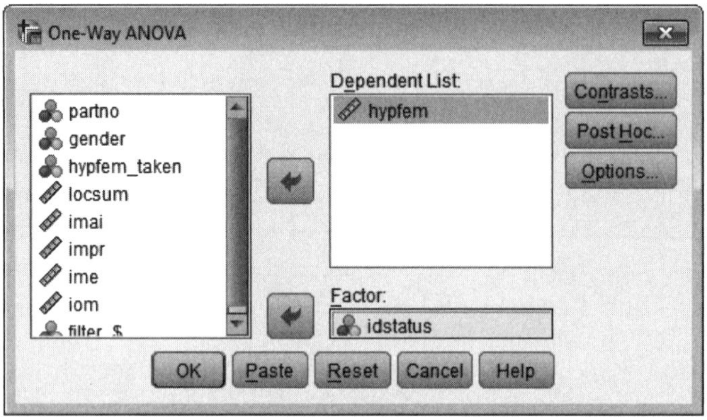

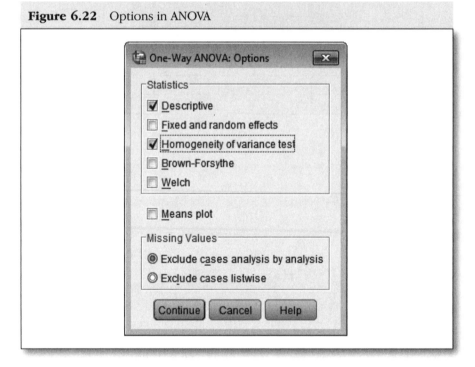

Figure 6.22 Options in ANOVA

Three tables of output appear. Table 6.12 includes the means and standard deviations for each *idstatus* group on *hypfem*. The standard deviations will be useful if Levene's test is rejected.

Results for the Levene's test in Table 6.13 indicate that variances are not equal ($p = .027$) at the .05 significance level. The largest group, moratorium

Table 6.12 SPSS Descriptive Statistics Output for hypfem by idstatus

Descriptives

hypfem

	N	Mean	Std. Deviation	Std. Error	95% Confidence Interval for Mean	
					Lower Bound	Upper Bound
diffusion	71	9.87	4.466	.530	8.82	10.93
foreclosure	45	8.82	3.921	.585	7.64	10.00
moratorium	133	7.32	3.324	.288	6.75	7.89
achievement	36	7.19	3.702	.617	5.94	8.45
Total	285	8.18	3.921	.232	7.72	8.63

Table 6.13 SPSS Output Evaluating the Assumption of Homogeneity of Variance

Test of Homogeneity of Variances

hypfem

Levene Statistic	df1	df2	Sig.
3.092	3	281	.027

($n = 133$), has the smallest variance (the standard deviation of 3.324 squared). This may lead to an increased risk of Type I error.

The significance value in Table 6.14 ($p < .001$) indicates that the null hypothesis for the F-test is rejected, thus concluding there is at least one significant difference among the pairs of *idstatus* groups for *hypfem*. However, it is possible that the result is not valid. The F-test may be falsely rejecting the null hypothesis because variances are not equal across groups.

Table 6.14 SPSS Output for One-Factor ANOVA on hypfem

ANOVA

hypfem

	Sum of Squares	df	Mean Square	F	Sig.
Between Groups	356.415	3	118.805	8.324	.000
Within Groups	4010.813	281	14.273		
Total	4367.228	284			

SPSS Tip 6: It would not be legitimate for a researcher to conduct an analysis several different ways simply to find the desired answers to a research question. Here, Dr. Novak is conducting the three additional analyses for a different reason, to determine whether or not her original probability results are valid. If results from all analyses lead to the same conclusion (rejection of the null hypothesis), then she can rest assured that her conclusion about the *idstatus* means for *hypfem* is valid.

At this point, there are several options for Dr. Novak to consider. She could simply report the results of the ANOVA, because the distribution is not terribly skewed and Levene's test was significant at the .05 level, not the .01 or .001 level. However, she is not completely satisfied with this option. Instead, she conducted a few other analyses and compared results to find out if they all led to the same conclusion regarding the mean differences in *hypfem*. ****SPSS Tip 6** First, she ran the Welch and Brown-Forsythe modifications of the *F*-test. Next, she ran the nonparametric Kruskal-Wallis test. Third, she conducted an ANOVA on a square root transformation of *hypfem*.

To obtain modifications of the *F*-test, Dr. Novak conducted the one-factor ANOVA again. This time, in the **Options** window shown in Figure 6.23, she selected **Brown-Forsythe** and **Welch**.

Figure 6.23   Options in ANOVA

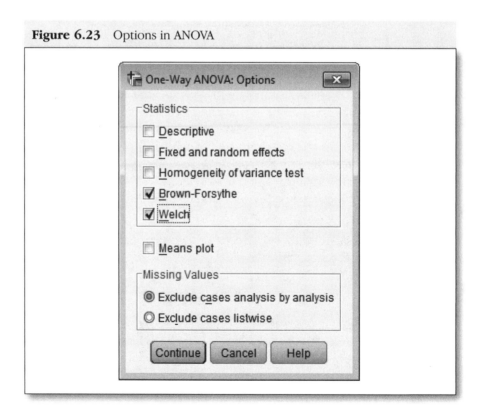

The output in Table 6.15 indicates rejection of the null hypothesis at the .001 level for both tests, which is to say that at least one pair of *idstatus* group means for *hypfem* differs significantly.

Table 6.15   SPSS Output for Alternate Tests of the *F*-Statistic

Robust Tests of Equality of Means

hypfem

	Statistic[a]	df1	df2	Sig.
Welch	7.149	3	99.851	.000
Brown-Forsythe	7.784	3	184.359	.000

[a.] Asymptotically F distributed.

Next, Dr. Novak obtained the Kruskal-Wallis test in a similar fashion as the Mann-Whitney test for the motivation subscales. Under the **Analyze menu**, she selected **Nonparametric Tests**, **Legacy Dialogs**, and **K Independent Samples**. In the **Test Variable List** box, she placed *hypfem*, and in the **Grouping Variable** box, she placed *idstatus* (see Figure 6.24).

Figure 6.24   Analyze → Nonparametric Tests → Legacy Dialogs → K Independent Samples

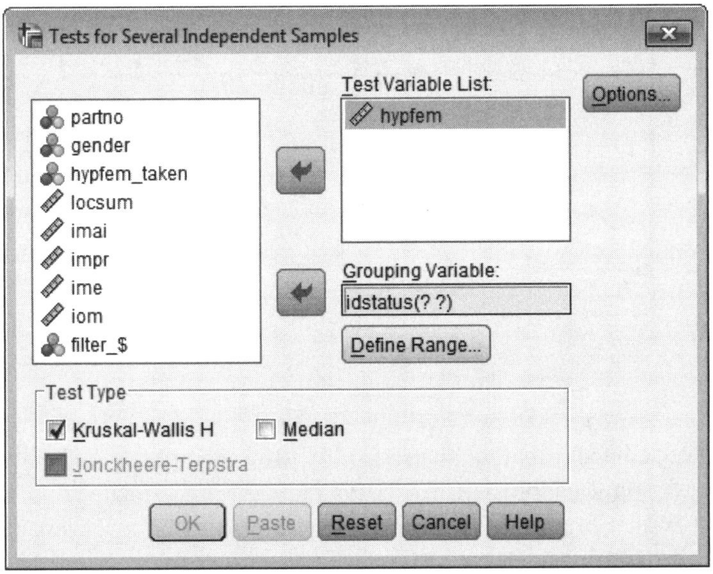

She clicked the **Define Range** button in order to specify the codes for the first and last group of *idstatus*, which are 1 and 4 (see Figure 6.25).

Figure 6.25   Codes for Grouping Variable

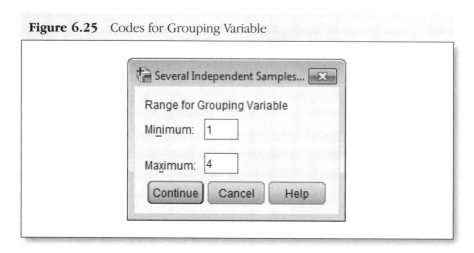

After she clicked **Continue** and **OK**, two output tables were produced. Table 6.16 shows the mean ranks for *idstatus* on *hypfem*.

Table 6.16   SPSS Descriptive Statistics Output for the Kruskal-Wallis Test

Ranks

	idstatus	N	Mean Rank
hypfem	diffusion	71	178.67
	foreclosure	45	153.77
	moratorium	133	126.22
	achievement	36	121.19
	Total	285	

Results in Table 6.17 indicate that the null hypothesis for the nonparametric Kruskal-Wallis test is rejected, which is to say that the shapes of the *hypfem* distributions for the four *idstatus* groups are similar.

Dr. Novak's final step to examine the validity of the original ANOVA results was to create a square root transformation of *hypfem*, reevaluate the assumptions, and rerun the one-factor ANOVA. To begin, she selected

Table 6.17 SPSS Inferential Statistics Output for the Kruskal-Wallis Test

Test Statistics[a,b]

	hypfem
Chi-square	22.261
df	3
Asymp. Sig.	.000

a. Kruskal Wallis Test

b. Grouping Variable: idstatus

Compute Variable under the **Transform menu**. She created a new name for the transformed variable, *hypfem_sqroot*, and typed it in the **Target Variable** box. Then, under **Function group**, she selected **Arithmetic**, scrolled down the list of **Functions and Special Variables**, then double-clicked **Sqrt**. SQRT(?) appears in the **Numeric Expression** box (see Figure 6.26). In place of the question mark, she placed the original variable name, *hypfem*, clicked **OK**, and the new variable was added to her data set. The file *module6_lifedomains_final.sav* contains the transformed variable.

Figure 6.26 Transform → Compute Variable

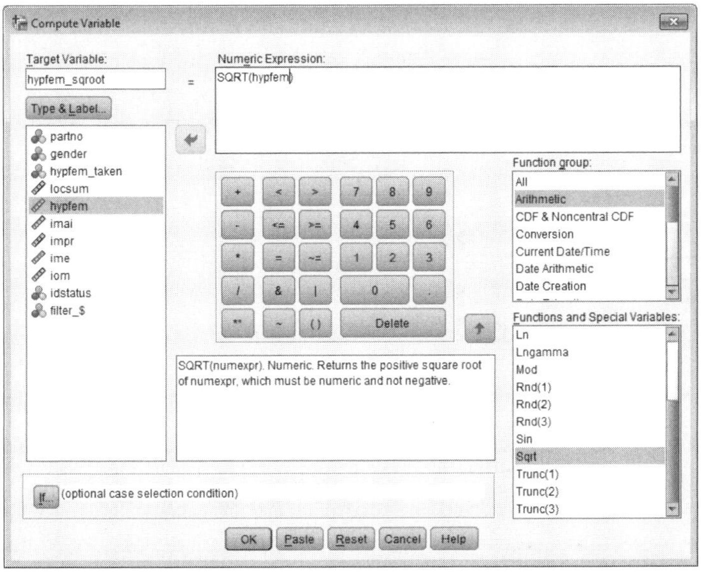

To reevaluate the assumptions, Dr. Novak used the same procedures as before. In terms of skewness and kurtosis, results were mixed. The square root transformation improved the distributions of some groups that were originally non-normal, but a few of the somewhat normal groups are now showing non-normal results. The standardized skewness values for diffusion, foreclosure, moratorium, and achievement are –3.751, 1.218, –1.152, and .687, respectively. Standardized kurtosis values are 3.222, –.521, .118, and .449, respectively. Tests of normality also showed mixed results. Thus, the transformation did not unequivocally satisfy the assumption of normality. However, it did fix the problem of unequal variances. The Levene's test had a p value of .227, indicating that the variances across groups were equal, and the result of the ANOVA was $F(3, 281) = 6.403, p < .001$. There is a significant difference among the group means on the transformed hyperfemininity variable.

When comparing the three alternate analyses (Welch and Brown-Forsythe, Kruskal-Wallis, and ANOVA on the square root transformation of *hypfem*), they all converged on the same statistical decision as the original ANOVA, which was to reject the null hypothesis. Therefore, Dr. Novak's conclusion that there is at least one significant difference among the pairs of *idstatus* means for *hypfem* is a valid one.

Evaluating Assumptions for a Two-Factor ANOVA on Locus of Control

The final statistical test Dr. Novak evaluated is a two-factor ANOVA. The independent variables are *gender* and *idstatus*, and the dependent variable is *locsum*. Before evaluating the assumptions, she removed the **Select Cases** on *hypfem_taken*. This analysis required the entire data set. Then, she split the file by *gender* and *idstatus*. Using the same procedures as before, she began by obtaining skewness and kurtosis for *locsum*. ****SPSS Tip 7** The standardized values were low—only 4 out of the 16 had an absolute value between 1.00 and 2.00. The histograms looked quite close to normal, and the Shapiro-Wilks tests showed only three normality rejections using a significance level of .05. Kolmogorov-Smirnov p values were lower, especially for the groups with large sample sizes, but Dr. Novak knows that these tests are sensitive to large samples.

SPSS Tip 7: When you run the analysis, you may notice that the skewness and kurtosis output for males and females by *idstatus* contains an extra row showing a dot. This indicates that some cases in the data file had a missing value for *idstatus*. In the output, the *N* column shows that 8 females and 6 males were missing *idstatus*.

To measure homogeneity of variance using the Levene's test, she conducted the two-factor ANOVA so that the results from this test of the assumption would be produced. First, she removed the **Split File**, then under the **Analyze menu** she selected **General Linear Model** and **Univariate**. In the **Dependent Variable** box, she placed *locsum*, and in the **Fixed Factor(s)** box, she placed *gender* and *idstatus* (see Figure 6.27).

Figure 6.27 General Linear Model → Univariate

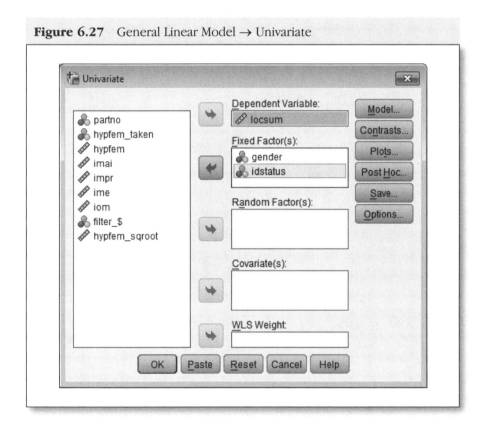

She clicked the **Options** button in order to request the **Homogeneity tests** as well as the **Descriptive statistics** (see Figure 6.28).

Results in Table 6.18 show that the variances are equal ($p = .666$). No further analysis needs to be conducted because both the normality and homogeneity of variance assumptions are satisfied. The probability results for the two-factor ANOVA shown in Table 6.19 are valid. The main effects of *gender* and *idstatus* are significant, but the interaction between them is not.

Figure 6.28 Options in Univariate Analyses

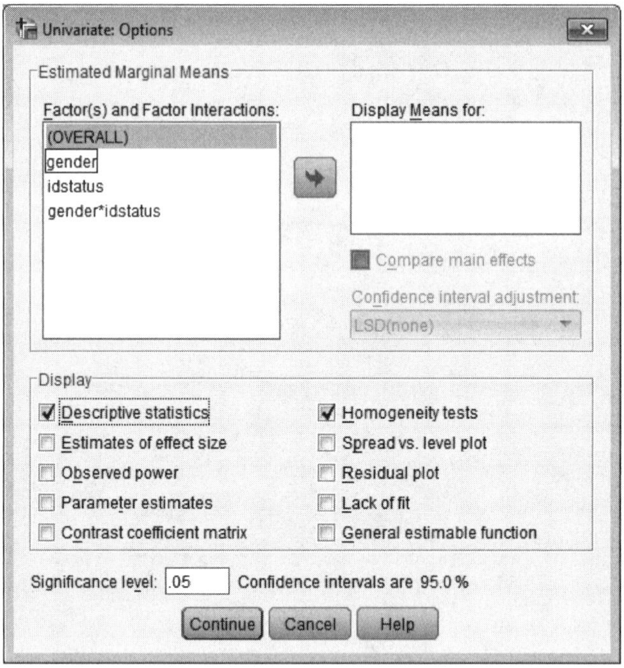

Table 6.18 SPSS Output for Levene's Test in the Two-Factor ANOVA Analysis

Levene's Test of Equality of Error Variances[a]

Dependent Variable:locsum

F	df1	df2	Sig.
.707	7	1061	.666

Tests the null hypothesis that the error variance

of the dependent variable is equal across groups.

[a.] Design: Intercept + gender + idstatus + gender

Table 6.19 SPSS Output for the Two-Factor ANOVA

Tests of Between-Subjects Effects

Dependent Variable:locsum

Source	Type III Sum of Squares	df	Mean Square	F	Sig.
Corrected Model	613.662[a]	7	87.666	6.645	.000
Intercept	99700.433	1	99700.433	7557.277	.000
gender	222.292	1	222.292	16.850	.000
idstatus	301.624	3	100.541	7.621	.000
gender * idstatus	26.080	3	8.693	.659	.577
Error	13997.391	1061	13.193		
Total	156320.000	1069			
Corrected Total	14611.053	1068			

a. R Squared = .042 (Adjusted R Squared = .036)
* idstatus

E. Reflection and Additional Decision Making △

Dr. Novak realizes that examining assumptions involves a great deal of preliminary analysis before answering her research questions. However, she feels it is worth spending the time necessary to ensure that the statistical decisions that lead to conclusions about her sample of college students are valid. When another researcher or a practitioner in her field reads the results from her study, she wants them to know that they are solid. For publication in empirical research journals, she knows editors are increasingly requiring authors to include both a description of the assumptions that apply to the particular model and statements about how the assumptions were evaluated and addressed.

This module presented only a portion of the assumption analysis that Dr. Novak needed to carry out for each of her continuous variables. Results from the analysis of a depression variable (not shown in this module) were especially interesting. For each of the four *idstatus* groups, the distributions on this variable were positively skewed with standardized values of 7.748, 8.044, 13.325, and 13.000. Positive kurtosis was also problematic, with values as high as 31.877. After conducting a square root transformation, the results were dramatically improved for all groups.

Standardized skewness and kurtosis values ranged from .198 to 1.207 across groups, tests of normality were not rejected, and the homogeneity of variance assumption was satisfied. She found these results interesting because the outcome of the transformation was markedly different from what occurred when the hyperfemininity variable was transformed using the square root function, as shown in this module. This supports what some researchers have said about the use of transformations. They work well in some cases, but not in others.

Now Dr. Novak will focus her attention on interpreting results of her *t*-tests and ANOVAs that indicate the extent to which mean scores on the dependent variables vary by participant characteristics in her study. For *t*-tests with significant results, she knows automatically which group had the higher scores because there are only two genders. But for the significant ANOVAs, post hoc analysis will be necessary to determine which pair(s) of groups means are significantly different. Many post hoc tests are available. She will need to decide which ones are appropriate for each situation. Some tests, such as the Games-Howell, are intended for use when equal variances are not assumed.

△ F. Writing It Up

The first set of paragraphs below include Dr. Novak's summary of her evaluation of the model assumptions described in this module. She will place them within the Methodology section of a manuscript. Outcomes from the alternate analyses she conducted (such as nonparametric tests) are typically inserted into the appropriate places in the Results section so that comparisons among all tests used to answer a research question can be made. Both summaries are rather lengthy. Depending upon the purpose for sharing the information, it might be necessary to create an abbreviated version.

Paragraphs for Methodology Section

"For each *t*-test and analysis of variance (ANOVA), three model assumptions were evaluated. Due to the type of research design and data collection method, the independence assumption was satisfied. Observations are independent of each other. It is not likely that one participant's score on an instrument is influenced by another participant's score on the same instrument. To examine the normality assumption for each group of the independent variable, skewness and kurtosis values, results from normality tests, and visual displays of data using histograms and normal Q-Q plots were examined. Levene's test was used to determine whether the homogeneity of variance assumption was satisfied.

"For *t*-tests on the motivation subscales, most of the distributions for males and females on the four dependent variables were shown to have some amount of negative skewness and either positive or negative kurtosis. The Kolmogorov-Smirnov and Shapiro-Wilks tests of normality were rejected for all groups on all variables. This was not surprising, however, because of the sensitivity of these tests to large sample sizes. Histograms and normal Q-Q plots showed that the motivation effort subscale deviated the most from normality for both genders. With regard to homogeneity of variance, results from Levene's test showed that only the motivation effort scale had unequal variances across the two genders. The non-parametric Mann-Whitney test was conducted on this subscale as well as the others due to their non-normality and unequal sample sizes for males and females. Outcomes from the parametric and non-parametric tests will be compared in the Results section.

"The same procedures were used to examine assumptions for the two analyses of variances. For the two-factor ANOVA on locus of control, both assumptions were satisfied. The data was normal across all subgroups of both independent variables and the homogeneity of variance assumption was satisfied. For the one-factor ANOVA, distributions for only a few of the ideology identity status groups on the hyperfemininity variable were slightly non-normal, and the homogeneity of variance assumption was not satisfied at the .05 level. Due to the largely unequal sample sizes, a ratio of nearly four to one for the largest versus the smallest group size, the validity of the probability statements for the ANOVA may be compromised. Several alternate analyses were conducted and compared to the *F*-test results. They include two modifications of the *F*-test, the Kruskal-Wallis test, and a square root transformation of the dependent variable."

Paragraphs for Results Section

"Probability results were the same for the non-parametric Mann-Whitney U test and the parametric *t*-test for the motivation effort subscale. The *p* values were both < .001. Furthermore, results from the parametric and nonparametric tests did not differ for the other three motivation subscales. The *p* values for *t*-tests on academic interest, personal responsibility, and overall motivation subscales were .016, .034, and < .001, respectively. Mann-Whitney *p* values were .017, .046, and < .001, respectively. Both tests led to the same conclusions about mean differences in gender.

"When examining mean differences in hyperfemininity scores across ideology identity status groups, results from the alternate analyses were the same as the result of the original ANOVA, which was to reject the null hypothesis at $p < .001$. The Welch and Brown-Forsythe modifications, the non-parametric Kruskal-Wallis test, and an ANOVA on the square root transformation of hyperfemininity variable all had p values less than .001. Thus, the conclusion that hyperfemininity scores differed significantly across the identity status groups is valid."

△ Reflective Questions

- Why is it important to evaluate the assumptions of a statistical model?
- How is the independence assumption evaluated?
- What procedures are used to evaluate the normality assumption, and how are the results interpreted?
- What procedures are used to evaluate homogeneity of variance, and how are the results interpreted?
- Why is it beneficial to conduct alternate analyses (nonparametric tests, modifications of the F-test statistic) if a model assumption is violated?
- How are these alternate analyses conducted?
- What is the process for creating a square root transformation of a variable?

△ Extensions

- Certain portions of the output for the ANOVAs on hyperfemininity and locus of control were not displayed in the module. On your own, produce skewness and kurtosis values, normality tests, and visual displays of data (such as histograms and normal Q-Q plots), and compare your results to those described in the text of the module.
- Discuss transformations of variables. Locate information from statistics textbooks or published articles that describes the common types of transformations and how they may be useful when certain model assumptions are violated.

- Discuss the meaning of Type I error and power in the context of this study.
- Statisticians are continually examining the impact of violating model assumptions on the validity of test results. They also continue to investigate the tests used to evaluate assumptions (e.g., Levene's test and Kolmogorov-Smirnov). Find information in other sources, such as textbook and journal articles, on these topics and discuss the most current findings.
- Using variables in other data files, practice testing the normality and homogeneity of variance assumptions for t-tests and ANOVAs to determine whether the validity of results may be compromised.
- Because the purpose of this module is to focus on the evaluation of model assumptions, it does not include detailed descriptions of results for the t-tests and ANOVAs that were conducted. Write your own interpretations of the results that compare mean differences across groups and make conclusions about the overall outcomes of the t-tests and ANOVAs. Discuss whether follow-up analyses (such as post hoc tests) need to be conducted, and, if so, perform the procedures and interpret the results.

Evaluating Model Assumptions for Multiple Regression Analysis

---

&✄✦

DATA FILES FOR THIS MODULE

module7_lifedomains.sav
module7_lifedomains_final.sav

&✄✦

KEY LEARNING OBJECTIVES

The student will learn to

- examine model assumptions for a multiple regression analysis (independence, normality, and homoscedasticity of residuals and linear relationships among variables)
- produce and interpret various statistics to evaluate the assumptions
- produce and interpret visual displays of data to evaluate the assumptions
- determine whether multicollinearity exists among the predictors
- produce and interpret measures that identify outliers and influential data points in the regression analysis

A. Description of Researcher's Study △

Dr. Novak continues her investigation of life domain constructs in this module. Module 6 demonstrated how she examined model assumptions for tests of mean differences that she plans to conduct in the first aspect of her study.

Now she is ready to begin the second aspect of her study, which investigates the nature of relationships among a set of life domain constructs. One research question requires a multiple regression analysis to determine the amount of variance in female depression scores explained by measures of locus of control, hyperfemininity, masculinity, femininity, and three subscales from an aggression instrument.

This module describes how she evaluated the multiple regression assumptions of linearity among the predictor variables, independence of residuals, normality of residuals, and homoscedasticity of residuals. In addition to these assumptions, Dr. Novak examined other important aspects of the model to ensure that her regression analysis will produce valid results. These include measuring the extent of multicollinearity among predictor variables and identifying outliers and influential data points.

With regard to outliers, you may recall that Module 5 in Section 2 described how a researcher used boxplots and other procedures to identify outliers in the distributions of two continuous variables. Here, in this module, Dr. Novak uses several measures to identify outliers and influential data points that are specific to the multiple regression model and can help to determine their impact on the regression equation.

△ B. A Look at the Data

Dr. Novak's file (*module7_lifedomains.sav*) contains 283 cases and 10 variables. This represents a subset of her full sample, namely, female students who were administered the hyperfemininity scale. The first two variables shown in Table 7.1 indicate the participant number and gender (which is a constant in this file). The remaining eight variables represent the set of continuous variables used in the regression analysis.

Table 7.1 Variables in the Life Domains Study Data File

Variable Name	Description
partno	numerical identifier for each study participant
gender	gender is a constant (1 = female) for this subset of the full data file
locsum	total score on items from a locus of control survey. There were 29 total items on the survey, 6 of which were filler items with responses not included in the sum. Each item on the survey had two options, 0 and 1, thus the possible range for *locsum* is 0 to 23.

Variable Name	Description
hypfem	total score on items for the Hyperfemininity Scale. There were 26 items on the survey. Each item had three options, 0, 1, and 2, so the possible range for *hypfem* is 0 to 52.
masc	total score on 20 items regarding masculine characteristics on the Bem Sex Role Inventory (BSRI). Each item had seven options (1 to 7), so the possible range for *masc* is 7 to 140.
fem	total score of 20 items regarding feminine characteristics on the Bem Sex Role Inventory (BSRI). Each item had seven options (1 to 7), so the possible range for *fem* is 7 to 140.
yrelaggr	total score on the relational aggression subscale of the Young Adult Social Behavior (YASB) instrument. Each of the five items in this subscale had five options (1 to 5), so the possible range for *yrelaggr* is 5 to 25.
ysocaggr	total score on the social aggression subscale of the Young Adult Social Behavior (YASB) instrument. Each of the five items in this subscale had five options (1 to 5), so the possible range for *ysocaggr* is 5 to 25.
yintmat	total score on the interpersonal maturity subscale of the Young Adult Social Behavior (YASB) instrument. Each of the four items in this subscale had five options (1 to 5), so the possible range for *yintmat* is 4 to 20.
bdisum	total score on the Beck Depression Inventory II. There were 21 total items on the inventory. Each item had four options (0, 1, 2, and 3), so the possible range for *bdisum* is 0 to 63.

C. Planning and Decision Making △

To evaluate the regression model, Dr. Novak reflected on what she knew about the model assumptions and other diagnostics, their impact on validity, the approach she will take to examine the data, and what she will do if there is a problem. Her regression analysis incorporates seven independent variables or predictors, which are *locsum, hypfem, masc, fem, yrelaggr, ysocaggr,* and *yintmat*. The dependent variable is *bdisum*. The following sections describe her planning and decision making regarding the assumptions of the regression model, multicollinearity, outliers, and influential data points.

The Assumptions

There are assumptions about variables and assumptions about residuals (Mertler & Vannatta, 2005). Some are related to the research design and cannot be tested, per se, whereas others are data-related. The three assumptions about variables are as follows:

1. The independent variables are fixed, not random, so the measurement scale cannot change from one analysis to another.
2. The independent variables are measured without error.
3. There is a linear relationship among the independent and dependent variables.

> ****1** Dr. Novak says: "Usually when someone says they conducted a multiple regression, they typically are referring to a regression that was carried out using the ordinary least squares approach. If there are nonlinear relationships among variables, then a different approach to analyzing the data should be taken, such as using a polynomial regression model."
>
> ****2** Dr. Novak says: "This is true, of course, for all types of statistical tests. When reliability is low, it means there is a large degree of measurement error."

Multiple regression analysis was developed to handle neither random variables nor nonlinear relationships among variables. Therefore, if Assumptions 1 and 3 are not satisfied, then this type of analysis is not the appropriate choice for analyzing the data. ****Dr. Novak (1)** If Assumption 2 is not satisfied, then results will be meaningless. Scores from all instruments must have a high degree of reliability. ****Dr. Novak(2)** In a regression, error will make it more difficult to measure accurately the amount of variance in the dependent variable that is explained by the set of independent variables.

Assumptions 1 and 2 are design related. Assumption 3 (linearity) is data-related and can be tested. Dr. Novak will create a matrix of bivariate scatterplots for all variables in the regression. This is one way to examine efficiently whether relationships are linear. For variables with moderate to high correlation coefficients, the plots should resemble ellipses where most of the points cluster around a diagonal from lower left to upper right (for a positive correlation) or from upper left to lower right (for a negative correlation). Scatterplots that show points following a curved path are likely to be nonlinear.

There are also three assumptions about residuals:

4. Residuals are independent.
5. Residuals are normally distributed.
6. Residuals have constant variance (homoscedasticity).

Assumption 4 is design-related. If there is no reason to believe that one participant's responses on an instrument influence another participant's responses, then the assumption is satisfied. However, there is a way to empirically test the assumption. The Durbin-Watson statistic provides a measure of the serial correlations among the residuals. This is typically used for time series applications, but can be computed for other samples as well. The range of the statistic is 0 to 4. Critical tables are available for use in comparing calculated values. There are also general guidelines for interpreting the statistic. Some statisticians say that if the value is less than 1, the residuals are positively correlated. If the value is larger than 2, the residuals are negatively correlated. Other statisticians (Osborne & Waters, 2002) state that values between 1.5 and 2.5 indicate no dependency among residuals.

Assumptions 5 and 6 are similar to the normality and heterogeneity of variance assumptions for tests of mean differences among groups (described in Module 6), except they refer to the residuals of the regression model. Residuals are the differences between the actual value and the predicted value for the dependent variable. Dr. Novak will examine Assumption 5, normality, by obtaining standardized skewness and kurtosis values for the distribution of residuals as well as histograms and normal Q-Q plots.

To examine homoscedasticity, Assumption 6, she will create a residual plot where the x-axis represents standardized predicted values and the y-axis represents standardized residuals. The data points in the plot should be dispersed randomly around the horizontal line at zero, from the lower end to the upper end of the scale. Small residuals (near 0) will be close to the line and larger residuals will be further from the line (above the line for a positive residual and below the line for a negative residual). An example of violating this assumption would be if residuals clustered close to the line at the lower end of the x-axis (i.e., smaller predicted values) and grew increasingly further away from the line toward the upper end of the x-axis (i.e., larger predicted values).

The residual plot can also be used to detect violations of normality (Assumption 5) and linearity of relationships (Assumption 3). When the distance of residuals from the 0 line is greater above the line than it is below the line (or vice versa), the distribution may be non-normal. A violation of linearity may show up in a plot that looks as though there is a curve in the pattern of residuals. In other words, the residuals might gradually increase from negative to positive in the lower part of the scale and then gradually decrease from positive to negative in the upper part of the scale. Generally speaking, if normality, homoscedasticity, and linearity are satisfied, the residuals should be randomly distributed in a rectangular fashion around the horizontal line at 0.

There are several paths to take if the model assumptions are not met. Similar to some of the assumptions in Module 6, if the sample size is large, moderate violations are most likely not a big concern, especially with regard to non-normality. So one option is to do nothing. A second option is to delete variables that may be causing the problem. Third, the problematic variables could be transformed. Finally, if there is a violation of the linearity assumption, a nonlinear regression model should be used (Stevens, 2009).

Multicollinearity

This exists when there are moderate to high relationships among the independent variables (or predictors). It is a problem because it limits the multiple correlation coefficient (R), the regression equation is less stable (because the variances of regression coefficients are large), and the effects of the predictors are confounded.

Dr. Novak will use two types of evidence to determine if multicollinearity exists in her data. First, an intercorrelation matrix will indicate the strength of relationships among the predictors. Then, she will request tolerance values and variance inflation factors for all predictors. They are available through the regression command in SPSS. Tolerance is the proportion of variance in an independent variable that is not explained by its relationship with the other independent variables. It ranges from 0 to 1. Small values of .1 or less indicate multicollinearity. The variance inflation factors (VIFs) are the inverse of tolerance values. They measure the relationship between the independent variable and all other independent variables. VIFs greater than 10 indicate multicollinearity. **Dr. Novak(3)** If multicollinearity is a problem, Dr. Novak could remove one of the variables that correlates highly with others from her analysis. Another possibility is to combine variables into one measure, if appropriate. **Dr. Novak(4)**

**3 Dr. Novak says: "If these measures show that multicollinearity may be a problem, then I will further examine collinearity diagnostics, which include the eigenvalue condition index and variance proportions. They are also available in SPSS."

**4 Dr. Novak says: "Alternative paths other researchers have taken are to conduct factor analysis and reduce the number of predictors, use a stepwise regression in order to highlight the importance of 'entry order' of predictors into the model, or conduct an alternative to multiple regression, such as ridge regression (Stevens, 2009)."

Outliers and Influential Data Points

Regression is extremely sensitive to outliers. In multiple regression, there can be outliers on the outcome variable or outliers on the set of the predictors. In the first situation, a case with a predicted value that is very different from the actual value may be identified as an outlier. In the regression procedure, Dr. Novak will request a table of output listing cases having a standardized residual greater than an absolute value of three standard deviations from the mean of 0. For a normal distribution with no outliers, 99% of residuals should be within ±3 standard deviations and 95% of residuals should be within ±2 standard deviations.

In the second situation, cases that are different from the rest of the sample on the set of predictors are considered outliers. For each case, Dr. Novak will obtain leverage (h) values from the Regression procedure. Values greater than $3(k + 1)/n$, where k is the number of predictors and n is the sample size, are considered large. Mahalanobis distance, D^2, is another measure available in SPSS that identifies this type of outlier. It tells how far the case is from the centroid (vector of means) of all other cases. In order to determine whether D^2 is too large, it is compared against values in a critical table. **Dr. Novak(5)**

**5 Dr. Novak says: "When the sample size is large (greater than 50), h and D^2 have been shown to be quite similar in their identification of outliers."

A case can be an outlier as described above, but may or may not be an influential data point, and vice versa. Three measures are available to determine the magnitude of the impact each case has on the predicted regression equation: Cook's distance, DfFit, and DfBetas. Cook's distance evaluates the entire regression equation and measures the extent of change in the set of regression coefficients if the case was deleted. One value per case is given. It is sometimes thought of as a measure of the combined influence of an outlier on Y and an outlier on the set of predictor variables.

A DfFit value measures how much the predicted value for a case will change when that case is deleted. In other words, it measures the impact of the outlier on the predicted value. Specifically, it indicates the number of estimated standard errors that the predicted value changes when the case is deleted. An absolute value of 2 is considered large. As with Cook's distance, it evaluates the entire regression equation, and one value per case is given. However, unlike Cook's distance, the sign of the value is preserved.

The third measure of influential data points is actually a set of measures. The DfBetas determine how much each regression coefficient changes when a case is deleted. They are also measured in terms of estimated standard errors. As with the DfFit, absolute values of 2 are considered large. Unlike Cook's distance and DfFit, it measures the separate effect for each predictor, so a DfBeta value is produced for each predictor variable and the constant in the regression equation.

Now to Begin

Most of the procedures that Dr. Novak needs to conduct are available within the **Statistics, Plots,** or **Save** portions of **SPSS regression**. In **Statistics**, she will obtain the tolerance and variance inflation factors by requesting collinearity diagnostics, the Durbin-Watson statistic for evaluating independence of residuals, and casewise diagnostics for examining outliers outside two or three standard deviations. In **Plots**, she will request histograms and normal probability plots for the standardized residuals as well as a scatterplot of standardized residuals. In **Save**, she will add new variables to her file (e.g., Cook's distance, DfFit) to identify potential outliers and influential data points. ****Dr. Novak(6)**

> **6 Dr. Novak says: "Of course, all of these procedures could be run in one or two steps, but I perform them separately so that I can place my full attention on examining one assumption at a time."

△ D. Using SPSS to Address Issues and Prepare Data

Multicollinearity

Dr. Novak decided to begin by examining multicollinearity, because if it exists, she may need to remove or combine predictors in her regression model, which would then impact the evaluation of model assumptions. To obtain the intercorrelation matrix for all variables, she selected **Correlate** and **Bivariate** under the **Analyze menu**. She moved the dependent variable and all seven independent variables (predictors) into the **Variables** box (see Figure 7.1).

After she clicked **OK**, the matrix in Table 7.2 was produced. She examined the upper right triangle of correlation coefficients. ****SPSS Tip 1** All correlations are

> **SPSS Tip 1: Dr. Novak could also examine the lower left triangle of results in the matrix. They are the same coefficients.

Figure 7.1   Analyze → Correlate → Bivariate

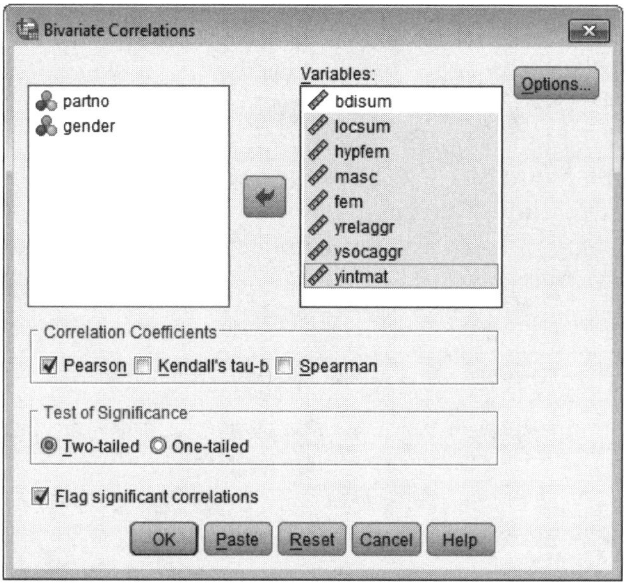

Table 7.2   SPSS Intercorrelation Matrix for All Variables in the Regression

Correlations

		bdisum	locsum	hypfem	masc	fem	yrelaggr	ysocaggr	yintmat
bdisum	Pearson Correlation	1	.211**	.170**	-.159**	-.112	-.276**	-.122*	.122*
	Sig. (2-tailed)		.000	.004	.007	.059	.000	.041	.040
	N	283	283	283	283	283	283	283	283
locsum	Pearson Correlation	.211**	1	.256**	-.125*	-.140*	-.236**	-.180**	.082
	Sig. (2-tailed)	.000		.000	.036	.018	.000	.002	.170
	N	283	283	283	283	283	283	283	283
hypfem	Pearson Correlation	.170**	.256**	1	-.117	-.093	-.327**	-.457**	.205**
	Sig. (2-tailed)	.004	.000		.050	.120	.000	.000	.001
	N	283	283	283	283	283	283	283	283
masc	Pearson Correlation	-.159**	-.125*	-.117	1	-.006	.116	.023	-.197**
	Sig. (2-tailed)	.007	.036	.050		.915	.050	.701	.001
	N	283	283	283	283	283	283	283	283
fem	Pearson Correlation	-.112	-.140*	-.093	-.006	1	.199**	.280**	-.182**
	Sig. (2-tailed)	.059	.018	.120	.915		.001	.000	.002
	N	283	283	283	283	283	283	283	283
yrelaggr	Pearson Correlation	-.276**	-.236**	-.327**	.116	.199**	1	.493**	-.359**
	Sig. (2-tailed)	.000	.000	.000	.050	.001		.000	.000
	N	283	283	283	283	283	283	283	283
ysocaggr	Pearson Correlation	-.122*	-.180**	-.457**	.023	.280**	.493**	1	-.214**
	Sig. (2-tailed)	.041	.002	.000	.701	.000	.000		.000
	N	283	283	283	283	283	283	283	283
yintmat	Pearson Correlation	.122*	.082	.205**	-.197**	-.182**	-.359**	-.214**	1
	Sig. (2-tailed)	.040	.170	.001	.001	.002	.000	.000	
	N	283	283	283	283	283	283	283	283

**. Correlation is significant at the 0.01 level (2-tailed).

*. Correlation is significant at the 0.05 level (2-tailed).

rather low. Only 4 of the 28 coefficients are above an absolute value of .300. The largest correlation ($r = .493$) is between the two aggression scales, *yrelaggr* and *ysocaggr*. The next largest ($r = -.457$) is between *hypfem* and *ysocaggr*. The other two coefficients represent relationships between *yrelaggr* and *yintmat* ($r = -.359$) and *hypfem* and *yrelaggr* ($r = -.327$).

Next, she investigated the tolerance and variance inflation factors for the model by using a feature in the **Regression** procedure. Under the **Analyze menu**, she selected **Regression** and **Linear**. She placed *bdisum* in the **Dependent** box and the seven predictors (*locsum*, *hypfem*, *masc*, *fem*, *yrelaggr*, *ysocaggr*, and *yintmat*) in the **Independent(s)** box (see Figure 7.2).

Figure 7.2 Analyze → Regression → Linear

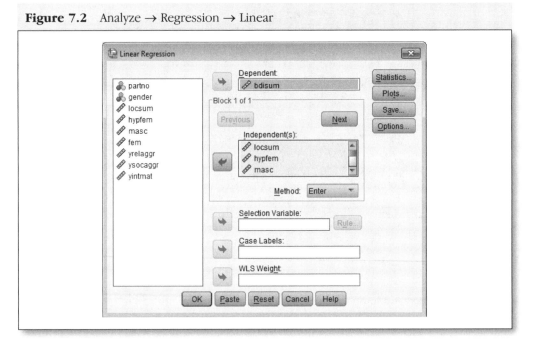

She selected the **Statistics** button to get the window shown in Figure 7.3. **Estimates** and **Model Fit** are the default options. She deselected both of them and selected **Collinearity diagnostics** to get the values for tolerance and VIF.

After she clicked **Continue** and **OK**, several tables of output were produced. At this point in her preliminary analysis, Dr. Novak is interested only in the output shown in Table 7.3. Values for tolerance are greater than .1 and the VIFs are less than 10. This information, along with the correlations in

Figure 7.3 Statistics in Regression

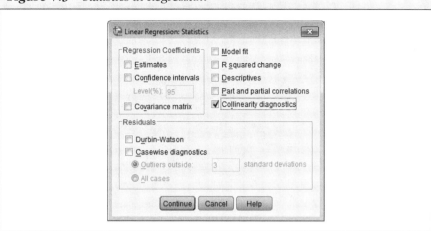

Table 7.3 Portion of SPSS Output From Regression Analysis That Includes Collinearity Statistics

Coefficients[a]

Model		Collinearity Statistics	
		Tolerance	VIF
1	locsum	.891	1.123
	hypfem	.738	1.356
	masc	.939	1.065
	fem	.891	1.122
	yrelaggr	.665	1.503
	ysocaggr	.625	1.601
	yintmat	.825	1.212

[a.] Dependent Variable: bdisum

Table 7.2, indicate that multicollinearity is not a problem in her regression model. ****SPSS Tip 2**

Assumption of Linear Relationships Among Variables

Now Dr. Novak begins her evaluation of the model assumptions. First, she obtained a matrix scatterplot to determine

**SPSS Tip 2: Another table, labeled Collinearity Diagnostics, also appears in the SPSS output. Because there is no multicollinearity among the variables, Dr. Novak did not need to look further. These diagnostics are helpful when tolerance values or VIF indicate a possible problem.

whether relationships among the variables are linear. This type of plot is essentially a compilation of all bivariate scatterplots that visually display the relationships between each pair of variables. Under the **Graphs menu**, she selected **Legacy Dialogs** and **Scatter/Dot**. The default plot is the **Simple Scatter.** For her purposes, she clicked on **Matrix Scatter** instead (see Figure 7.4).

Figure 7.4   Graphs → Legacy Dialogs → Scatter/Dot

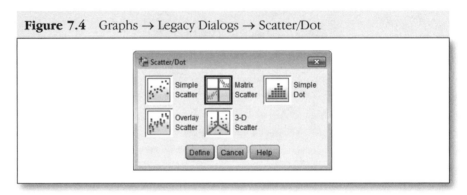

After she clicked **Define**, the window shown in Figure 7.5 opened. Here, she placed all variables (dependent and independent) in the **Matrix Variables** box and clicked **OK**.

Figure 7.5   Variables in Scatterplot Matrix

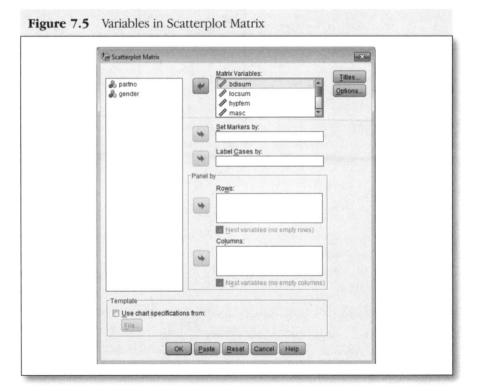

Figure 7.6 shows the complete matrix scatterplot. Not surprisingly, many plots are rather circular due to the relatively low correlations among variables. If there were stronger relationships, the plots would be elliptical from lower left to upper right for a positive relationship and from upper left to lower right for a negative relationship. She noticed that the

> ****SPSS Tip 3:** Dr. Novak also evaluated the linearity assumption through the use of standardized residual scatterplots which are produced later in the "Evaluating Homoscedasticity of Residuals" section.

plot for *yrelaggr* and *ysocaggr*, which had the highest correlation of .493, was the most elliptical in shape. Dr. Novak's purpose for obtaining this output, however, was to identify whether scatterplots show a curvilinear pattern. None of them do, so the linearity assumption appears to be satisfied based on this visual evidence. ****SPSS Tip 3**

Figure 7.6 SPSS Matrix Scatterplot for All Variables in the Multiple Regression

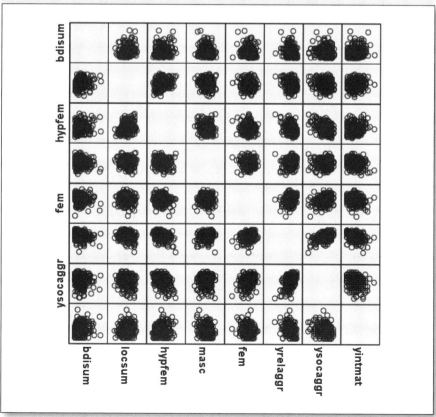

Evaluating Independence of Residuals

Dr. Novak has no reason to suspect that the residuals in her analysis are correlated. One participant's scores are not likely to be related to another participant's scores. Also, there is no time aspect in her research design. However, because the Durbin-Watson statistic is an available procedure under the **Statistics** button in the **Linear Regression procedure**, she decided to run the analysis to evaluate this assumption. In Figure 7.7, she deselected the **Estimates** and **Model fit** default options and selected only **Durbin-Watson** under **Residuals**.

Figure 7.7 Statistics in Linear Regression

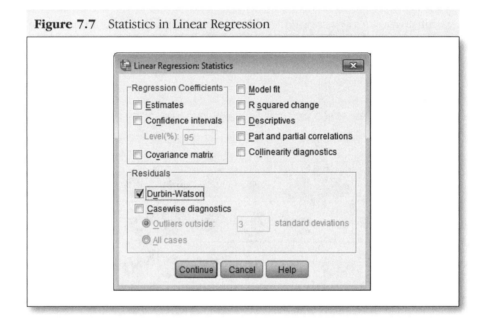

In addition to the other regression output produced by SPSS, the Durbin-Watson statistic appears in the **Model Summary** output shown in Table 7.4. This statistic is a test of serial correlations among residuals and ranges from 0 to 4. The value for Dr. Novak's regression is 1.911. Because it is greater than 1 and less than 2, she confirmed that residuals in her regression are not dependent and thus the assumption is satisfied.

Evaluating Normality of Residuals

In order to obtain skewness and kurtosis values for the residuals, Dr. Novak first needed to add a variable that contained the model's residuals. This can be done in the **Linear Regression procedure** under the **Save** button. In Figure 7.8, she selected **Unstandardized** under **Residuals**. After

Table 7.4 Portion of SPSS Regression Output That Includes the Durbin-Watson Statistic

Model Summary[b]

Model	R	R Square	Adjusted R Square	Std. Error of the Estimate	Durbin-Watson
1	.345[a]	.119	.097	9.168	1.911

a. Predictors: (Constant), yintmat, locsum, fem, masc, hypfem, yrelaggr, ysocaggr

b. Dependent Variable: bdisum

Figure 7.8 Save Variables in Linear Regression

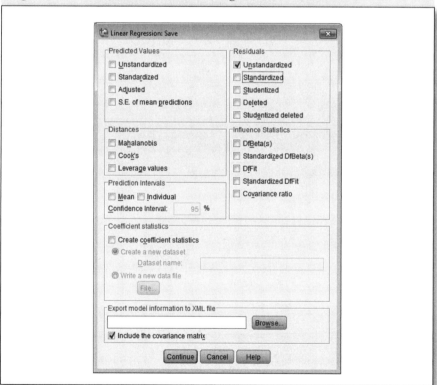

she clicked **Continue**, SPSS added a new variable to her file called *RES_1*, which contains the unstandardized values for each residual.

To examine the residuals, she requested **Descriptives** under the **Analyze menu** as shown in Figure 7.9. In the dialog box, she placed *RES_1* in the **Variable(s)** box.

Figure 7.9 Analyze → Descriptive Statistics → Descriptives

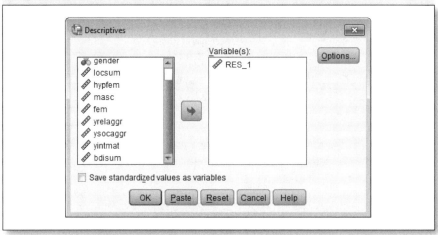

After clicking the **Options** button, she selected only **Kurtosis** and **Skewness** (see Figure 7.10).

Figure 7.10 Options in Descriptive Statistics

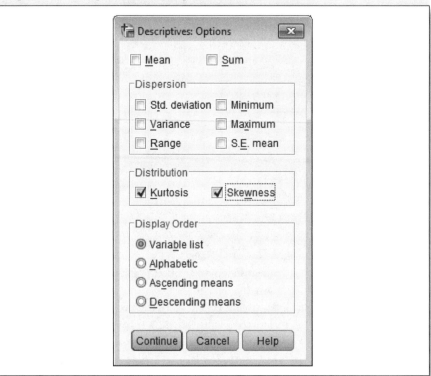

This produced the values in Table 7.5. Dr. Novak divided each statistic by its standard error to obtain a standardized skewness value of 8.94 and a standardized kurtosis value of 9.15. ****SPSS Tip 4** Therefore, this evidence says the distribution of residuals is somewhat

> **SPSS Tip 4: Dr. Novak could also have run the analysis on the standardized residuals. The skewness and kurtosis values would be identical to those in Table 7.5.

Table 7.5   SPSS Skewness and Kurtosis Values for Residuals

Descriptive Statistics

	N	Skewness		Kurtosis	
	Statistic	Statistic	Std. Error	Statistic	Std. Error
RES_1	283	1.297	.145	2.644	.289
Valid *N* (listwise)	283				

positively skewed and is leptokurtic (positive kurtosis) with a somewhat peaked and narrow distribution.

Next, Dr. Novak produced visual displays of residuals using the **Plots** button within the **Linear Regression procedure**. She selected **Histogram** and **Normal probability plot** in the window shown in Figure 7.11.

Figure 7.11   Plots in Linear Regression

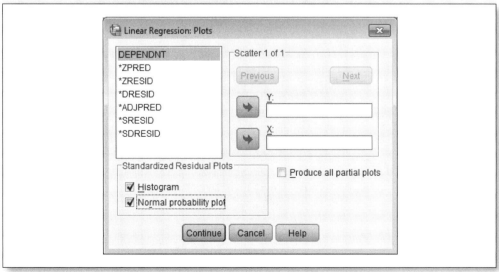

The histogram of standardized residuals for *bdisum* is shown in Figure 7.12. There appears to be some positive skewness because the tail is longer in the upper end of the scale. It is somewhat peaked as well, indicating positive kurtosis.

Figure 7.12 SPSS Histogram of Standardized Residuals for the Depression Scores

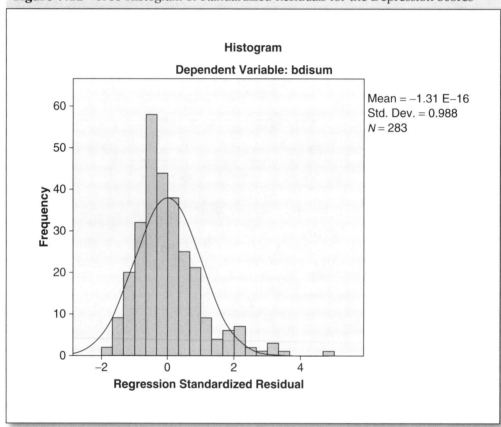

Normal P-P plots are similar to the normal Q-Q plot Dr. Novak used to evaluate the normality assumption for her model in Module 6. Here, the plot in Figure 7.13 shows that the actual probability values stray somewhat from a diagonal line that represents the expected probabilities for a normal distribution. Dr. Novak concluded that there is some deviation from normality, but it is not severe.

Figure 7.13 Normal Probability Plot of the Standardized Residuals for Depression Scores

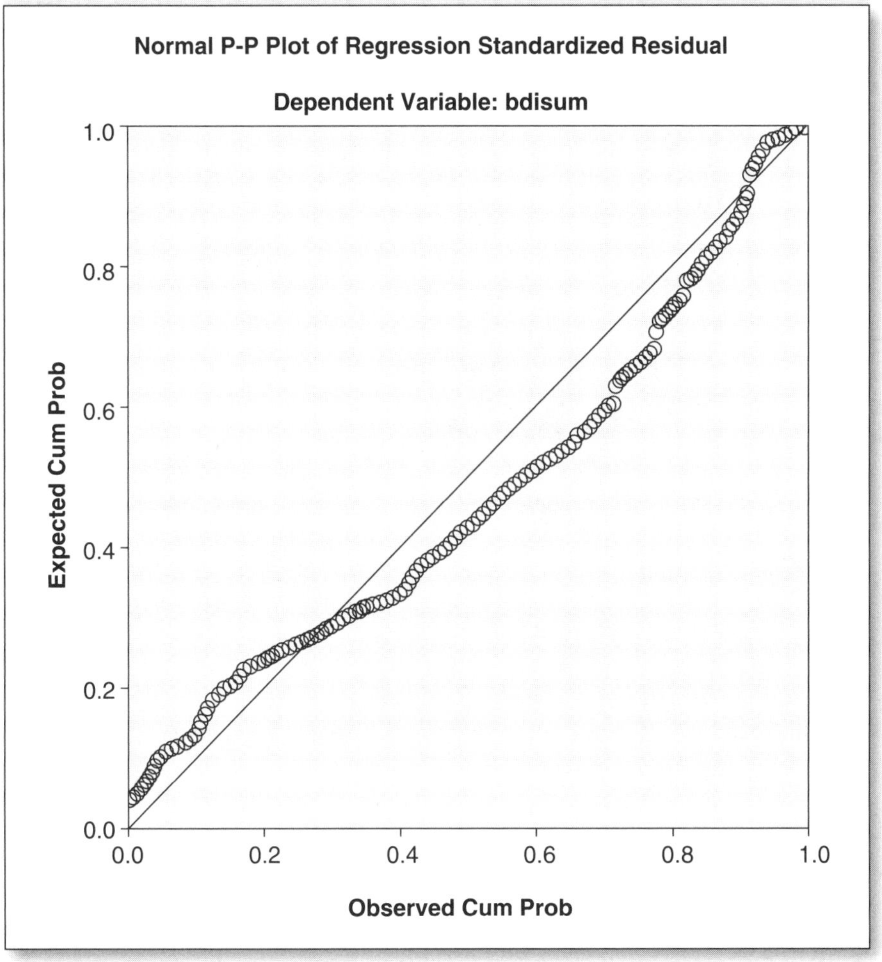

Evaluating Homoscedasticity of Residuals

Dr. Novak used a scatterplot of standardized predicted values by standardized residuals to evaluate the homoscedasticity assumption, which is the constant variance of residuals. To get the plot, she selected the **Plots** button within the **Linear Regression procedure**. The standardized predicted values, ZPRED, are placed under **X** (which represents the *x*-axis), and the standardized residuals, ZRESID, are placed under **Y** (which represents the *y*-axis) (see Figure 7.14).

Figure 7.14 Plots in Linear Regression

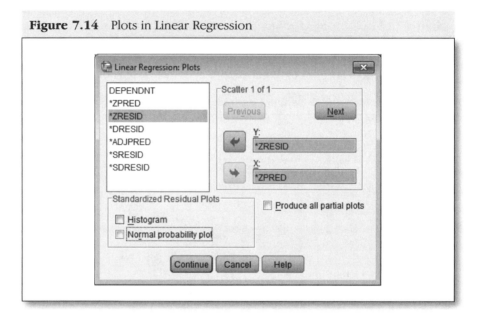

The points in the plot should be scattered randomly above and below the horizontal zero line in a rectangular fashion if the assumption is satisfied. Figure 7.15 does not show random scatter. Rather, residuals in the lower end of the scale for predicted depression scores are small (close to the zero line), but as the predicted depression scores increase, the magnitude of the residuals increases (moves further from the zero line). This is an indication of homoscedasticity of residuals.

This plot can also be used to evaluate the linearity assumption and the normality assumption. A curvilinear pattern in data points would indicate a nonlinear relationship among the variables. No curvilinear pattern is observed in this plot. This confirms Dr. Novak's previous results, which indicated that the linear assumption was satisfied.

With regard to the normality assumption, Dr. Novak noticed that the positive residuals extend further away from the zero line (up to about +4) compared to the negative residuals (down to about −2). This is an indication of non-normality, which is similar to what she found using skewness and kurtosis values and visual displays of the distribution.

Outliers on the Residuals

To begin examining outliers on the prediction of *bdisum*, Dr. Novak selected the **Statistics** button in the **Linear Regression procedure**. Under **Residuals**, she selected **Casewise diagnostics** and **Outliers outside 3 standard deviations** (see Figure 7.16).

Figure 7.15 Standardized Residual Plot for the Dependent Variable of Depression

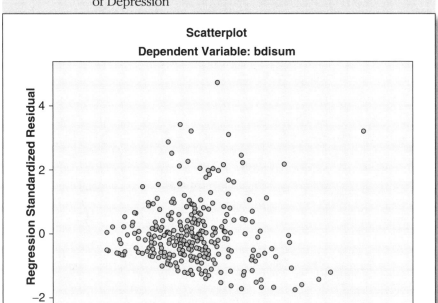

Figure 7.16 Statistics in Linear Regression

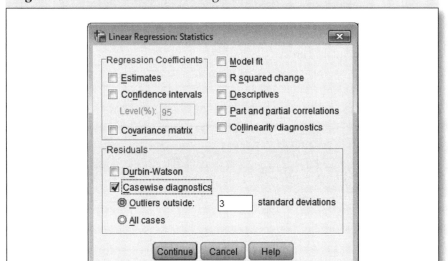

**SPSS Tip 5: Be careful when you look at cases in the data file. In Table 7.6, the Case Number is the row in SPSS that represents that participant's value. If you have an ID variable in your file (similar to the *partno* in Dr. Novak's file), the ID number may not be the same as the case number.

The output in Table 7.6 shows that five standardized residuals are above an absolute value of 3.000. Dr. Novak knows it is okay for a few residuals to be above 3, but not too many. About 99% of residuals should be within 3 standard deviations of the mean, above or below, and about 95% of residuals should be within ±2 standard deviations of the mean. In her distribution, 278 out of 283 (98.2%) are within ±3 standard deviations. The highest standardized residual was 4.727. Although the output is not shown here, she ran the procedure again, and 15 residuals were outside of ±2 standard deviations, thus 94.7% were within these limits. These results indicate that there are probably no extreme outliers on the residuals. **SPSS Tip 5**

Table 7.6 SPSS Standardized Residuals Above an Absolute Value of Three Standard Deviations

Casewise Diagnostics[a]

Case Number	Std. Residual	bdisum	Predicted Value	Residual
31	3.216	41	11.52	29.482
145	3.100	43	14.58	28.421
157	4.727	57	13.66	43.340
196	3.423	42	10.61	31.385
217	3.205	55	25.62	29.381

[a] Dependent Variable: bdisum

**SPSS Tip 6: If you want to examine the predicted values for all cases, a variable can be added to your file similar to the way Dr. Novak added a variable that included residuals for all cases. To do so, go to Save under the Linear Regression procedure.

Dr. Novak noticed that all residuals in Table 7.6 were positive, meaning that these cases are underestimated by the regression model. That is, the actual depression score is higher than the predicted regression score. For example, case number 157 has an actual score of 57, but the predicted score is 13.66. The residual, sometimes called the prediction error, is 43.34 (57.00 – 13.66). **SPSS Tip 6**

Outliers on the Set of Predictors

Under the **Save** button within the **Linear Regression procedure**, Dr. Novak selected several measures that would provide her with information about outliers on the set of predictors in this section (**Leverage values** and **Mahalanobis** under the **Distances** section) and information about influential data points in the next section (**Cook's** under **Distances** as well as **DfFit** and **DfBeta(s)** under **Influential Statistics**) (see Figure 7.17). These measures will be added as variables to her data file. They are included in *module7_lifedomains_final.sav*, which also contains the residual variable, *RES_1*, added previously.

Figure 7.17 Save in Linear Regression

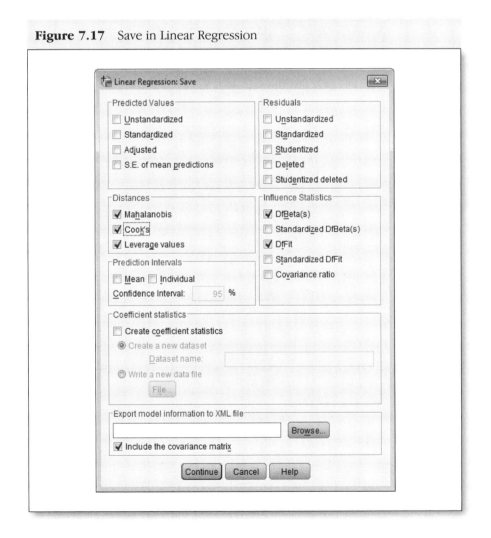

**SPSS Tip 7: The convention in SPSS for naming variables created by the Linear Regression procedure is to end the variable name in "_1" for the first time a regression analysis has been run on the data. If Dr. Novak were to run the regression again and request to Save the same variables, then the variable names would end in "_2" and so on. This convention allows the user to easily distinguish among the saved variables, which is why Dr. Novak does not typically rename these variables.

SPSS creates a default name for each variable added to the file. **SPSS Tip 7** To examine outliers on the set of predictors, Dr. Novak looks at the leverage values, *LEV_1* and Mahalanobis D^2, *MAH_1*. Values of leverage greater than $3(k + 1)/n$, where k is the number of predictors and n is the sample size, are considered large and identified as outliers. For her regression, the value would be .08481. One way to quickly determine whether any leverage values are greater than this value is to sort by the variable. Under the **Data menu**, Dr. Novak selected **Sort Cases** and sorted *LEV_1* in **Ascending order** as shown in Figure 7.18. In her data file, she found the lowest value for *LEV_1* at the top of the file (.00337). At the bottom of the file, the two highest values for *LEV1* were above the cutoff of .08481. They were .09192 for *partno* = 1009 and .13009 for *partno* = 787.

Figure 7.18 Sorting Cases

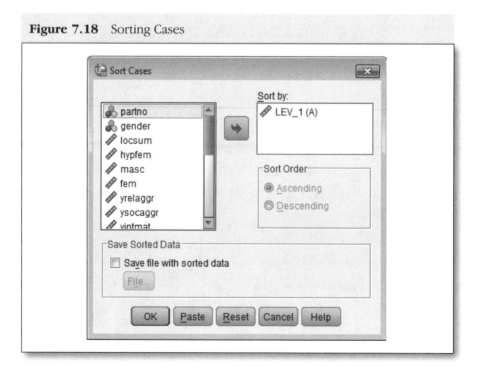

Next, Dr. Novak sorted the file by *MAH_1* to look at values for Mahalanobis D^2. To obtain a point of comparison, she looked in a table of critical values for D^2 and found that the cutoff for her data was about 23.600 (Stevens, 2009). Two values in *MAH_1* are above this number: 25.92284 for *partno* = 1009 and 36.68509 for *partno* = 787. These are the same two cases identified by the leverage measure. ****SPSS Tip 8**

> ****SPSS Tip 8:** It is not surprising that both measures of outliers on the set of predictors identified the same cases. Leverage and Mahalanobis D^2 are about equal for large sample sizes ($n > 50$). D^2 can be expressed as $(n - 1)$ h, where h is the leverage value.

Influential Data Points

For Cook's distance, a value greater than 1 is considered large. It is a measure of change in the regression coefficient if the case is deleted and is sometimes thought of as a measure of the combined influence of the outlier on the dependent and independent variables. It evaluates the entire regression equation, and as such, one value per case is given. Dr. Novak sorted her file by *COO1* and found that the highest value was .13196. Therefore, no influential data points are identified by this measure.

The DfFit values measure how much (in terms of the number of estimated standard errors) a predicted value will change when the case is deleted. Positive and negative values are produced. An absolute value of 2 standard errors is considered large. Like Cook's distance, the entire regression equation is evaluated, so one value per case is produced. Dr. Novak sorted her file by the DfFit variable *DFF_1* and examined the lowest and highest values. The lowest value was just under an absolute value of 2 (–1.99345). The highest value was 2.76072 for *partno* = 974. No other values were greater than 2 standard errors.

The last measure of influential data points are the DfBetas, which indicate how much each regression coefficient changes (in terms of estimated standard errors) when the case is deleted. Once again, an absolute value of 2 is considered large. Unlike Cook's distance and DfFit, DfBetas provide a value for each regression coefficient. Rather than sorting her data file eight times, once for each DfBeta value, Dr. Novak decided it would be more efficient to request minimum and maximum values for each variable using the **Descriptives procedure** under the **Analyze menu** shown in Figure 7.19.

Then, because she was interested only in maximum and minimum values, she selected only **Minimum** and **Maximum** in the **Options** window (see Figure 7.20).

Figure 7.19 Analyze → Descriptive Statistics → Descriptives

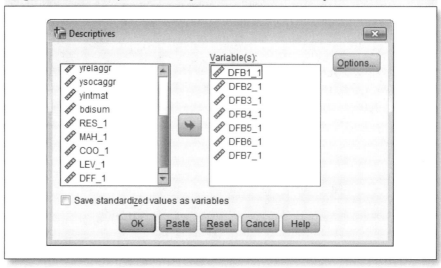

Figure 7.20 Options in Descriptive Statistics

As Table 7.7 indicates, all values were quite low. None were above an absolute value of 2 or even 1. Therefore, no influential data points were identified.

Table 7.7 SPSS Minimum and Maximum Values for DfBeta Measures of Influential Data Points

Descriptive Statistics

	N	Minimum	Maximum
DFB1_1	283	-.04711	.04643
DFB2_1	283	-.05396	.06231
DFB3_1	283	-.03487	.01940
DFB4_1	283	-.02934	.02561
DFB5_1	283	-.07570	.08465
DFB6_1	283	-.06130	.05068
DFB7_1	283	-.12084	.08740
Valid *N* (listwise)	283		

E. Reflection and Additional Decision Making △

Although Dr. Novak conducted the linear regression procedure many times up to this point, she has not yet examined the regression results to answer her research question about the amount of variance in depression that is explained by locus of control, hyperfemininity, gender roles, and aggression. Before doing so, she wants to take a step back and reflect on her evaluation of the model and its diagnostics to look at the big picture and how it may guide her next steps.

According to tolerance and VIFs, there was no multicollinearity among her variables. However, there was a moderate intercorrelation between *yrelaggr* and *ysocaggr*. Because they are two subscales of an instrument that measures aggression, she may want to combine them into one variable and compare results when she examines her regression output.

The assumptions of independent residuals and linear relationships among variables were both satisfied. However, the normality and homoscedasticity assumptions were not satisfied. The distribution of residuals was somewhat positively skewed, and the variances were unequal across the score scale for the depression dependent variable. One option here could be to compute a square root transformation of depression and run the regression again. It might make the residual distribution more closely approximate normal and stabilize the variance.

As for outliers and influential data points, five cases were identified as outliers on the standardized residuals and two cases were identified as outliers on the set of predictors. Only one case, however, was flagged as an influential data point. For the DfFit values, which measure the change in the predicted value, *partno* = 974 had an estimate of standard error larger than 2. It was also identified as an outlier in terms of standardized residuals. Therefore, *partno* = 974 is the only problematic case. The other outliers were not considered to be influential data points in the creation of the regression equation. She decided to try running the analysis again without this case to find out how much of an impact it has on the regression, although she suspects that it will not alter the results drastically.

Finally, Dr. Novak reflected on her dependent variable, *bdisum*. She believes one problem is that the predictor variables all have relatively low correlations with the dependent variable. One reason might be that *bdisum* is a constrained variable. The scale for the depression instrument ranges from 0 to 63, but for her data, 90% of the participants had a score in the range of 0 to 23. When variables are constrained, it leads to difficulties in estimating the regression equation. Her sample was selected from a normal population of college students, and the depression scores were at the low end of the scale. If the sample was chosen from a population of people with depressive symptoms, then the scale for the depression variable would less likely be constrained. When designing her next research study, she will consider studying the more specific population. By doing so, she might be able to obtain regression results that lead to a better determination of how much variance in depression can be explained by the constructs of locus of control, hyperfemininity, masculinity, femininity, and aggression.

△ F. Writing It Up

Dr. Novak's summary paragraphs, shown here, will be placed in a methodology section of a future manuscript under the heading "Evaluation of the Regression Model."

"Multiple regression assumptions for the particular model used in this study were examined. The assumptions of linearity and independence of residuals were met. First, bivariate scatterplots that displayed the relationships between all pairs of variables were examined for the linearity assumption. None of the plots showed curvilinear relationships. A standardized residual plot also indicated that the assumption of linear relationships was satisfied. Second, due to the design of the study, residuals were expected to be independent. A Durbin-Watson statistic of 1.911 provided numerical evidence that this assumption was satisfied.

"However, normality and homoscedasticity of residuals were violated to some extent. A histogram and normal probability plot of residuals showed a somewhat positively skewed distribution. Skewness and kurtosis for the residuals were between standardized values of 8 and 10, both positive. A standardized residual plot showed that the variance of residuals was not equal across the depression score scale. Lower values of predicted depression had small residuals. As the predicted depression score increased, residuals became larger. In an attempt to stabilize the variance and improve upon normality, a square root transformation of depression was computed. The assumption of normality was met, and standardized skewness and kurtosis values were low. Although there was an improvement in the equality of residual variance, the homoscedasticity assumption was still not met.

"Two additional aspects of the regression analysis were evaluated, multicollinearity and influential data points. Most intercorrelations of variables were low. The highest coefficient ($r = .498$) was between two of the aggression subscales (relational and social). An examination of tolerance and VIF indicated that multicollinearity was not a problem for the data. With regard to influential data points, although two cases were identified as outliers on the set of predictors and five cases were identified as outliers in terms of residuals, only one case was identified by the DfFit measure as an influential data point."

After presenting the results from her regression model in the Results section, Dr. Novak will compare results from a regression on the transformed depression variable. Overall, the outcomes from both regressions were quite similar. She will also provide regression results when the influential data point was removed and after combining the two aggression subscales. There were few differences.

Reflective Questions △

- What are the assumptions about variables and about residuals in a multiple regression model?
- What procedures are used to evaluate the assumption of linearity among variables, and how are the results interpreted?

- What is the Durbin-Watson statistic, and what assumption does it evaluate?
- What descriptive statistics and visual displays of data are used to evaluate the normality of residuals, and how are they interpreted?
- What is a standardized residual plot, and how is it created? How would the plot look if certain assumptions were violated?
- How is multicollinearity examined?
- What are the processes for obtaining measures that identify outliers and influential data points, and how are their values interpreted?

△ Extensions

- Locate critical value tables for the Durbin-Watson statistic, which evaluates the independence assumption, and for the Mahalanobis distance, which identifies outliers on the set of predictors. Determine the critical values for Dr. Novak's analysis.
- In statistics books or journal articles, look for examples of standardized residual plots that show violations of each assumption and discuss the visual patterns of the residuals.
- Find a data set that is appropriate for conducting a multiple regression analysis. Perform the evaluations of assumptions and diagnostics that Dr. Novak performed in this module. Present your analyses and discuss the implications of the results.
- In the Reflection section, Dr. Novak mentioned a few additional analyses that she would like to conduct. Perform these analyses and discuss their results.

△ Additional Resources for Section 3: Model Assumptions

Field, A. (2009). *Discovering statistics using SPSS* (3rd ed.). Thousand Oaks, CA: Sage. (See Chapter 5 on exploring assumptions.)

Howell, D. C. (2002). *Statistical methods for psychology* (5th ed.). Duxbury, CA: Pacific Grove. (See Section 11.8 for violations of assumptions and Section 11.9 for data transformations.)

Glass, G. V, & Hopkins, K. D. (1996). *Statistical methods in education and psychology* (3rd ed.). Boston: Allyn & Bacon. (See Sections 12.9 through 12.12, 15.24, 15.25, and 15.30 for assumptions, their consequences, and alternative analyses.)

Holcomb, Z. C. (2009). *SPSS basics: Techniques for a first course in statistics* (2nd ed.). Glendale, CA: Pyrczak.

IBM. (2011). *SPSS Statistics 20 core systems user's guide*. Author. (A pdf version can be obtained from http://www.ibm.com)

Kinnear, P. R., & Gray, C. D. (2009). *SPSS 16 made simple*. Sussex, UK: Psychology Press.

Kulas, J. T. (2009). *SPSS essentials: Managing and analyzing social sciences data*. San Francisco: Jossey-Bass.

Mertler, C. A., & Vannatta, R. A. (2005). *Advanced and multivariate statistical methods: Practical application and interpretation* (3rd ed.). Glendale, CA: Pyrczak. (See Section 7.2 on assumptions and limitations of multiple regression.)

Osborne, J., & Waters, E. (2002). Four assumptions of multiple regression that researchers should always test. *Practical Assessment, Research, and Evaluation, 8*(2). Available: http://pareonline.net/getvn.asp?v=8&n=2

Stevens, J. (2009). *Applied multivariate statistics for the social sciences* (5th ed.). New York: Taylor & Francis. (See Chapter 6 on assumptions in MANOVA.)

Tabachnick, B. G., & Fidell, L. S. (2007). *Using multivariate statistics* (5th ed.). Boston: Pearson. (See Chapter 4 for more information on model assumptions, multicollinearity, outliers, and data transformations.)

INTRODUCTION TO SECTION 4

Missing Data

This section illustrates how two researchers examined missing data in their studies. When the percentage of data missing in a data set is high, it can lead to serious consequences within the research (McKnight, McKnight, Sidani, & Figueredo, 2007). Internal validity may be compromised due to the instability or inaccuracy of estimated relationships between variables. Variables may not accurately measure the underlying theoretical construct, which leads to a lack of construct validity. Finally, results may not generalize well to other samples from the same population.

A large body of research has been generated on how to detect, classify, and handle missing data. Statisticians are in agreement regarding the importance of detection and classification but have developed a wide variety of procedures, from simple to highly complex, for dealing with it in a data set. Modules 8 and 9 in this section merely skim the surface of this important topic area. The purpose of these research scenarios is to provide readers with a basic introduction to missing data and to increase their awareness of the need to quantify and describe it in a study. There are many reasons why missing data occur. Participants drop out of a study, errors in data collection are made, some survey items are not applicable to all respondents, and individuals choose not to respond for unknown reasons. These modules describe how each researcher quantified the missing data, determined its nature, and diagnosed patterns. However, the modules do not demonstrate how to replace missing values. Broadly speaking, there are two ways to handle missing data. One is to delete the cases or variables, the other is to replace the missing values. A variety of procedures for data replacement exist and are quite complex, going beyond the scope of this book. Excellent resources are provided at the end of this section on diagnosing and replacing missing values.

Module 8: Faculty administered an assessment of knowledge and skills to students in a graduate nursing program. They also asked students to complete a survey indicating their level of satisfaction with several aspects of the program. Dr. Atwood, the program director, intends to use the data to determine strengths and weaknesses of the program. However, she noticed that a few application tasks had several missing values and other tasks had none. After quantifying the amount of missing data for each task and searching for patterns across tasks, she discovered that one task was not working well. She decided not to include this task in a composite score variable to evaluate students' level of knowledge of skills, but will use its results to inform the program. She also detected missing data in various sets of survey items, and in one instance, it led to the identification of an error in data collection.

Module 9: Dr. Zaleski is implementing a program for autistic children in early elementary grades. The program focuses on behavior modification and cognitive language skills. His sample of 34 children came from two public schools. Data were collected from teachers, parents, and students in a wide variety of forms, such as interviews, questionnaires, observations of teacher and student sessions, and examination of artifacts from teacher/parent correspondence and student work samples. This module describes how Dr. Zaleski examined missing data from the quantitative portion of a parent questionnaire administered at the midpoint of the program. Missing values were quantified by cases, by variables, and across the entire set of data points. He further investigated two variables with high percentages of missing values by creating dummy variables to represent missing versus non-missing cases. Chi-square tests and t-tests were then used to identify whether relationships existed between the dummy variable and other questionnaire variables.

Determining the Quantity and Nature of Missing Data

─── ❧❧ ───

DATA FILES FOR THIS MODULE

module8_nursing.sav
module8_nursing_final.sav

─── ❧❧ ───

KEY LEARNING OBJECTIVES

The student will learn to

- determine the number and percentage of missing data for variables
- compare the score distributions of variables with missing data versus variables without missing data
- examine and interpret the pattern of missing data within cases
- compute a mean variable specifying the number of non-missing values that must be present

A. Description of Researcher's Study △

Dr. Atwood is the director of a graduate nursing program. She and her colleagues recently conducted an assessment of the program to determine how well it prepares students for the profession. To this end, they developed an assessment instrument containing performance-based tasks that gave students the opportunity to apply their knowledge and skills to realistic situations. A holistic rubric was created for each task. Graduate student assistants were trained to score the blinded responses to each task. A portion of responses was scored by two raters to ensure that interrater reliability was high.

The nursing faculty also wanted systematic feedback from students on how satisfied they were with the program. One way they collected the feedback was through a survey instrument developed by Dr. Atwood and her colleagues. Students rated their level of satisfaction with regard to several specific aspects of the program. In addition to the Likert-type data, the faculty incorporated fieldwork assessments and collected data in the form of exit interviews with each student. Their intention is to use both the quantitative and qualitative data to assess how well their program prepares students.

Currently, Dr. Atwood's data file includes scores on the application tasks and responses to the survey. This module illustrates how she examined variables and cases to determine the quantity and nature of missing values. It also describes how she plans to deal with the missing data when she begins her analyses to evaluate the program.

△ B. A Look at the Data

The quantitative data for Dr. Atwood's study is in *module8_nursing .sav*. This file consists of 26 variables and 73 cases (students). As shown in Table 8.1, the variables represent scores on the eight application tasks and responses to 13 items on the satisfaction survey. Previous experience, gender, and cohort identification for each student are also included in the file.

Table 8.1 Variables in the Data File for the Nursing Program Study

Variable Name	Description
id	numerical identifier for participants 1 to 73
cohort	represents the cohort to which each graduate student belonged (1, 2, or 3)
gender	1 = male, 2 = female
exper	indicates whether the student had previous nursing experience (0 = no, 1 = yes)
app1	scores for this application task on the assessment. Possible scores were 1, 2, 3, or 4.
app2	same as above
app3	same as above
app4	same as above
app5	same as above
app6	same as above

Variable Name	Description
app7	same as above
app8	same as above
app_avg	mean scores on the set of eight application tasks
item1	responses for this item on the survey. Options were 1, 2, 3, or 4
item2	same as above
item3	same as above
item4	same as above
item5	same as above
item6	same as above
item7	same as above
item8	responses for this item on the survey. Options were 1, 2, or 3.
item9	same as above
item10	same as above
item11	responses for this item on the survey. Options were 0 or 1.
item12	same as above
item13	same as above

C. Planning and Decision Making △

Dr. Atwood knows there are no missing data for *cohort*, *gender*, or *exper* because these variables were obtained from the program's records. Upon scrolling through the file to get an overall feel for the completeness of her data, she noticed several missing values within some of the application tasks and survey items. Several descriptive procedures in SPSS provide summaries of missing cases as well as valid cases (non-missing cases) for each variable. Because her data values are integers, with the exception of *app_avg*, she decided to use the **Frequency procedure** to obtain the percentage of missing data. ****Dr. Atwood(1)**

**1 Dr. Atwood says: "Not only will the frequency procedure show me the number of missing cases per variable, it also produces frequency tables that may come in handy if I want to compare scores on tasks with no or few missing values versus scores on tasks with a lot of missing values."

**2 Dr. Atwood says: "Rubrics for scoring responses to each task were structured so that if a student wrote something on the task page (i.e., he or she attempted to respond to the task), the student received a score from 1 to 4. The score would be a '1' if the response showed very little or no knowledge. Thus, missing data on a task occurred when the student left the task completely blank. There are a variety of reasons why a student might not respond to a task: content was not covered in the coursework, content was too difficult, prompt or directions were confusing, or lack of time."

Her next step will be to further inspect each variable that has missing data for 5% or more of the cases. She knows that if less than 5% of data are missing, then the consequences on validity and generalizability are not so dire. If the variable is an application task, she will examine the distribution of non-missing scores to roughly determine its difficulty level. Tasks with a majority of high scores (3 or 4) could be classified as easy, and tasks with a majority of low scores (1 or 2) could be considered difficult. Then she will compare the difficulty level of tasks with missing values to tasks with complete data. If more than one task has missing data, Dr. Atwood will examine the pattern of student responses to determine if there is a relationship among the tasks. For example, if a student does not answer one application task, is it likely that he or she does not answer another application task? **Dr. Atwood(2)**

Dr. Atwood will also create a mean variable that contains the average application score only for those students who responded to at least 75% of the tasks. Her file currently contains a mean variable, *app_avg*, but it shows a mean score for all students regardless of how many items they left blank. She plans to use the **Mean function** under the **Transform menu** in SPSS to compute the new variable. It will allow her to create a mean for each student who has a score on at least six of the eight application tasks. Means for students with more than two missing scores will not be computed.

Dr. Atwood knows that there are several ways to compute a mean in SPSS, and they can potentially lead to three different values for a particular case. Her original *app_avg* was created using the mean function without any specification as to how missing values would be handled. This procedure sums all non-missing values for a student and divides by the total number of non-missing values. For example, if the sum of a student's scores on seven of eight tasks was 22 and he left one task blank, then his mean would be 3.14 (22 divided by 7). SPSS automatically adjusts the denominator for each student based on the number of non-missing values.

If Dr. Atwood used the sum function and divided by 8 (the total number of application tasks), each missing value would be treated as a score of "0." Therefore, this method produces lower mean scores for cases with missing data compared to the mean procedure described in the previous paragraph. The denominator for calculating the mean would be 8 for all students, even if they left a task blank. The student in the previous example would have a mean of 2.75 (22 divided by 8) if this method was used.

A third way to compute a mean is to create the arithmetic equation for the mean, which is (app1 + app2 + app3 + app4 + app5 + app6 + app7 + app8)/8. Using this method, the mean will not be calculated for cases with at least one missing score and will be displayed as a missing value. So the student in the example above who was missing only one of the eight tasks would have a missing mean. **Dr. Atwood(3)** (See Module 3

**3 Dr. Atwood says: "I always use the Mean function rather than the other two methods for calculating the average score across variables. The second method (the sum function) produces an incorrect mean because it essentially replaces a missing case with a value of 0. Missing and '0' represent two different types of responses. The third method is also not desirable because the mean will not be computed unless the case has complete data across all variables. This method may discount too many cases, especially if the mean composite score variable is composed of a large number of variables (e.g., 30). I prefer the first method, using the Mean function, because it allows me to specify how I want to handle missing data each time I use it."

in Section 2 for another research scenario in which the mean of a set of variables is computed.)

Dr. Atwood will use similar steps to examine the quantity and nature of missing data for the 13 student survey items. However, she will not create a mean variable for the survey items.

D. Using SPSS to Address Issues and Prepare Data △

Missing Data in the Application Tasks

To determine the percentage of missing data for the eight application tasks, Dr. Atwood selected **Descriptive Statistics** and **Frequencies** under the **Analyze menu**. Then, she placed each of the variables in the **Variable(s)** box (see Figure 8.1).

Figure 8.1 Analyze → Descriptive Statistics → Frequencies

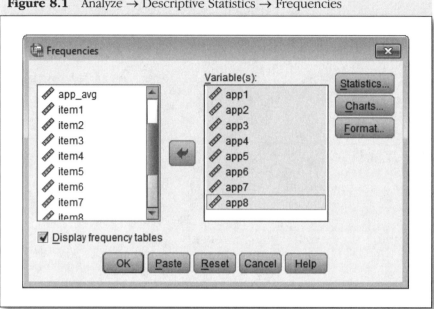

Table 8.2 is the first table of output produced by SPSS. It shows the number of **Valid** (non-missing) and **Missing** cases for each application task. Dr. Atwood noticed that four variables had no missing data (*app1, app3, app4*, and *app5*). The other four variables ranged from having two missing cases (*app6*) to 13 missing cases (*app2*).

Table 8.2 SPSS Output Showing the Number of Missing Values for Each Application Task

Statistics

		app1	app2	app3	app4	app5	app6	app7	app8
N	Valid	73	60	73	73	73	71	69	66
	Missing	0	13	0	0	0	2	4	7

A frequency table is also produced for each application task. Dr. Atwood began her further investigation of missing data by comparing the distribution of non-missing cases on *app2* to the distributions of other tasks. First, as shown in the **Missing** row of Table 8.3, 17.8% of the cases are missing a value for *app2*.

Table 8.3 SPSS Frequency Output for the Second Application Task

app2

		Frequency	Percent	Valid Percent	Cumulative Percent
Valid	1	40	54.8	66.7	66.7
	2	9	12.3	15.0	81.7
	3	6	8.2	10.0	91.7
	4	5	6.8	8.3	100.0
	Total	60	82.2	100.0	
Missing	System	13	17.8		
Total		73	100.0		

Looking under the **Valid Percent** column, Dr. Atwood noticed that the majority of scores were a 1 (66.7%). Furthermore, the **Cumulative Percent** column indicated that 81.7% of students received a score of 1 or 2, the two lowest scores. Upon examining all of the frequency distributions, this task appeared to be more difficult than the other tasks. The cumulative percentage for scores of 1 or 2 on each of the other seven application tasks were much lower, ranging from 22.7% for *app8* to 36.6% for *app6*. These results show that *app2* appears to be functioning differently from the rest of the tasks. It contained more missing data, and the majority of students had low scores.

Next, she examined *app6, app7,* and *app8*, which also had missing data. Because all three tasks were at the end of the knowledge and skills assessment instrument, Dr. Atwood wondered whether students might not have answered them because they ran out of time. The percentage of missing data increased with each successive task (2.7% for *app6*, 5.5% for *app7*, and 9.6% for *app8*. To examine whether there was a pattern of missing data across the variables, she first sorted the file by *app6* in ascending order. She used the **Sort Cases procedure** under the **Data menu** (see Figure 8.2).

Figure 8.2   Data → Sort Cases

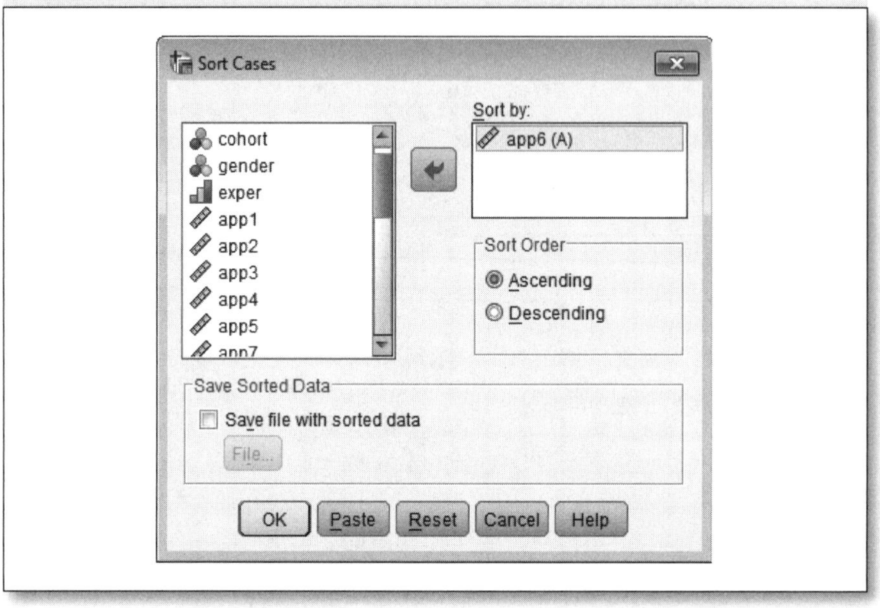

SPSS Tip 1: Dr. Atwood's procedure of multiple sorts in ascending order places the cases with missing values on several variables at the top of the data file so they can be seen easily. There are other methods for looking at the pattern of missing data (Boslaugh, 2005; McKnight et al., 2007). Dr. Atwood used this method because it was easy and efficient for her relatively small data set.

After the sort, Dr. Atwood saw that the first two cases at the beginning of the data file (*id*=7 and *id*=73) also had missing data for *app7* and *app8*.

Then she conducted the **Sort Cases procedure** again, but sorted only by *app7* in ascending order. Now there are two additional cases at the beginning of the file (*id*=11 and *id*=65) that have missing values on *app7* as well as *app8*. Finally, she conducted the **Sort Cases procedure** one last time, sorting only by *app8* in ascending order. There were an additional three cases (*id*=57, *id*=43, and *id*=66) with missing values on *app8*. ****SPSS Tip 1**

The first seven cases in her sorted data file contain all the missing data on the last three tasks of the application assessment. These cases represent the two missing values for *app6*, the four missing values for *app7*, and the seven missing values for *app8*. ****SPSS Tip 2** This tells Dr. Atwood that there is a relationship between missing data on the final three tasks. Possibly, the students ran out of time and were not able to complete the assessment.

Now she wants to create a variable, *app_avg_r*, that will produce an application mean only for cases with at least 75% non-missing data. Because there are eight tasks, this means that at least six out of eight values must be non missing in order for the mean to be computed. Under the **Transform menu**, she selected **Compute Variable** (see Figure 8.3). First, she typed the new variable name in the **Target Variable** box. Then, under the **Function group** box, she selected **Statistical**. This produces a list under the **Functions and Special Variables** box that includes the **Mean function**. When she clicked on **Mean**, it placed **MEAN(?,?)** in the

SPSS Tip 2: If this procedure did not capture all of the missing data on the three variables, Dr. Atwood could have identified the remaining cases using the Find procedure under the Edit menu. By typing a dot (.) in the Find box and clicking the Find button, it would take her directly to the case with a missing value. This method is useful when there is only a small amount of missing data. In large data files with high percentages of missing data, other methods would be preferred.

Figure 8.3 Transform → Compute Variable

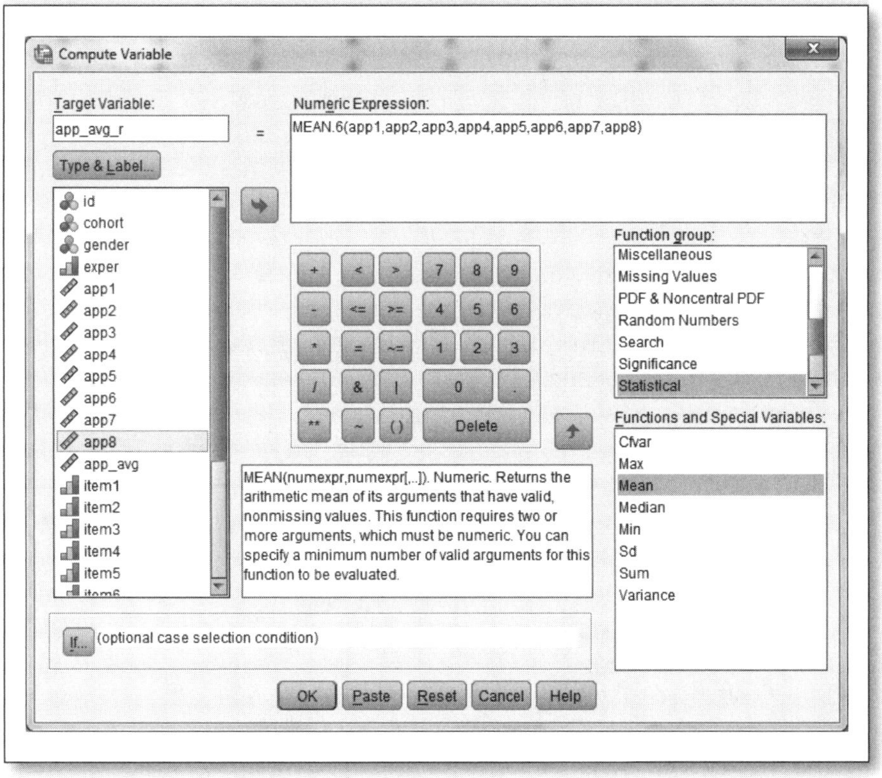

SPSS Tip 3: In order to compare mean scores across the two variables (*app_avg* and *app_avg_r*), Dr. Atwood moved the newly created variable (*app_avg_r*) from the end of the file and placed it immediately after the original mean variable (*app_avg*). This allows her to more easily examine values on both mean variables for each case.

Numeric Expression box. In place of the question marks, she listed each variable name inside the parentheses and separated them by commas. Finally, in order to tell SPSS to calculate the mean only if the case has at least six valid values, she typed **.6** after **MEAN** as shown in Figure 8.3. (See Module 3 in Section 2 for another scenario that describes the various ways to calculate a mean variable.)

After she clicked **OK**, the new variable, *app_avg_r*, was added to the file. When she looked at the data for this new variable, only two cases had a missing mean (*id*=7 and *id*=73). Both cases are missing values on four of the eight variables (*app2*, *app6*, *app7*, and *app8*). The file *module8_nursing_final.sav* contains this new mean variable. ****SPSS Tip 3**

Missing Data in the Survey Items

The first portion of missing survey data that Dr. Atwood noticed upon looking at her data set was at the end of the file. When the data were sorted in ascending order by *id*, all cases with *id* values from 55 through 73 had missing data for *item11*, *item12*, and *item13*. Because this situation is highly unlikely to have happened by chance, she searched for a reason. When she examined other variables to see what the cases might have in common, she discovered that the cases represented all 19 students who were in Cohort 3. After talking with the graduate assistants responsible for data entry, she discovered that all copies of the survey administered to Cohort 3 were missing the last page. Therefore, these students did not have the opportunity to respond to the final three items. Although this was a very unfortunate circumstance, nothing can be done about it at this point in time. It was a data collection error, and care will be taken next time to ensure that all instruments are accurate and complete prior to administration.

To determine whether there were missing values on these items from students in other cohorts, Dr. Atwood ran the **Frequencies procedure** as she did for the application tasks. The first table of output, shown in Table 8.4, indicated no additional missing data on the final three survey items for the 54 students who were in Cohorts 1 and 2.

Table 8.4 SPSS Output Showing the Number of Missing Cases for the Last Three Survey Items

Statistics

		item11	item12	item13
N	Valid	54	54	54
	Missing	19	19	19

Now Dr. Atwood turned her attention to the other portion of missing data she noticed in the file. She suspects it was due to the design of the survey instrument. Items 1 through 7 were statements for which all students responded in terms of their level of satisfaction. However, Items 8, 9, and 10 were intended only for students with previous nursing experience. Thus, Dr. Atwood believes that most, if not all, of the missing values in this set of items are for students who did not have experience.

There are a number of ways to determine whether the missing values occur only for students without prior nursing experience. Dr. Atwood decided to split the file by *exper* and run the **Frequencies procedure** for each of the three items. First, under the **Data menu**, she selected **Split File**. This opened a dialog box in which she selected **Compare groups** and placed *exper* in the **Groups Based on** box and clicked **OK** (see Figure 8.4). (For an additional description and example of the Split File procedure, see Module 2 in Section 1.)

Figure 8.4 Data → Split File

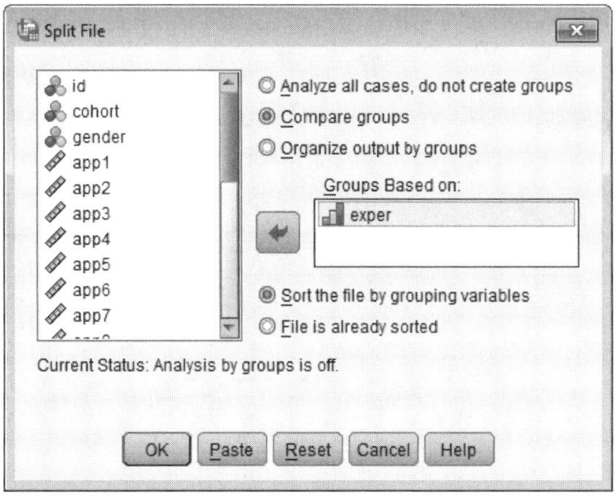

After running the **Frequencies procedure** for Items 8, 9, and 10, Table 8.5 shows that all students ($n = 23$) who did not have prior nursing experience (*exper* = 0) did not respond to this set of three items. The table also shows that two additional students with prior nursing experience (*exper* = 1) did not respond to *item10*. One case (*id* = 26) was a female student in Cohort 1, and the other case (*id* = 56) was a female student in Cohort 3.

Table 8.5 SPSS Output Showing the Number of Missing Cases for a Set of Three Survey Items

Statistics

exper			item8	item9	item10
0 no	*N*	Valid	0	0	0
		Missing	23	23	23
1 yes	*N*	Valid	50	50	48
		Missing	0	0	2

SPSS Tip 4: Dr. Atwood remembered to turn off the Split File by selecting "Analyze all cases" before running the Frequency procedure. She did not want to examine the output by the experience variable because all students were asked to answer this set of items.

Finally, Dr. Atwood used the **Frequencies procedure** again to check Items 1 through 7. ****SPSS Tip 4** There were only two missing values, as shown in Table 8.6. For *item4*, the case with *id*=36 was a male student in Cohort 2 with no prior nursing experience. For *item5*, the case with *id*=28 was a female student in Cohort 2 with prior nursing experience.

Table 8.6 SPSS Output Showing the Number of Missing Cases for the First Seven Survey Items

Statistics

		item1	item2	item3	item4	item5	item6	item7
N	Valid	73	73	73	72	72	73	73
	Missing	0	0	0	1	1	0	0

E. Reflection and Additional Decision Making △

Based on her missing data analysis, Dr. Atwood deemed application task 2 (*app2*) to be problematic. Compared to other tasks, it was difficult for students. Only 15% of all students received the two highest scores of 3 or 4. Also, it was not answered at all by 18% of students. Now she needs to determine why this task functioned so differently from the others. One reason may be that the wording was unclear or awkward and the students did not know what was being asked of them. Another possibility could be that students did not have the opportunity to learn the knowledge and skills in their nursing classes. In this situation, the task itself may not be problematic, but there is a lack of align-ment between the task and the course cur-riculum. Therefore, she decided to delete *app2* from all analyses of the assessment's composite scores. ****Dr. Atwood(4)** However, when presenting results for individual tasks, she will include *app2*. She believes the results for this task can provide good data for discussion among faculty members.

> ****4 Dr. Atwood says:** "To delete *app2* from the composite scores, I will need to create yet another new application mean variable! I will use the same mean function procedure I used when creating *app_avg_r*, except *app2* will not be included in the function. I will still indicate that 6 values must be non-missing, which is actually 86% of the data. But if I used a cutoff value of 5, the percentage would be below 75%."

The analysis of missing data for *app6*, *app7*, and *app8* caused Dr. Atwood to question whether they allowed stu-dents enough time to respond to the assessment. Results showed a pattern for these last three tasks. Students who left *app6* blank also left *app7* and *app8* blank. Students who answered *app6*, but left *app7* blank, also left *app8* blank. Now she needs to discover the reason. Maybe the amount of time allotted was not enough, or maybe they spent too much time on the task that did not work well (*app2*). Another possibility is that students were not told up front to manage their time and therefore did not pace themselves well.

In the future, Dr. Atwood thinks it may be a good idea to define miss-ing scores in different ways depending on where they occurred in the assessment. She could use a code of "8" for missing scores on a task that was "skipped," meaning that tasks before and after it were answered. A code of "9" could be used for missing scores on tasks at the end of the assessment when no further tasks were answered by the student. These user-defined missing values may be especially helpful with larger data sets because they would allow her to detect patterns more easily.

Regarding the missing page on the survey instrument for Cohort 3, Dr. Atwood realizes that she needs to institute a double-check of all instruments and surveys prior to data collection. When giving directions to assistants, she will also stress the importance of paying careful attention to all details related to carrying out the study.

△ F. Writing It Up

If there is something of interest to say about missing data, it is typically included in the Methodology section. The following paragraphs include Dr. Atwood's description of missing data for her study of the nursing program. She will place it in her Data and Variables subsection of Methodology.

"Missing data occurred on four of the eight application tasks in the student knowledge and skills assessment. Three of these tasks were at the end of the assessment. Based on the pattern of missing responses, it appeared that 10% of all students ran out of time and were not able to complete the assessment. Two of the 73 students (3%) did not answer the last three tasks, two students (3%) did not answer the last two tasks, and 3 students (4%) did not answer the last task.

"Another application task with the largest amount of missing data was Task 2. It was essentially skipped by 13 of the 73 students (18%). In addition, the majority of students who responded to the task received low scores. A decision was made not to include this task when calculating and analyzing the overall composite mean for the assessment. However, its results are included when presenting descriptive statistics individually for each task. A later section in this report provides information from exit interviews in which students were asked about their response, or lack of one, to Task 2. Students with missing values, as well as other students with low scores, provided useful information about the content of this task compared to other tasks on the assessment instrument.

"With regard to the student survey, all 73 students were asked to respond to the first seven items. Missing data were minimal (only 2 data points out of more than 500 data points). Items 8, 9, and 10 were intended only for those students who had prior nursing experience, so the total sample (by design) was only 50 for each item. Once again, the amount of missing data was minimal (only two data points across all three items). Finally, although Items 11, 12, and 13 were intended for all students, an error in data collection led to a reduced sample of 54 students. Students in Cohort 3 inadvertently did not receive these last three items. There were no additional missing data."

Reflective Questions △

- What is the process for obtaining the number and percentage of missing data for a variable? How are the results interpreted?
- Why is it useful to compare the data distributions for variables with missing data versus variables without missing data?
- What are some reasons why missing data might occur in a research study? Can missing data be prevented? If so, how?
- How do the various procedures used to create mean variables differ in terms of their resulting values?
- Which procedure for creating mean variables is best to use when a researcher wants to specify how to treat missing data?

Extensions △

- The complete set of frequency tables for the application tasks was not presented in the module. Obtain the tables on your own and compare the distributions of non-missing scores across the tasks as Dr. Atwood did.
- Compare students' averages for Dr. Atwood's two mean variables for the application tasks. Discuss the differences in their values.
- As described in the Additional Decision Making section, Dr. Atwood plans to create a third mean variable. Create the variable and compare its values to those in the existing two mean variables.
- Find a data set that contains missing values. Using some of the same procedures as Dr. Atwood, describe the amount of missing data, determine if any patterns might exist, and discuss possible reasons why the data are missing.
- Look through several statistics textbooks for information about missing data. Discuss what you find. Then, obtain a few books or journal articles that focus specifically on missing data. Describe the type of information that is covered in this broad field of statistics.

Quantifying Missing Data and Diagnosing Their Patterns

❧❧

DATA FILES FOR THIS MODULE

module9_autism.sav
module9_autism_final.sav

❧❧

KEY LEARNING OBJECTIVES

The student will learn to

- quantify the missing data in cases, in variables, and across the entire data set
- evaluate the nature and pattern of missing data by creating and examining a variable that contains dummy codes
- use statistical procedures to evaluate the relationship between the dummy variable and other variables in the data set.

A. Description of Researcher's Study △

Dr. Zaleski is a social science researcher who has worked with autistic children and their families for several years. One of his current projects is a collaboration with two public schools to institute a program for autistic children in the early elementary grades. As of now, the program focuses on behavior modification and cognitive/language skills. Autistic children, their parents, and their teachers were asked to participate from October to February during the past academic year.

Although the sample of children in the study is small, Dr. Zaleski has a large amount of and variety of data. Over the past 5 months, he collected information from the teachers, parents, and students. A small portion of the data obtained from parents is used in this module. Other types of data include qualitative responses to questionnaires and interviews, observations of teacher and student sessions, and examination of artifacts such as teacher/parent correspondence and student work samples.

Participation was optional and did not affect students' grades or other evaluations in any way. Parents could remove their students from the program at any time. The majority of the students (29 out of 34) remained in the program the entire 5 months. Five students (15%) did not complete the program, dropping out in late December or early January.

Dr. Zaleski's overall goal is to determine the successfulness of the program and to identify its strengths and weaknesses. He is also interested in knowing if there were any differences in the two schools with respect to how the program was implemented and how it may have changed over time.

Prior to answering his many specific research questions, which require a compilation of all data types, his first step is to identify and examine missing data in the quantitative data obtained from parents at the midpoint of the study before any students dropped out of the program. Specifically, the survey asked parents to rate their level of satisfaction within three dimensions: the behavioral modification aspect of the program, the cognitive/language aspect of the program, and support provided by the school. A final set of items asked parents about their level of stress. This module describes how Dr. Zaleski quantified missing data for cases and variables and how he diagnosed patterns of missing data across variables.

△ B. A Look at the Data

Dr. Zaleski's data file (*module9_autism.sav*) contains 13 variables and 34 cases and is described in Table 9.1. It represents data collected in mid December from a survey administered to parents of the 34 autistic children who initially participated in the program at two public schools. The file consists of parents' mean scores on three dimensions of the survey (support, cognitive/language skills, behavior modification) and parents' responses to six individual items that measure stress. All 34 parents took the survey, but five of them eventually removed their child from the program at some point afterwards. The variable named *completion* identifies data for these parents. Two other background variables describe the grade level of the child and the school system he or she attended.

Table 9.1 Variables in the Data File for the Autism Study

Variable Name	Description
parent	numerical identifier for parent responding to survey (1 to 34)
sch_syst	identifies the school system in which the child was enrolled, either 1 or 2
grade	grade level of child (0 = kindergarten, 1 = 1st grade, 2 = 2nd grade, 3 = 3rd grade)
completion	indicates whether the child and parent participated during the entire length of the program (0 = did not complete the program, 1 = did complete the program)
support	average scores for the first dimension on the program survey. Items that make up this dimension asked parents to rate the *level of support they received from their school* during the program.
cog_lang	average scores for the second dimension on the program survey. Items that make up this dimension asked parents to rate their *satisfaction with the cognitive and language aspect* of the program.
beh_mod	average scores for the third dimension on the program survey. Items that make up this dimension asked parents to rate their *satisfaction with the behavioral modification aspect* of the program.
item1	responses to the item on the *parental stress* portion of the questionnaire. Options were 1, 2, 3, 4, or 5.
item2	same as above
item3	same as above
item4	same as above
item5	same as above
item6	same as above

C. Planning and Decision Making △

Dr. Zaleski will begin his inspection of missing data by determining its quantity. He plans to examine it in three ways. For each case, he wants to know how many missing values occur across all variables; for each variable, he wants to know the percentage of cases with missing values; and for the entire data set, he wants to know the percentage of total data points (number of cases multiplied by the number of variables) that are missing.

**1 Dr. Zaleski says: "The reason some cases have missing values for a dimension is that the parent answered less than 75% of the items that make up the dimension. After the survey was administered in December, I conducted a factor analysis to examine the factor loadings of items on dimensions. Internal consistency, measured by Cronbach's alpha, was high for each dimension. Once this analysis was completed, I produced a mean composite score for each parent who responded to at least 75% of items in the dimension." (See Module 8 in this section for a detailed description of how to use the mean function with missing data.)

**2 Dr. Zaleski says: "You may be familiar with the phrase 'dummy coding' if you have ever done, or read about, regression analysis. It refers to a procedure by which you create dichotomous variables that represent nominal or categorical predictors in a regression. Here, in my missing data analysis, I will use dummy coding in order to transform a continuous or categorical variable into a dichotomous variable so that I can determine whether the 'missingness' of data on a particular variable is related to other variables in the data set."

For the first examination, he needs to create a new variable that will provide the number of missing values across the three survey dimensions and the six stress items for each case. Then, he will conduct a **Frequency procedure** to obtain the percentage of cases with complete data versus the percentage of cases for which some values are missing.

There are many ways to obtain the total number of missing values for each variable. Most of the descriptive and inferential procedures in SPSS provide this information in some format. Because data for the dimension variables (*support*, *cog_lang*, and *beh_mod*) are continuous, Dr. Zaleski will use the **Descriptives procedure**. In addition to producing the means and standard deviations for each variable, it provides missing data summaries. ****Dr. Zaleski(1)** For the stress items, Dr. Zaleski will run a frequency procedure because the values for these variables are integers from 1 to 5 on an ordinal scale.

Finally, obtaining the percentage of total data points that are missing is quite simple. Dr. Zaleski will divide the total number of missing values by the total number of cells across all 12 variables in the file, excluding *parent*, which is the id variable.

After investigating the quantity of missing data, his next step will be to evaluate it for patterns. For variables with more than 5% missing data, Dr. Zaleski will create a new variable with dummy codes (0 = not missing, 1 = missing). ****Dr. Zaleski(2)** Then, he will conduct analyses to determine if the dummy variable is related to other important variables in the data set. To evaluate the relationship between the dummy variable and each categorical variable (*sch_syst*, *grade*, and *completion* as well as the stress item variables), he will use the **Crosstabs procedure** and calculate the chi-square test. For continuous variables (i.e., the survey dimension variables), Dr. Zaleski will conduct *t*-tests in which the independent variable is the dummy-coded variable and the dependent variables are *cog_lang* and *beh_mod*.

D. Using SPSS to Address Issues and Prepare Data △

Quantity of Missing Data for Each Case

To determine the number of missing values across all variables for each case, Dr. Zaleski selected **Compute Variable** under the **Transform menu**. He created a new variable name, *miss_per_case*, in the **Target Variable** box. Next, in the **Function group** box, he chose **Missing Values** and selected the **Nmiss** function. In the **Numeric Expression** box, he placed the three dimension variables (*support*, *cog_lang*, and *beh_mod*) and the six stress item variables (*item1* through *item6*) in the parentheses after **NMISS** (see Figure 9.1).

Figure 9.1   Transform → Compute Variable

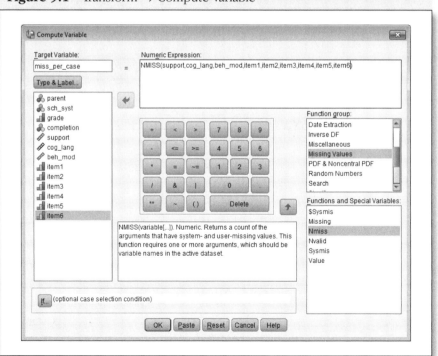

After he clicked **OK**, the new variable was added to the end of the file. Dr. Zaleski obtained a frequency distribution for the new variable by using the **Frequencies procedure** under the **Analyze menu** (see Figure 9.2).

Figure 9.2 Analyze → Descriptive Statistics → Frequencies

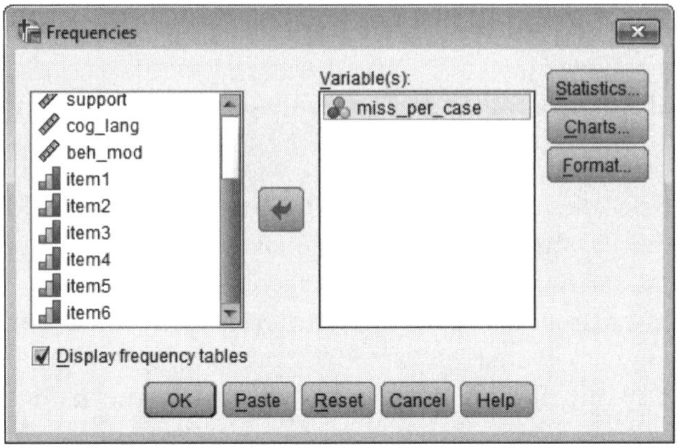

The output in Table 9.2 shows that 58.8% of cases had complete data across the nine variables. The remainder of cases (14 out of 34) had one or two missing data points across the nine variables.

Table 9.2 SPSS Frequency Output for Missing Data Across All Survey Dimensions and Items

miss_per_case

		Frequency	Percent	Valid Percent	Cumulative Percent
Valid	0	20	58.8	58.8	58.8
	1	11	32.4	32.4	91.2
	2	3	8.8	8.8	100.0
	Total	34	100.0	100.0	

Quantity of Missing Data for Each Variable

To determine the number of missing values within each of the three dimension variables, Dr. Zaleski selected **Descriptives Statistics** and **Descriptives** under the **Analyze menu**. He placed the three variables (*support*, *cog_lang*, and *beh_mod*) in the **Variable(s)** box and clicked **OK** (see Figure 9.3).

Figure 9.3 Analyze → Descriptive Statistics → Descriptives

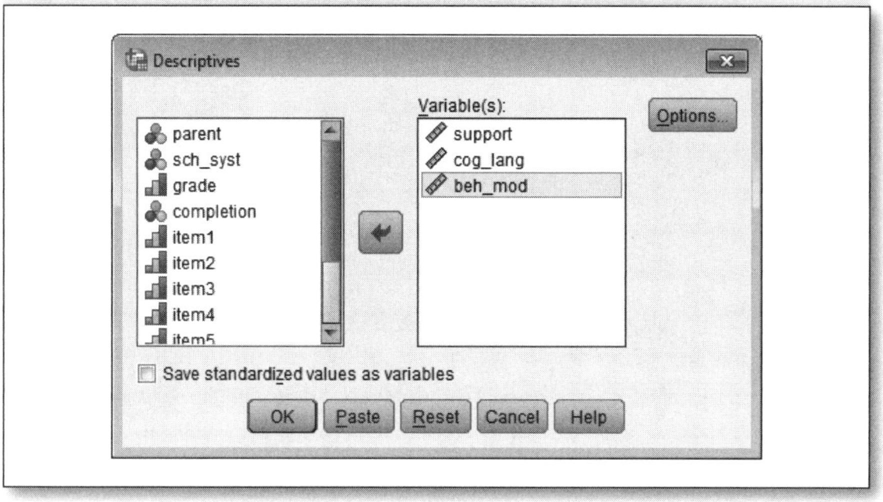

In addition to the means and standard deviations presented in Table 9.3, the total number of cases (*N*) is provided in the first column for each of the three variables. The values for *N* in each of the first three rows indicate the total number of valid cases; that is, cases with non-missing values for that particular variable. Recall that there are 34 cases in Dr. Zaleski's file. There were no missing cases for *cog_lang*; 34 out of the 34 cases had a value. Only one case had missing data for *beh_mod* (which represents only 3% of all cases). For *support*, however, seven cases (21% of all cases) had missing data. Dr. Zaleski made note of this potentially problematic variable for further analysis.

Table 9.3 SPSS Descriptive Output Showing the Number of Valid Cases for Each Variable

Descriptive Statistics

	N	Minimum	Maximum	Mean	Std. Deviation
support	27	1.50	4.00	2.4525	.60519
cog_lang	34	1.33	4.00	3.0392	.68921
beh_mod	33	1.48	4.00	2.8232	.61036
Valid N (listwise)	26				

Now, Dr. Zaleski conducted the **Frequencies procedure** to examine the quantity of missing data on the six parental stress items as shown in Figure 9.4.

Figure 9.4 Analyze → Descriptive Statistics → Frequencies

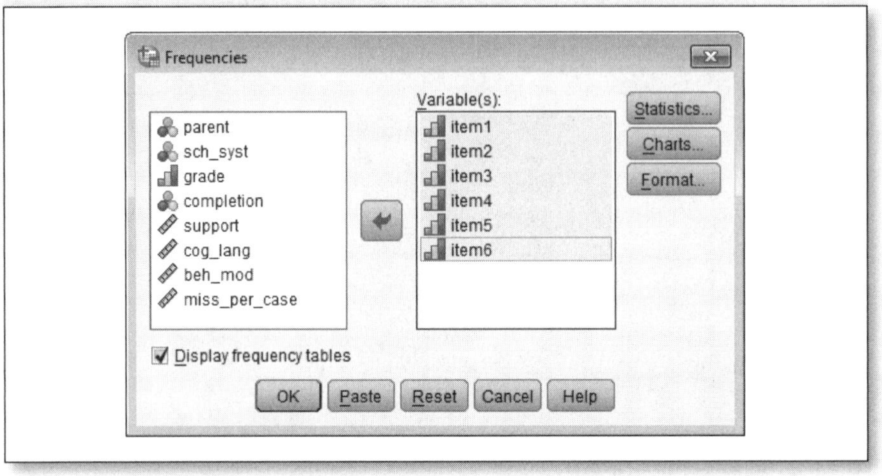

At this point, he was only interested in the first section of output. Table 9.4 displays the number of missing cases for each variable. No cases have missing data for *item1* or *item6*. For *item2*, *item4*, and *item5*, only one case has missing data (3% of total cases for each variable). The potentially problematic variable is *item3*, with six missing cases (18% of total cases).

Table 9.4 SPSS Output Showing the Number of Missing Values for Each Stress Variable

Statistics

		item1	item2	item3	item4	item5	item6
N	Valid	34	33	28	33	33	34
	Missing	0	1	6	1	1	0

Overall Quantity of Missing Data

To find the percentage of missing data points across the entire data set, Dr. Zaleski first calculated the total number of data cells across the variables. Twelve variables times 34 cases is a total of 408 data cells. There were no missing data for the three background variables; however, eight missing data points occurred within the three dimensions and nine missing data points occurred for the six stress items. Dividing these 17 missing values by 408 results in only 4.2% of missing data points across the entire data set. Overall, this is a relatively low percentage. Dr. Zaleski is concerned, though, about its concentration within two variables (*support* and *item3*). He now wants to evaluate these variables to determine if patterns or relationships exist among the other variables' values.

Evaluating the Support Variable

The procedure to dummy code *support* is similar to the one he used to create *miss_per_case*. Under the **Transform menu**, he selected **Compute Variable**. In the **Target Variable** box, he typed the new variable's name, *support_missing*. In the **Numeric Expression** box, he placed the **NMISS** function and inserted *support* in the parentheses (see Figure 9.5).

Figure 9.5 Transform → Compute Variable

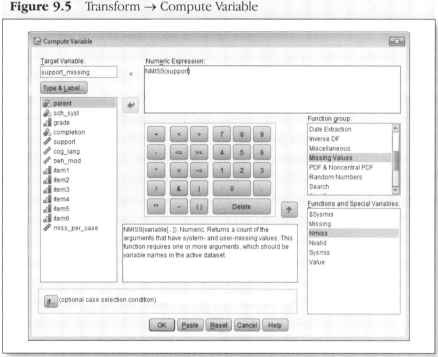

After he clicked **OK**, *support_missing* was added to the data file. He ran the **Frequencies procedure** to ensure that the new variable was created correctly. Table 9.5 shows seven cases with a code of "1." This is the same amount of missing data shown in Table 9.3 for *support*.

Now Dr. Zaleski was able to run a set of **Crosstab procedures** to determine if significant relationships existed between *support_missing* and the three categorical background variables. The detailed steps are provided here for *sch_syst*. Under the **Analyze menu**, he selected **Descriptive Statistics** and

Table 9.5 SPSS Frequency Output for the Dummy Coded Support Variable

support_missing

		Frequency	Percent	Valid Percent	Cumulative Percent
Valid	0	27	79.4	79.4	79.4
	1	7	20.6	20.6	100.0
	Total	34	100.0	100.0	

SPSS Tip 1: Dr. Zaleski could have placed *sch_syst* in the Column(s) box and *support_missing* in the Row(s) box. The results would be identical. For ease of interpretation, however, consistency across all analyses is helpful. For instance, when examining the relationships with *grade* and *completion*, Dr. Zaleski will keep *support_missing* in the Column(s) box and place the background variables in the Row(s) box.

Crosstabs. He placed *sch_syst* in the **Row(s)** box and *support_missing* in the **Column(s)** box (see Figure 9.6). ****SPSS Tip 1**

Dr. Zaleski wanted the output table to include observed counts (frequencies) as well as column percentages so that he could examine the percentage of total cases within each missing code. To get this information, he clicked the **Cells** button and another window opened (see Figure 9.7). He kept the default selection of **Observed Counts** and added **Column Percentages**.

Figure 9.6 Analyze → Descriptive Statistics → Crosstabs

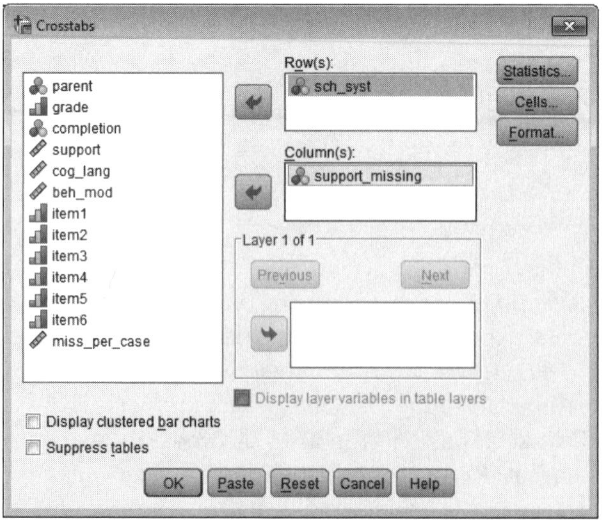

Figure 9.7 Display in Crosstabs

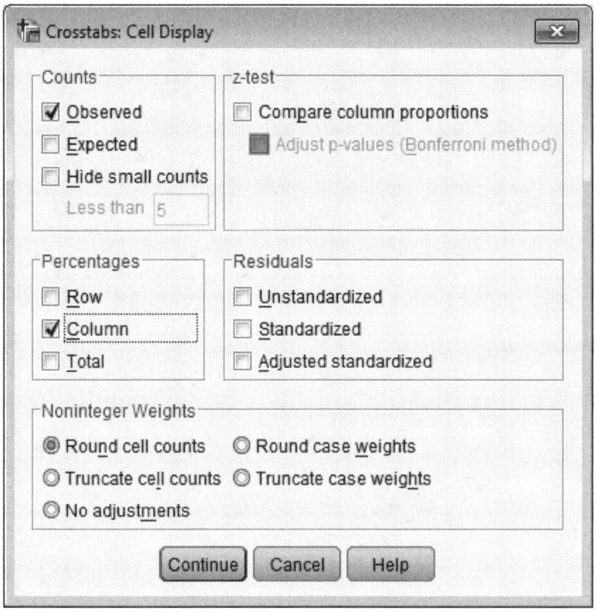

Also in the **Crosstabs** dialog box, Dr. Zaleski clicked the **Statistics** button to display the window shown in Figure 9.8. He selected **Chi-square**, then ran the **Crosstabs procedure**.

Figure 9.8 Statistics in Crosstabs

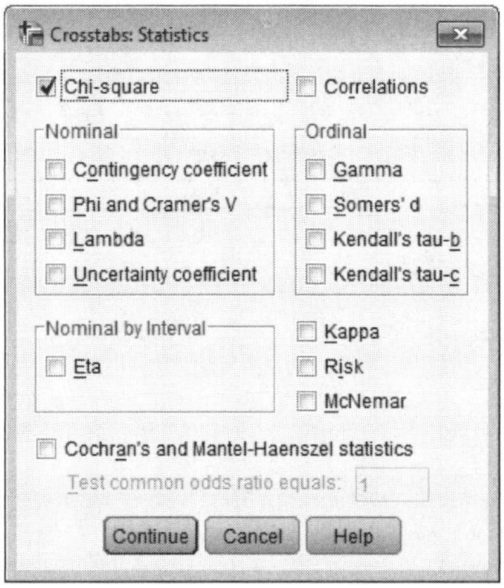

The output in Table 9.6 shows that the majority of cases with missing data on *support* (85.7%) are from school system 1 (6 out of 7). There appears to be a relationship between these two variables. (See Module 4 in Section 2 for more information on interpreting row and column percents in Crosstabs output.)

Table 9.6 SPSS Crosstabs Output for School System by Missing Data on Support

sch_syst * support_missing Crosstabulation

			support_missing 0	support_missing 1	Total
sch_syst	1	Count	10	6	16
		% within support_missing	37.0%	85.7%	47.1%
	2	Count	17	1	18
		% within support_missing	63.0%	14.3%	52.9%
Total		Count	27	7	34
		% within support_missing	100.0%	100.0%	100.0%

The chi-square test result shown in Table 9.7 indicates that the relationship is significant at the .05 level [$\chi_{(1)} = 5.287, p = .021$]. This statistical result indicates that a higher proportion of cases with missing data on the support dimension are from School System 1.

Table 9.7 SPSS Chi-Square Output for School System by Missing Data on Support

Chi-Square Tests

	Value	df	Asymp. Sig. (2-sided)	Exact Sig. (2-sided)	Exact Sig. (1-sided)
Pearson Chi-Square	5.287[a]	1	.021		
Continuity Correction[b]	3.514	1	.061		
Likelihood Ratio	5.680	1	.017		
Fisher's Exact Test				.035	.029
Linear-by-Linear Association	5.131	1	.023		
N of Valid Cases	34				

[a.] 2 cells (50.0%) have expected count less than 5. The minimum expected count is 3.29.

[b.] Computed only for a 2x2 table

Dr. Zaleski tested the other two relationships using the same steps as above. For *grade*, the majority of cases (85.7%) with missing support values were in the two lower grades. Two out of seven (28.6%) were in kindergarten, and four out of seven (57.1%) were in Grade 1. However, the relationship between *support_missing* and *grade* was not statistically significant $[\chi_{(3)} = 5.542, p = .136]$. There was also no significant relationship between *support_missing* and *completion* $[\chi_{(1)} = .001, p = .972]$.

Because the survey items for stress were not considered to be continuous variables in this study, Dr. Zaleski also used the **Crosstabs procedure** to examine the relationships between *support_missing* and each of the six items. The results indicated no significant relationships between responses to any of the items and missing data on *support*. The *p* values for the chi-square results were all above a significance level of .05.

Moving forward, Dr. Zaleski conducted a set of *t*-tests to determine whether missing versus non-missing cases for *support* had significantly different mean scores on the other two dimension variables. Under the **Analyze menu**, he selected **Compare Means** and **Independent-Samples T Test**. He placed *support_missing* in the **Grouping Variable** box and *cog_lang* and *beh_mod* in the **Test Variable(s)** box (see Figure 9.9).

Figure 9.9   Analyze → Compare Means → Independent-Samples T Test

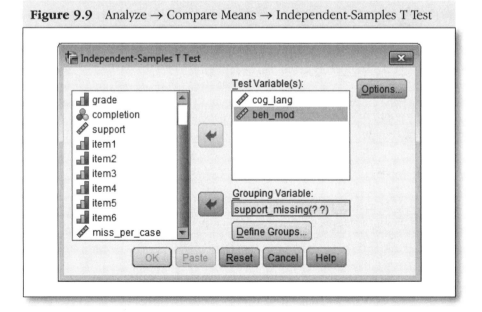

He needed to tell SPSS the codes for *support_missing*, so he clicked the **Define Groups** box and typed his codes of 0 and 1 (see Figure 9.10).

Figure 9.10   Codes for Grouping Variable

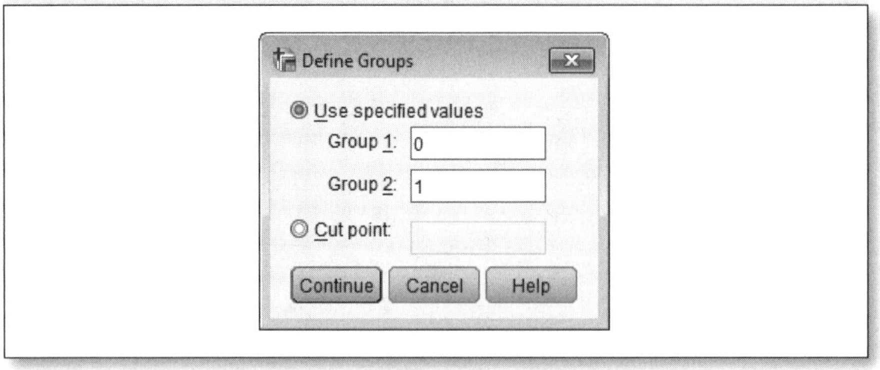

SPSS Tip 2: Levene's test for the assumption of equal variances is automatically provided in the output. For each *t*-test, two test statistics and two *p* values are provided. When variances are equal (i.e., Levene's test is not rejected), the first *t*-test, which represents "equal variances assumed," should be reported. When Levene's test is rejected, then the second *t*-test result for "equal variances not assumed" should be reported. Notice also that the degrees of freedom differ for the two *t*-tests; the degrees of freedom are not integers for the second *t*-test.

After running the procedure, Dr. Zaleski examined results from Levene's test of the homogeneity of variances assumption and results from the *t*-test. **SPSS Tip 2** Portions of the output are shown in Tables 9.8 and 9.9. The assumption of equal variances was satisfied for both variables as evidenced by the nonsignificant *p* values for Levene's test in Table 9.8. The *t*-test results were not significant, and the *p* values in Table 9.9 indicate that there was no difference in mean scores on *cog_lang* or *beh_mod* for cases with missing *support* data versus cases with no missing *support* data. Although the descriptive output is not shown here, the *cog_lang* means were 3.19 and 3.00, respectively. The *beh_mod* means were 2.84 and 2.82, respectively. (See Module 6 in Section 3 for a detailed explanation and example of this model assumption and its interpretation in a *t*-test.)

Evaluating Item 3

Dr. Zaleski's final set of analyses was for *item3*, in which 18% of the data was missing. He computed a dummy variable, *item3_missing*, just as he did for *support*. When examining output from the crosstabs and chi-square procedures, he found no relationship between *item3_missing* and *sch_syst*,

Table 9.8 SPSS *t*-Test Output Showing Levene's Test Results

		Levene's Test for Equality of Variances		*t*-test for Equality of Means	
		F	Sig.	t	df
cog_lang	Equal variances assumed	.150	.701	-.646	32
	Equal variances not assumed			-.669	9.816
beh_mod	Equal variances assumed	.074	.788	-.067	31
	Equal variances not assumed			-.072	10.487

Independent Samples Test

Table 9.9 Part 2 of the *t*-Test Results for Missing Support Values

Independent Samples Test

		t-test for Equality of Means			
		Sig. (2 -tailed)	Mean Difference	Std. Error Difference	95% Confidence Interval of the Difference
					Lower
cog_lang	Equal variances assumed	.523	-.19048	.29494	-.79125
	Equal variances not assumed	.519	-.19048	.28465	-.82633
beh_mod	Equal variances assumed	.947	-.01767	.26404	-.55618
	Equal variances not assumed	.944	-.01767	.24638	-.56319

grade, or *completion*. The significance levels for the chi-square test were .874, .319, and .156, respectively.

Using *t*-tests to determine if means on the three survey dimensions differed by *item3_missing* initially uncovered one significant result for *beh_mod* ($p = .026$). The mean score on the behavior modification dimension was lower for cases with missing data on *item3* compared to cases with non-missing data (2.33 and 2.93, respectively). However, the homogeneity of variances assumption was not satisfied for *beh_mod*, and the adjusted *p* value for equal variances not assumed was .119, which no longer indicates a significant result.

Finally, the chi-square results produced by the crosstabs procedure indicated no significant relationships between cases with missing values on *item3* and responses to the other five survey items. Each *p* value for the five chi-square tests was above a significance level of .05.

△ E. Reflection and Additional Decision Making

**3 Dr. Zaleski says: "SPSS handles missing data in one of two ways. In listwise exclusion, SPSS excludes all cases with missing data on any of the variables in the analysis. For example, if I was obtaining a correlation matrix for the six stress survey items, the listwise method would calculate the correlations based only on cases with complete data across all six variables. Not only does this method delete the missing values, it also deletes actual values from the analysis. The number of cases used to calculate each correlation is equal. On the other hand, the pairwise (or casewise) method excludes only those cases with missing data on the pair of variables that is being correlated. In this method, the number of cases used for each correlation can vary from pair to pair."

Overall, the quantity of missing data in Dr. Zaleski's data set was rather small. Only 4.2% of all data points across the variables were missing. However, the small amount of missing data was concentrated within *support* and *item3*. Now Dr. Zaleski must decide what to do about these two variables, if anything. Deleting the variables entirely from the data set is one option, but it is not a desirable one. He would lose a great deal of important information about the level of support parents received from the school system and about parental anger, which is measured by *item3* on the stress survey. Another possibility is to make a choice about how data are deleted based on the particular analysis to be conducted. SPSS excludes cases with missing data on a listwise or pairwise basis. **Dr. Zaleski(3)** The disadvantage of deleting data in this manner is that it can decrease the sample size to a point where statistical power is reduced, making it difficult to find significant results that truly exist.

Rather than deletion, Dr. Zaleski could replace the missing data with actual values. There is no shortage of methods for doing so. The most basic is mean substitution. It simply replaces the missing data with the overall variable mean or a group mean calculated based on categories in a different variable. **Dr. Zaleski(4)** Another method is to replace missing values with predicted values from a multiple regression. The variable with missing data is the dependent variable, and the predictors are variables that have relationships with the dependent variable. The regression equation created by running the procedure without the missing cases is used to create predicted values to replace the missing values.

**4 Dr. Zaleski says: "If you are using regression analysis to answer a research question, you don't have to do the mean substitution on your own. Instead, SPSS has an option allowing you to request that missing values be replaced with the variable's mean. Thus, all cases are retained for the regression. The means, however, are not written into the data file."

There is no general agreement regarding the best method for replacing missing values, but most statisticians believe that mean substitution and the regression method are less desirable than other procedures such as maximum likelihood, expectation maximization, and weighting, to name a few. Dr. Zaleski is especially concerned about one of his variables, *support*, because his analysis showed that a relationship existed between missing data on the support dimension and the school system the child attended. He is aware that procedures for replacing missing data are quite complex and may require specialized programs that he does not have. Therefore, he decides to call upon a colleague who has a great deal of knowledge and experience in this area. Together they will decide how to handle the missing data.

Recall that Dr. Zaleski collected additional information from parents, students, and teachers. Possibly, the interview responses will shed light on missing data for *support* and why it might be related to the school system. **Dr. Zaleski(5)** As far as answering the study's many research questions and reporting the results, Dr. Zaleski and his colleague may decide to run two analyses, one with the missing data and one without the missing data. Results from the two analyses will be compared to determine the extent to which the test statistics and

**5 Dr. Zaleski says: "This is another reason why it's useful to diagnose patterns in missing data. It can help a researcher uncover important information that would otherwise have gone unnoticed."

p values differ. If results are similar, then the missing data did not impact the analysis. If they are different, he and his colleague will need to determine which is the best representation of reality. (See Module 5 in Section 2 for a research scenario that conducts two analyses, one with outliers and one without outliers, and compares the results.)

△ F. Writing It Up

Dr. Zaleski wrote the following paragraphs about missing data to include in the methodology section of a paper or report. After he combines the parent questionnaire data with the other types of data collected in his study and he and his colleague decide how to handle the missing data, then he will also include that information.

"Only 4.2% of the 408 data points across all 12 variables in the file were missing. The amount of missing data for each case across all variables was also low. Approximately 59% of cases had complete data for all variables. The majority of other cases (32%) had one missing value. Only three cases had two missing values. They each were missing a different stress survey item (*item2*, *item3*, and *item5*) and had a missing value for either *support* or *beh_mod*.

"Although the overall quantity of missing data was small, it appeared to be concentrated within two variables. First, the variable representing mean composite scores for the support dimension was missing 21% of the data (7 out of 34 cases). Items in this dimension asked parents to indicate the degree to which they felt the support provided to them by their school was adequate. The other variable was item 3 on the parental stress survey. The content of the item was anger. Parents were asked to indicate how often they felt this emotion.

"After dummy coding the missing data for the support dimension and item 3, relationships between these dummy variables and other variables in the study were examined. A chi-square test was used if the variable's scale of measurement was categorical (e.g., the background variables and the stress item variables), and a *t*-test was used if the measurement scale was continuous (mean scores on the dimension variables). Only one significant result occurred. A relationship [$\chi_{(1)} = 5.287, p = .021$] was found between the school system the child attended and whether the parent had a missing score for support. Six of the seven missing support cases were from school system 1."

△ Reflective Questions

- What are the processes for quantifying missing data in cases, in variables, and across the entire data set?
- How is a dummy variable used to describe missing data?
- What statistical procedures are useful for evaluating relationships between the dummy variable and other categorical variables in the data set?
- What statistical procedures can be used to evaluate mean differences on continuous variables by missing versus non-missing cases?

Extensions △

- Discuss the row versus column percentages produced in the Crosstabs procedure and the unique information these values provide about the two variables being compared.
- The results for the analysis of item 3 were summarized but not completely presented in the module. Obtain the output that Dr. Zaleski produced and interpret it.
- Discuss why deleting cases with missing data from all analyses of the research questions may not be the best choice in some circumstances. Incorporate statistical power issues in your discussion.
- Obtain a data set with missing data and conduct various statistical analyses in SPSS using listwise deletion and pairwise deletion. Compare the two results for each analysis you conduct.
- Browse through statistics books and journal articles to get a sense of the broad topic of missing data analysis. Discuss some of the additional aspects of missing data that were not illustrated in this module.

Additional Resources for Section 4: Missing Data Δ

Abu-Bader, S. H. (2010). *Advanced and multivariate statistical methods for social science research*. Chicago: Lyceum. (See section on missing data in Chapter 2, pp. 28–43.)

Boslaugh, S. (2005). *An intermediate guide to SPSS programming: Using syntax for data management.* Thousand Oaks, CA: Sage. (See Chapter 17 on missing data.)

Holcomb, Z. C. (2009). *SPSS basics: Techniques for a first course in statistics* (2nd ed.). Glendale, CA: Pyrczak.

IBM. (2011). *SPSS Statistics 20 core systems user's guide*. Author. (A pdf version can be obtained from http://www.ibm.com)

Kinnear, P. R., & Gray, C. D. (2009). *SPSS 16 made simple*. Sussex, UK: Psychology Press.

Kulas, J. T. (2009). *SPSS essentials: Managing and analyzing social sciences data*. San Francisco: Jossey-Bass.

McKnight, P. E., McKnight, K. M., Sidani, S., & Figueredo, A. J. (2007). *Missing data: A gentle introduction.* New York: Guilford.

Tabachnick, B. G., & Fidell, L. S. (2007). *Using multivariate statistics* (5th ed.). Boston: Pearson Education. (See Section 1.3 on missing data in Chapter 4, pp. 62–71.)

INTRODUCTION TO SECTION 5

Working With Multiple Data Files

O ver the past few years, Dr. Salerno, an education professor, has been in a partnership with a large school district. She works collaboratively with personnel in the central administration office to produce annual reports of quantitative data and to conduct additional data analyses that address more specific district concerns. Recently, the district has been concerned about low math performance in their three high schools. They asked Dr. Salerno to examine students' high school mathematics performance using several different indicators. During their discussions, Dr. Salerno and the district personnel decided to investigate student achievement on a standardized math test (the state assessment administered to Grade 11 students); the total number of math courses students took from Grade 9 to Grade 12; the type of math courses students took each year (e.g., general math, algebra 1, geometry, algebra 2, and advanced math); the grades received in each math course; and the cumulative math grade point average over the 4 years. They wanted to know this information by school and by demographic subgroups.

The district maintains an extensive longitudinal database containing student information such as demographics, feeder school patterns, program participation, residential status, test scores, classroom information, coursework, attendance, mobility, and discipline. The three modules in this section describe the process Dr. Salerno went through to obtain the necessary data from the district's database and compile it in a format that she needed for her analyses.

Knowing that the study of math performance data involved gathering and analyzing a massive amount of student information over several years, Dr. Salerno decided to form three overarching questions to investigate, from least complex to most complex. The three modules in this section describe how she created the data file necessary for each set of analyses.

△ Module 10: Merging Files

Dr. Salerno's first broad question is, "How do average math scaled scores on the Grade 11 state math test in 2010–11 vary by school and by demographics (gender, ethnicity, and socioeconomic status)?" This module describes how she merged the district's demographic data file with the district's test score data file. Both files consisted of the same students in the same year, but each file contained a different set of variables. This required using a merge procedure for which variables are added.

△ Module 11: Aggregating Data and Restructuring Files

The second question in her study is, "What are the relationships between student performance on the Grade 11 state math test in 2010–11, the type of math course taken in Grade 11, and the grades received in the math course; and to what extent do these results vary across schools and demographic subgroups?" In this module, Dr. Salerno needed to conduct another merge of files that included the math coursework variables. Then, it was necessary to aggregate coursework data to produce an average numerical math grade for each student during the 2010–11 school year. Finally, she had to restructure the data file so that all information for a student was contained in one row (case) rather than multiple rows (cases).

△ Module 12: Identifying a Cohort of Students

The third question is, "For a cohort of students who attended the district's high schools in Grade 9 in 2008–09, Grade 10 in 2009–10, Grade 11 in 2010–11, and Grade 12 in 2011–12, what are the relationships between math achievement on a standardized test, total number of math courses taken, type of math courses taken, and overall cumulative math grade point average? And to what extent do results vary across schools and demographic subgroups?" This module describes the decisions Dr. Salerno made and the path she took to identify the cohort of students.

Merging Files

KEY LEARNING OBJECTIVES

The student will learn to

- conduct a procedure to determine why two similar files differ in their total number of cases
- merge two files containing different variables for the same sample
- perform a check to ensure that a matching variable is unique for all cases in a file

A. Description of Researcher's Study △

Dr. Salerno, an education professor, is in a partnership with a school district to examine data from their extensive longitudinal database in order to address areas of special interest. The district is interested in knowing more about students' high school mathematics performance in terms of scores on standardized math tests and coursework information such as the number and type of math courses taken in high school and the grades received in these courses.

This module describes Dr. Salerno's preparation for answering the first question in this study: How do average math scaled scores on the Grade 11 state math test in 2010–11 vary by school and by demographics (gender, ethnicity, and socioeconomic status)?

Dr. Salerno chose this question as a starting point in her study because of the value of examining scaled scores over performance levels. Personnel, parents, and other interested citizens in the community were well aware of the state test results in terms of performance levels. The annual reports displayed the percentage of students at each of the four levels, from below basic to advanced. In any given year, the percentage of students who scored at the proficient level or above on the math test was a well-known and talked about number, mainly due to accountability reasons. Conversely, discussions of scaled scores on the math test were rare, even though they are very useful and typically preferred in statistical analyses. First, they provide more information than a performance level. Two students with quite different scaled scores (e.g., 810 and 1020) can be classified at the same proficiency level (e.g., "proficient") if their scores fall between the cutoffs for that level. Second, scaled scores are interval variables but performance levels are not (even though some people incorrectly analyze them as such). Variables with an interval measurement scale allow for more powerful statistical techniques.

This module describes how Dr. Salerno combined information in two district files using a merging procedure. One file contained demographic data, and the other file contained test score data.

△ B. A Look at the Data

1 Dr. Salerno says: "It is easy to convert Excel files to SPSS files. First, under the File menu, I selected 'Open' and 'Data,' and a window opened. Under 'Files of Type,' I selected Excel (.xls) and located the folder in which my Excel files were stored. I highlighted the file I wanted to convert, then clicked 'OK.' Another window opened and I selected the box beside 'Read variable names from the first row of data' and clicked OK. A new SPSS file was created. I named the file and saved it."

Each table in the district's database is available in Excel format, which can then be converted into an SPSS file. In order to answer this research question, Dr. Salerno needed two tables from the database. The first table contained demographic information for all students enrolled in the district. When extracting the file from the database, she requested only Grade 11 data from the 2010–11 school year, then she converted to SPSS format. **Dr. Salerno(1)** There are 568 cases (students) in the SPSS file. The variables in the file (*module10_demographics.sav*) are described in Table 10.1. **Dr. Salerno(2)**

Table 10.1 Variables in the Grade 11 Student Demographic File for 2010–11

Variable Name	Description
studentID	5-digit unique student identification number
grade	11 (this is actually a constant, not a variable)
year	2011 (this is also a constant, not a variable)
school	2-digit unique school identifier
gender	1 = male; 2 = female
ethnicity	1 = Black; 2 = White; 3 = Other
SES	1 = free/reduced lunch; 2 = regular lunch

The second table in the database contained scaled scores on the state assessment. When extracting from the database, Dr. Salerno requested Grade 11 math results for 2010–11, but also decided to include reading scores as well in case there would be a future need to examine achievement results for all tested subjects ****Dr. Salerno(3)**. She converted to SPSS format. There are 535 cases (students) in the file. The variables in the file (*module10_tests.sav*) are described in Table 10.2.

**2 Dr. Salerno says: "Try to use the same (or at least very similar) variable names as in the original data file, especially if they are aligned with the SPSS variable naming rules. If you don't, you may become confused if you need to return to the original file at a later time, especially if you don't keep a codebook or data dictionary for your variables. This district used a particular convention to name variables of test results: 'S' is used to represent state tests, the subject area is next, and the type of information follows (e.g., took the test, performance level, or scaled score)." (See Module 1 in Section 1 for information on best practices in naming variables in SPSS and documenting their attributes.)

**3 Dr. Salerno says: "When extracting data from files in a database, think long and hard about variables you might need. You probably won't want to extract all variables because the file will be unwieldy. But try to project future needs or requests for information so you don't have to redo the extraction."

C. Planning and Decision Making △

After obtaining the two files, Dr. Salerno planned her next steps. First, she knew it was necessary to have all the demographic and test score data in one file. In other words, she needed to merge data from the two files together. Both files contained cases for Grade 11 students enrolled in the district during 2010–11, therefore the same students (cases) are in each

Table 10.2 Variables in the Grade 11 State Test File for 2010–11

Variable Name	Description
studentID	5-digit unique student identification number
grade	11 (this is actually a constant, not a variable)
year	2011 (this is also a constant, not a variable)
school	2-digit unique school identifier
Smath_took	1 = student took the state math test; 0 = student did not take the state math test
Smath_level	student's performance level on the state math test 1 = below basic; 2 = basic; 3 = proficient; 4 = advanced
Smath_scaled	student's scaled score on the state math test
Srdg_took	1 = student took the state reading test; 0 = student did not take the state reading test
Srdg_level	student's performance level on the state reading test 1 = below basic; 2 = basic; 3 = proficient; 4 = advanced
Srdg_scaled	student's scaled score on the state reading test

**4 Dr. Salerno says: "Another scenario for merging files is when they have different cases but the same information (variables). One example would be merging a file that has demographic information for Grade 10 students in 2010–11 with a file that has demographic information for Grade 11 students in 2010–11."

file. However, the files contain different information (variables) for the students. This represents a merge of files with the same cases but different information. **Dr. Salerno(4)

Another matter Dr. Salerno wanted to investigate was to find out why the two files had differing numbers of cases. She noticed that the demographic file had slightly more students than the test score file.

△ D. Using SPSS to Address Issues and Prepare Data

Before merging the data, Dr. Salerno explored why the demographic file had 568 cases and the test file had only 535 cases. The common variables in each file were *studentID*, *grade*, *year*, and *school*. Because *grade* and *year* were constants, her best bet was to obtain frequencies for *school* in each file to find out if there were any differences. Under the **Analyze menu**, she selected **Descriptive Statistics** and **Frequencies** to obtain the dialog box shown in Figure 10.1. She transferred *school* to the **Variable(s)** box.

Figure 10.1   Analyze → Descriptive Statistics → Frequencies

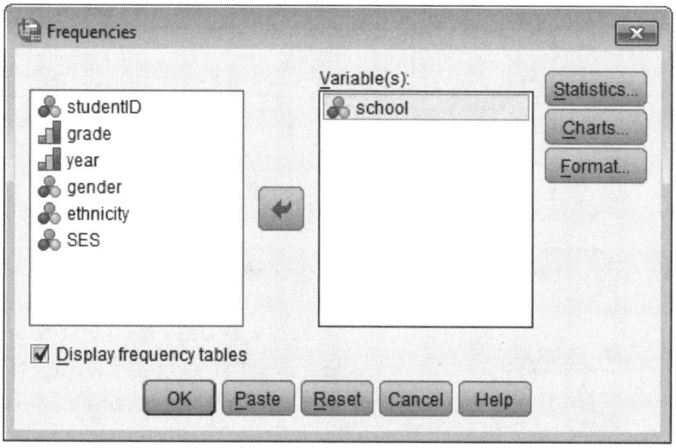

The output is shown in Tables 10.3 and 10.4. Both files contain the same number of students in each of the three district high schools (Schools 31, 32, and 33), but the demographics file also contained a school code of 41 that listed 33 students. When sharing her results with district personnel, Dr. Salerno discovered that this school code represented an alternative education center to which students from multiple districts were sent for behavioral reasons. The 33 students were in the center for the majority of the school year and thus were not listed as attending one of the district's three high schools. They took the state test, but their results were not included in the database table from which the data were extracted. A decision was made not to include these students in the study at this time.

Table 10.3   SPSS Output for the School Variable in the Demographics File

school

		Frequency	Percent	Valid Percent	Cumulative Percent
Valid	31	172	30.3	30.3	30.3
	32	198	34.9	34.9	65.1
	33	165	29.0	29.0	94.2
	41	33	5.8	5.8	100.0
	Total	568	100.0	100.0	

Table 10.4 SPSS Output for the School Variable in the Test File

school

		Frequency	Percent	Valid Percent	Cumulative Percent
Valid	31	172	32.1	32.1	32.1
	32	198	37.0	37.0	69.2
	33	165	30.8	30.8	100.0
	Total	535	100.0	100.0	

SPSS Tip 1: In this context, *studentID* was a unique identifier, but in other situations, you may need to ensure that the matching variable is truly unique for all cases. So it's wise to run a check for Duplicate Cases. Under the Data menu, select "Identify Duplicate Cases." Place the variable you want to check in the box "Define matching cases by" and click OK. This procedure will add a new variable to your file that contains a "1" if the case is unique and a "0" if the case is a duplicate. An output table is also produced. It shows the total number of cases that are unique (hopefully all of them in your data file) and the number of cases that are duplicates.

SPSS Tip 2: You can begin the merge with either file, but it's useful to think about the order in which you want your variables to appear in the merged file. Variables in the second file are added at the end of the variable list in the first file.

Now it was time to start the merge process. The first step is to identify the variable that will match cases from the two files. In this case, it was *studentID*. **SPSS Tip(1)** Next, both files must be sorted in ascending order by the matching variable. SPSS will give a warning that the merge will not work if the files are not sorted. Previously, Dr. Salerno conducted a **Sort** on *studentID* under the **Data menu** so she knew both files were appropriately sorted.

To begin the merge, Dr. Salerno opened the dialog box shown in Figure 10.2 by selecting **Merge Files** and **Add Variables** under the **Data menu**. Because she had only the demographics file open in SPSS, she chose the second option in the dialog box, **An external SPSS Statistics data file,** and used the **Browse** button to locate the file. If the test file was already open in SPSS, then she would have chosen the first option, **An open dataset**. **SPSS Tip(2)**

After pressing the **Continue** button, another dialog box opens (see Figure 10.3). On the right side is a box called **New Active Dataset.** It is a list of all variables that will be included in the newly merged file. Variables with an asterisk (*) are those that came from the first file (demographics). Variables with a plus (+) are those that came from the second

Figure 10.2 Data → Merge Files → Add Variables

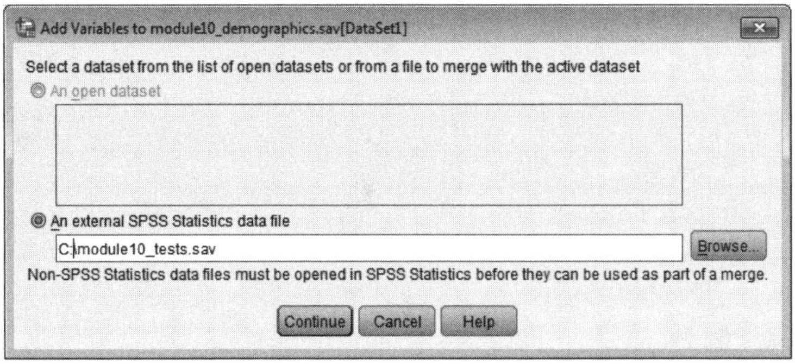

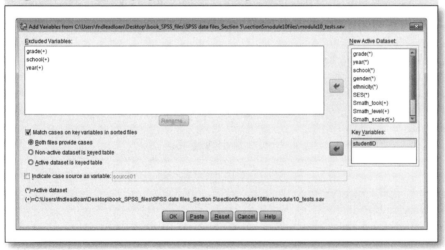

Figure 10.3 Identifying Variables in Merged File

file (tests). On the left side is a box called **Excluded Variables.** These variables from the second file were automatically excluded by SPSS because they are common to both data files. The *studentID* variable had also been in the **Excluded Variables** box, but because it is the matching variable, Dr. Salerno clicked **Match cases on key variables in sorted files** and moved it to the **Key Variables** box. SPSS will use it to match cases from both files.

Dr. Salerno also decided to include *school* from the test file into the new merged file so she could make sure that the school information was the same for each student in both files. To do this, she renamed *school* to *school_from_test_file* (by clicking the **Rename** button) and moved it to the **New Active Dataset** box as shown in Figure 10.4.

Figure 10.4   Identifying Variables in Merged File

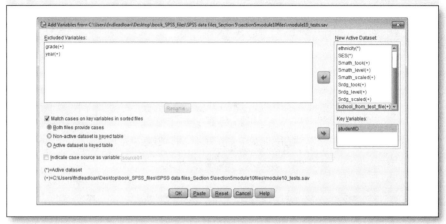

After clicking the **OK** button, the following warning appears as a reminder about the importance of sorting on the matching variable (see Figure 10.5).

Figure 10.5   A Warning Before the Merge

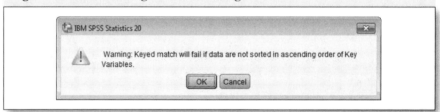

SPSS Tip 3: When working with multiple files and creating new ones, it's helpful to attach a brief description to each file stating its contents, when it was created, where the data were obtained, and anything else that is important to remember. Under the "Utilities menu," select "Data File Comments." Write the comments in the text area. Check the box "Display comments in output" to include the data description in the output. (See Module 1 in Section 1 for more information on best practices for naming and describing data files.)

A final click of the **OK** button will conduct the merge procedure. Variables from the test file are now added to the demographics file. Dr. Salerno preferred to save the newly merged file under a different file name because she wanted to retain the original demographics file. Therefore, immediately after the merge, she selected **Save As** under the **File menu** to create a new file name for the merged data (*see Module10_merged.sav*). As a final step, Dr. Salerno added the following descriptive comments to the new file: ****SPSS Tip(3)**

"Merged file created on 7/20/12. Contains data from two files extracted from the district database on 7/18/12: 1) demographics for Grade 11 students in 2010–2011, and 2) state test results for Grade 11 students in 2010–11."

E. Reflection and Additional Decision Making   △

Dr. Salerno inspected the new file to ensure the merge was successful and contained all appropriate variables. The file had 568 cases. When she sorted by *school* and looked at the test variables, she confirmed that students in School 41 had no data. Because of the decision she made with the district not to include students in the alternative education center in the current study, she decided to delete these 33 cases from the file. They are not necessary for her analyses, and the results will be easier to examine without the missing data. However, she saved her new working file as *module10_merged_no41.sav* so that the center's demographic data would still be available in the original merged file if necessary at a later time.

She conducted a few exploratory analyses of the variables in *module10_merged_no41.sav* to possibly uncover any final data issues to address. First, she wanted to ensure that *school* from the demographics file and *school_from_test_file* in the test file contained the same data. Upon inspection of frequency analysis and sorting cases by the variables, Dr. Salerno was satisfied that both variables had identical school codes for students. Next, she ran frequency analyses for nominal variables. There were no missing data for *gender*, *ethnicity*, or *SES*. When examining subgroup percentages for these variables, *ethnicity* showed that 47.9% of students were Black, 47.5% were White, and 4.7% were Other. Because of the small number and varied nature of students' ethnicities in the Other subgroup, Dr. Salerno and the district agreed that this group would not be included ethnicity analyses. However, she did keep their data in the file so that these students would be reflected in other types of statistics.

Finally, when examining the interval scaled score variable for math, *Smath_scaled*, she found a small amount of missing data (24 out of the 535 students or 4.5% across all three schools). Frequencies for *Smath_took* showed that these students did not take the test. Absence on testing day was the typical reason, but a few students took an alternative assessment due to special education status. She will report descriptive statistics for their demographic data but not test data in her report. Now Dr. Salerno feels comfortable proceeding with her analysis of data to answer the first broad question in the study: "How do average math scaled scores on the Grade 11 state math test in 2010–11 vary by school and by demographics (gender, ethnicity, and socioeconomic status)?"

△ F. Writing It Up

Research papers and technical reports do not usually include information about how the researcher merged files. But in some situations, there are interesting discoveries about the data that are brought to light in the process. Here, Dr. Salerno provided a brief description of the merging process and what she found.

"Two files were extracted from the district's database. One file contained demographic data for each student, and the other file contained scaled test scores for the mathematics and reading state assessments. During the merging process for the two files, the researcher noticed that the demographic file contained data for more students than the test score file. In addition to the three high schools in the district, there is also an alternative education center. A portion of students (33) attended this center for the majority of the 2010–11 school year, thus their test scores were reported for the center and not for their home school. Since the overall performance of the three schools was the focus of the research study, a decision was made not to include this set of students in the analysis of the research question."

△ Reflective Questions

- What are the two types of merging procedures, and in what situations would they be conducted?
- What are the processes for conducting a merge of two files?
- What are the processes for ensuring that the key variable in a merge procedure is truly a unique identifier for all cases?
- Why is it especially important to document the description of each data file when a study involves merging data?

△ Extensions

- In your field of study, give a few examples of data files that may need to be merged for purposes of conducting data analysis. Determine which specific procedure would be appropriate, Add Cases or Add Variables.
- Discuss the information provided by performance levels and by scaled scores on a test of knowledge. What are some common misperceptions of these measures? What statistical tests are appropriate for each measure?
- Obtain data files that could be combined for the purposes of analyzing a research question and follow Dr. Salerno's steps for merging their data together. If it involves adding variables, ensure that the key variable for matching cases is truly a unique identifier.

Aggregating Data and Restructuring Files

❧❧

DATA FILES FOR THIS MODULE

module10_merged_no41.sav

module11_mathcourse.sav

module11_demotests_mathcourse.sav

module11_demotests_mathcourse_recodes_aggr.sav

module11_demotests_mathcourse_recodes_aggr_restructure.sav

❧❧

KEY LEARNING OBJECTIVES

The student will learn to

- aggregate data to obtain an average math grade and to determine the number of semesters math courses were taken
- restructure a file so that all data for a student are contained in one row/case rather than multiple rows/cases

A. Description of Researcher's Study △

This module describes Dr. Salerno's preparation for answering the second question in her collaborative study with the local school district: What are the relationships between student performance on the Grade 11 state math test in 2010–11, the type of math courses taken in Grade 11, and the grades received in the math courses; and to what extent do these results vary across schools and demographic subgroups?

This question is a natural second phase in the study on high school students' mathematics performance. It incorporates math coursework information with the already obtained math assessment scores. The district is interested in knowing if course-taking differs for students across schools, ethnicity, SES, and gender; and also if the type of math courses taken and grades received are related to students' scores on the Grade 11 state math test.

This module describes the process Dr. Salerno used to create a file that contains all demographic, test score, and coursework data for each student. In addition to conducting another merge of files, she had to aggregate coursework data and restructure the final data file.

△ B. A Look at the Data

To answer the question, Dr. Salerno needed two files. The first file is the one she created in Module 10 by merging the demographic information and state test scores for Grade 11 students in 2010–11 (*module10_merged_no41 .sav*). Based on her earlier decision (described in Module 10) not to include data from the alternative education center, School 41 data were removed. Table 11.1 describes the variables in this file. There are 535 cases, representing students from Schools 31, 32, and 33.

Table 11.1 Variables in the Grade 11 Student Demographics and Test File for 2010–11

Variable Name	Description
studentID	5-digit unique student identification number
grade	11 (this is actually a constant, not a variable)
year	2011 (this is also a constant, not a variable)
school	2-digit unique school identifier
gender	1 = male; 2 = female
ethnicity	1 = Black; 2 = White; 3 = Other
SES	1 = free/reduced lunch; 2 = regular lunch
Smath_took	1 = student took the state math test; 0 = student did not take the state math test
Smath_level	student's performance level on the state math test 1 = below basic; 2 = basic; 3 = proficient; 4 = advanced
Smath_scaled	student's scaled score on the state math test
Srdg_took	1 = student took the state reading test; 0 = student did not take the state reading test
Srdg_level	student's performance level on the state reading test 1 = below basic; 2 = basic; 3 = proficient; 4 = advanced
Srdg_scaled	student's scaled score on the state reading test

To obtain coursework information, Dr. Salerno extracted the math course and math grade data from the district database. She converted the appropriate coursework table from Excel to SPSS format as illustrated in Module 10. The variables are described in Table 11.2. Unlike the tables previously extracted from the database, this one is a bit more complex because it contains multiple rows for each student. Each row provides the name of the math course a student took in a particular semester as well as the grade he/she received. So, for example, a student who took Algebra 2 during the first and second semesters of Grade 11 (and took no other math course) would have two rows. This file (*module11_mathcourse.sav*) has a total of 1284 cases/rows.

Table 11.2 Variables in the Grade 11 Math Coursework File for 2010–11

Variable Name	Description
studentID	5-digit unique student identification number
grade	11 (this is actually a constant, not a variable)
year	2011 (this is also a constant, not a variable)
school	2-digit unique school identifier
semester	indicates the semester in which students took a math course (1 or 2)
math_course	string variable (name of math course)
math_grade	string variable (letter grade received in math course, A to E)

C. Planning and Decision Making △

After considering the nature of the files and the research question, Dr. Salerno outlined the following steps she needs to take in order to prepare her data for analysis.

Her first step will be to merge the coursework file with the previously merged demographics and test score file. She will use the same procedure as she did in Module 10.

Second, in order to analyze the course and grade data, she must recode these two string variables into numerical variables. The variable *math_grade* contains letter grades (A through E) that she will recode from 4 to 0, respectively. The district does not use a plus/minus system. For the *math_course* variable, there are several versions of Algebra 2 and geometry courses as well as general math and advanced math courses. In order to make an

**1 Dr. Salerno says: "The transpose option for restructuring simply means that a new data file will be created in which all the original rows (cases) become columns (variables) and the original columns (variables) become the rows (cases). Here is an example of the first option (restructuring variables into cases). Suppose I have a file with three columns of data (school30, school31, school32), and the data in each column represent the total number of discipline referrals during one school year for each student in that particular school. Thus, each row contains data from multiple students (a different student in each school). After restructuring using the first option in SPSS, the newly restructured file would have one variable that includes the total discipline referrals for each student and another variable that indicates the school each student attended (i.e., an index variable). Therefore, the new file would have data for only one student per row."

informed decision about assigning numerical codes, Dr. Salerno wants to run a frequency analysis for *math_course*.

Third, to obtain one average math grade for each student in Grade 11, she needs to aggregate the data. This step will also provide information on the number of semesters in which students took a math course (i.e., the number of rows of course data for each student). The new variables can be saved into a new aggregated file or added to the existing file with multiple rows per student.

Finally, in order to answer the research question, Dr. Salerno needs to create a file with only one row of data per student. This row must include data for all variables so that comparisons can be made across student demographics, and correlations can be obtained between the test scores and coursework. Restructuring the file will accomplish this.

SPSS restructures files in one of three ways: restructuring selected variables into cases, restructuring selected cases into variables, and transposing data. ****Dr. Salerno(1)** Dr. Salerno's context requires the second option. SPSS will create multiple variables to represent the math course(s) each student took and the math grade(s) each student received. Thus, the newly restructured file will contain all math course information in one row for each student.

△ D. Using SPSS to Address Issues and Prepare Data

Step 1: Merge

As she did in Module 10, Dr. Salerno merged the math coursework file (*module11_mathcourse.sav*) and the demographics and test score file (*module10_merged_no41.sav*) by adding variables. The newly created file has 1284 cases and several variables that represent demographics, test scores, and math coursework. She noticed that the new file has many empty cells for the demographics and test score variables. That's okay. The data for these variables are provided in only one of the students' multiple rows. She named the new file *module11_demotests_mathcourse.sav*.

Step 2: Recode

To recode the string variable (*math_grade*) into a new variable that is numerical (*math_numgrade*), Dr. Salerno selected **Recode into Different Variables** under the **Transform menu**. In the dialog box shown in Figure 11.1, she placed *math_grade* in the **Input Variable** box, typed *math_numgrade* in the **Output Variable** box, and clicked the **Change** button.

Figure 11.1 Transform → Recode Into Different Variables

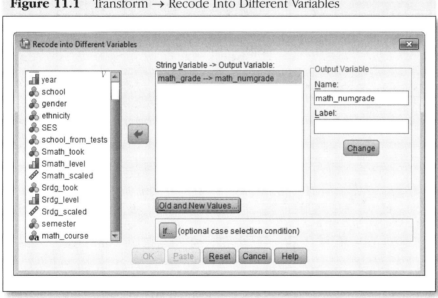

She clicked the **Old and New Values** button and typed the original letter grades (one at a time) in the **Value** box under **Old Value**. Then, she typed the numerical letter grades in the **Value** box under **New Value**. After each pair was entered, she clicked the **Add** button. Figure 11.2 shows that she recoded the letter grades A, B, C, and D to the numerical grades 4, 3, 2, and 1. She clicked **Add** one more time to complete the recode for E to 0. (See Module 3 in Section 2 for more details on recoding variables.)

Figure 11.2 Old and New Values

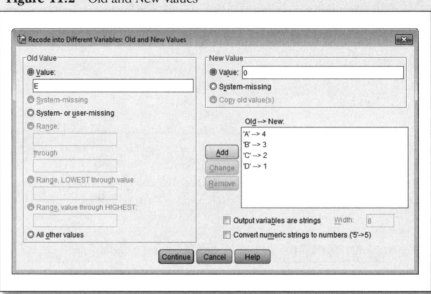

To ensure that the recoding of grades was successful, she obtained frequencies for *math_grade* (the original variable) and *math_numgrade* (the recoded variable). The results were the same for both variables. They were 199, 323, 336, 275, and 148, respectively, from A to E and 4 to 0. Three of the 1284 cases had missing grade data.

> ****2 Dr. Salerno says:** "It's not impossible to change your coding system, but if you can look ahead to what you might need in future analysis, it will save you time (and unnecessary aggravation) in terms of not having to rerun the procedures."

Next, she turned her attention to the math course data. The first column in Table 11.3 lists all math courses that appeared in the string variable *math_course*. She assigned a numerical code to each course as shown in the second column of Table 11.3. Lower codes represent lower-level math courses (e.g., general math) and higher codes represent higher-level math courses (e.g., calculus). Knowing that Grade 9, 10, and 12 data will be added to the file for the third research question in Module 12, she left a few gaps in the coding system so that additional courses can be added more easily. As an example, she reserved a code of 1 for General Math 1. ****Dr. Salerno(2)** Notice also that she assigned the State Prep course a code of 99. In her discussions with the district, she learned that this class was unlike the others in that it did not have a formal curriculum. Because the purpose of the prep course was simply to prepare students for the state math assessment administered in the spring, she is likely to exclude it from certain analyses of the research question.

Similar to the recoding procedure described earlier, she converted the string variable *math_course* into the numerical variable *math_numcourse*. Once again, she double-checked the recodings to ensure that the frequencies for both variables matched. They did, and the frequencies are shown in the third column of Table 11.3. Four of the 1284 rows did not contain a course name. The file *module11_demotests_mathcourse_recodes_aggr.sav* contains both recoded variables.

Table 11.3 Math Course Names, Codes, and Frequencies

Course Name (math_course)	Course Code (math_numcourse)	Frequency
Gen Math 2	2	7
Gen Math 3	3	59
Alg1 Standard	6	16
Alg1 Honors	7	1
Alg1 Basic	8	2
Alg2 Standard	10	537
Alg2 Honors	11	110
Alg2 Basic	12	10
Geom Standard	13	57
Geom Honors	14	6
Geom Basic	15	8
Trig	16	224
Calculus	19	16
State Prep	99	227

Step 3: Aggregate

This step aggregates the numerical math grades across semesters by student. Thus, it produces a mean math grade for each student. To carry out the procedure, Dr. Salerno selected **Aggregate** under the **Data menu**. As shown in Figure 11.3, she placed *studentID* in the **Break Variable(s)**

Figure 11.3 Data → Aggregate

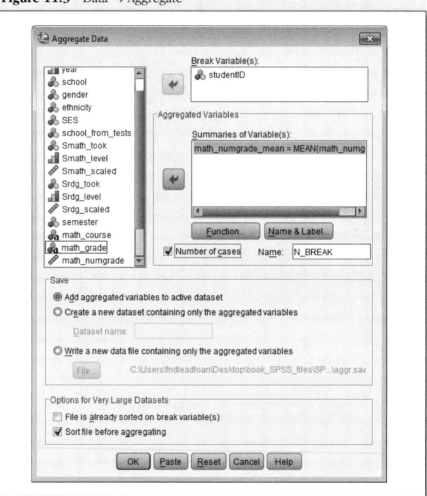

SPSS Tip 1: The aggregate function does not accommodate string variables, such as *math_course*, and the summary statistics are not meaningful for nominal variables, so *math_numcourse* is not examined using the Aggregate procedure.

box because it is the variable that will identify how to group the data. In other words, each unique *studentID* value will identify a new case.

She placed *math_numgrade* in the **Summaries of Variable(s)** box. ****SPSS Tip 1** This is the variable that will be aggregated. SPSS will provide a summary statistic of the numerical grades each student received and place it in a new variable called *math_numgrade_mean*. ****SPSS Tip 2**

She also checked the **Number of cases** box. It will create a new variable, with a default name, *N_BREAK*, that provides a total count of the number of numerical grades that went into the calculation of the mean grade for each student. This variable is useful to Dr. Salerno because it will tell her how many semesters of math were taken by each student.

The next choice to be made is where to place the two new variables. Dr. Salerno selected the option **Add aggregated variables to active dataset**. Her active data set is *module11_demotests_mathcourses_recodes*, which has 1284 cases. ****SPSS Tip 3**

Finally, in the **Options for Very Large Datasets** box, she selected **Sort file before aggregating**. Usually her file is sorted by *studentID*, but just to be sure, she chose this option.

SPSS Tip 2: The default summary statistic is the mean. The "Function" button allows for requesting many other descriptive statistics, such as median, standard deviation, minimum, maximum, and percentages above and below a particular value.

SPSS Tip 3: Another option is to create a new file that contains only the aggregated variables with the number of cases equal to the total number of students (i.e., 535). This file is useful for looking at the average math grade for each student and the total number of semesters they took math. However, it does not contain the demographic or test score variables.

After she clicked **OK** to run the **Aggregate** procedure, Dr. Salerno checked her file. The aggregated variables (*math_numgrade_mean* and *N_BREAK*) were added into the file, which still contained all 1284 cases. She scrolled through the file to ensure that the aggregate mean function worked properly. For instance, the first student in the file (*studentID*=10105) had two rows of course data as shown in Table 11.4. The mean accurately portrayed that the average of the two math grades was 1.00, and *N_BREAK* showed that there were two semesters listed for this student. The file *module11_demotests_mathcourse_recodes_aggr.sav* contains both aggregate variables.

Table 11.4 Math Coursework Data for Student 10105

math_course	math_grade	math_numgrade	math_numgrade_mean	*N_*BREAK
Alg2 Standard	C	2	1.00	2
Alg2 Standard	E	0	1.00	2

Step 4: Restructure

The final action of restructuring will reorganize the data file so that it contains one row (case) for each student with his or her complete information (demographics, test scores, and math coursework). Under the **Data menu**, Dr. Salerno selected **Restructure** to obtain the window shown in Figure 11.4. A **Data Wizard** walked her through the steps to restructure the file. The first step of the **Wizard** asked how she wanted the data to be restructured. There are three choices. The visuals accompanying the descriptions of each option are helpful in deciding how to proceed. For her purposes, she needs to **Restructure selected cases into variables**, the second option. This procedure will create several new variables for *semester*, *math_course*, *math_grade*, *math_numgrade*, and *math_numcourse*. For example, a student who took two semesters of Geometry will no longer have two rows that list the course information. Instead, the courses and grades for each semester will be displayed in multiple columns within one row.

Figure 11.4 Data → Restructure

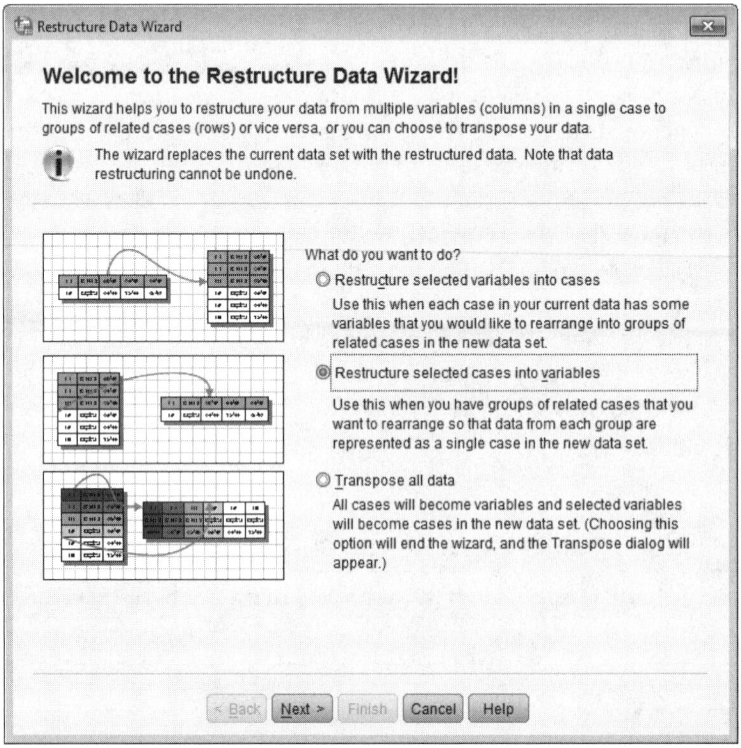

After she clicked the **Next** button, the **Data Wizard** asked her to select the variable that will determine the new rows. Similar to the **Aggregate procedure**, Dr. Salerno selected *studentID* as the **Identifier Variable** (see Figure 11.5). The **Index Variable** box is optional and allows users to select which variables in the file will be used to create the new variables. She does not specify an Index variable for her data. When the box is left unchecked, SPSS will automatically create new variables to accommodate all information in the file. ****SPSS Tip 4**

SPSS Tip 4: Choosing the *Index Variable(s)*, rather than automatically letting SPSS do it, does not always produce restructured results. For example, the restructuring procedure will not be performed if there are missing data in a variable or if values for variables were duplicated within a group. Therefore, leaving this box empty is necessary for some data sets, such as the one here.

Figure 11.5   Selecting Variables in Restructure

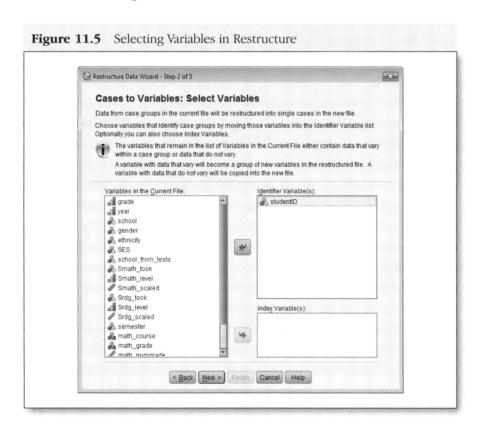

Step 3 in the **Wizard** refers to sorting. Dr. Salerno wants to be sure that the file was sorted properly, so she chose **Yes** for this step (see Figure 11.6).

Figure 11.6 Sorting in Restructure

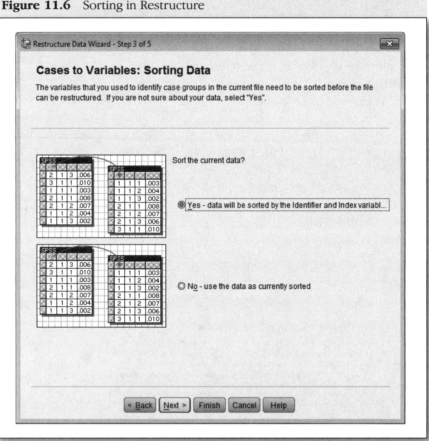

SPSS Tip 5: An Indicator variable can be created for each unique value of an Index variable. It uses values of 1 or 0 to indicate whether a value is present or absent for a case.

Step 4 asked her to specify several options (see Figure 11.7). Dr. Salerno retained the default **Order of New Variable Groups**, which is **Group by original variable**. This means that all *math_course* variables are grouped together and all *math_grade* variables are grouped together.

In the **Case Count Variable** box, she chose to create a new variable, named *cases_n*, that will provide a count of the number of semesters for each student. This variable will contain the same information as the *N_BREAK* variable created by the **Aggregate procedure**. She did not need to create an **Indicator Variable** because she had no Index variable. ****SPSS Tip 5**

Figure 11.7 Options in Restructure

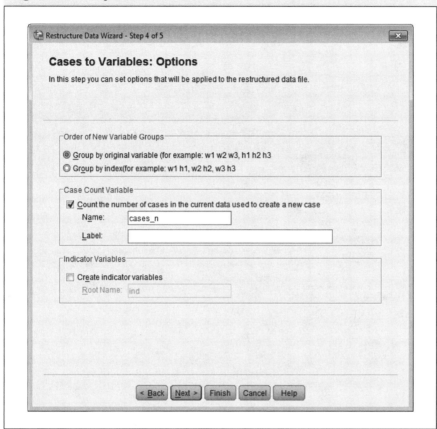

The final step in the **Data Wizard** is completed by selecting **Restructure the data now** (see Figure 11.8).

When she clicked **Finish**, a warning showed up on the screen (see Figure 11.9). This is only important if there were **Variable Sets** in the data file, but she did not have any. Therefore, she clicked **OK** and her data were restructured. She immediately saved the file under the new name: *module11_ demotests_mathcourse_recodes_aggr_restructure.sav*.

Once again, Dr. Salerno checked to ensure that the restructure procedure worked properly and did what she wanted it to do.

The file now contains only 535 cases, which matches the total number of students in the district's three high schools. There are 21 new variables: ***SPSS Tip 6

SPSS Tip 6: By default, a period is used to separate the original variable name from the number of the new variable.

Figure 11.8 Final Step in Restructure

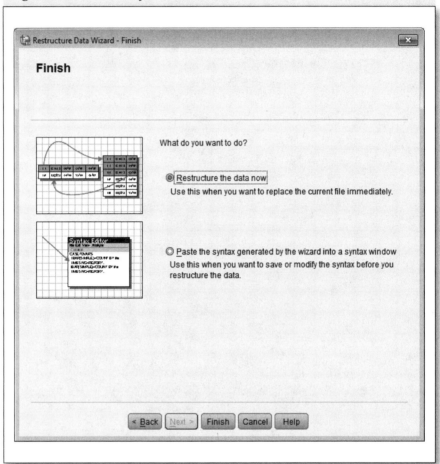

Figure 11.9

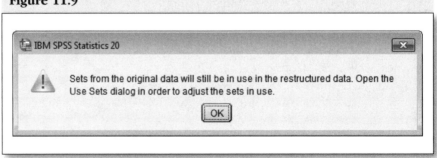

cases_n

semester.1 through *semester.4*

math_course.1 through *math_course.4*

math_grade.1 through *math_grade.4*

math_numgrade.1 through *math_numgrade.4*

math_numcourse.1 through *math_numcourse.4*

Because there are four newly created variables for each original variable (e.g., *math_course*), that means there was at least one student who took four semesters of math.

She ran a frequency analysis to summarize *cases_n*. The results in Table 11.5 indicate that 26 students had only one math course listed (thus only one semester of math). A total of 270 students had two semesters of math, and 238 students had three semesters. Only one student had four semesters of math. Frequencies for the *N_BREAK* variable produced by the **Aggregate procedure** were identical to those in Table 11.5. Thus, there are two ways to obtain the total semesters of math taken by students.

Table 11.5 SPSS Output for Number and Percent of Students Taking One, Two, Three, or Four Semesters of Math

cases_n

		Frequency	Percent	Valid Percent	Cumulative Percent
Valid	1	26	4.9	4.9	4.9
	2	270	50.5	50.5	55.3
	3	238	44.5	44.5	99.8
	4	1	.2	.2	100.0
	Total	535	100.0	100.0	

E. Reflection and Additional Decision Making △

Before Dr. Salerno can proceed to answer the research question in this phase of her study, a few decisions must be made. Some of the conversations she needs to have with district personnel are described next.

First, there is the issue of the State Prep math course. Most likely, the district will want to treat this course differently from other math courses. Although students receive a grade, the objective of the course is simply to prepare students for the state test in March. The district will probably want a summary of the students who took this course (demographically and by school), but it may not be included in other analyses of math courses taken. Furthermore, in her preliminary analysis, Dr. Salerno noticed that one school did not have any students listed as taking the State Prep course. She needs to find out why. Was it not offered in the school? Or were the results just not entered into the district database?

Second, decisions must be made on the level of detail for results. As an example, there are three different types of Algebra 2 (Standard, Honors, and Basic). For a first pass through the data, the district might want to combine the three versions into one. If so, then it may be helpful to have a new variable, called *algebra2*, that indicates whether a student did or did not take the course (a code of 1 or 0) regardless of the version. Dr. Salerno can use this newly created variable in analysis of the number of students who took Algebra 2 by school and by demographic subgroup as well as examine the grades received. Additional dichotomous variables can be created to represent the multiple versions of the other math courses.

A third issue is to decide how to treat the semesters of course-taking. There are many ways to proceed. One is to identify students who took the same math course over two semesters. During her preparation of the data files, Dr. Salerno noticed that most students appeared to be taking two semesters of the same course (e.g., Geometry in Semester 1 and Geometry in Semester 2) or two semesters of the same course plus a semester of State Prep. She can instruct SPSS to identify these cases by using **Select If** (*cases_n*=2 and (*math_course.1=math_course.2*) under the **Data menu**. This will identify students who took one math course over two semesters. Similar manipulations can be performed in order to identify the students who took a full year of one math course plus the State Prep course. She can also use these procedures if she decides to remove students' State Prep grades in certain analyses of the average math grade variable.

In summary, thoroughly answering the research question will require many types of descriptive and inferential analyses. Thus, the new variables in the restructured file will serve different purposes. They will allow for analyses that describe relationships between demographics, test scores, and coursework as well as for analyses that will identify similarities and differences in math course-taking patterns across demographics and schools.

E. Writing It Up △

Although detailed descriptions of merging, aggregating, and restructuring are usually not included in research papers or reports, Dr. Salerno created the following brief paragraph that describes how she produced her file from the district's database. After she and the district personnel make decisions about how to analyze the state prep course, how to analyze the two semesters of course-taking, and whether to combine all versions of a math course or analyze them separately, Dr. Salerno will state the specific operational definitions for all variables in the file under a Data or Variables subheading in the Methodology section.

"The math coursework variables were merged with the data file that contained demographic and state test score data for Grade 11 students in 2010–11. Next, data in the newly merged file were aggregated since the district's Excel file for coursework had multiple rows of data for each student. Each row included the type of math course the student took and the grade received during one semester of the school year. The aggregate procedure produced a new variable that contained the average math grade across all semesters of math taken by each student. The final step was to restructure the file so that it contained one row for each student which contained his/her complete information (demographics, test scores, and math coursework)."

Reflective Questions △

- What are the processes to aggregate data from groups of cases into a single case?
- What are the optional functions that can be used to calculate the aggregated values? When would they be useful?
- In what research situations might a person need to restructure a data file?
- What options are available for restructuring a file?
- What decisions must be made along the way to restructure a file?

Extensions △

- Run the procedures necessary to create a new average math grade variable that does not include the State Prep course grade in its calculation.
- Dr. Salerno chose to add the aggregated variable for mean math grades to her existing file. Run the aggregate procedure, creating

additional functions for the aggregated variable such as median or percent above/below a certain value. Also, choose the option that creates a new file for the aggregate variables, obtain descriptive statistics for the variables, and interpret results.

- Obtain multiple files that can be merged by adding either cases or variables. Examine the newly merged file to determine if other steps are necessary, such as aggregating or restructuring.

- Discuss what the Transpose Data option in the Restructure procedure does, and try it on a data file.

- Discuss the Variables into Cases option in the Restructure procedure, and describe a research situation in which it would be useful. If possible, find an appropriate data file and restructure it in this way.

Identifying a Cohort of Students

꒰ঌ

DATA FILES FOR THIS MODULE

module12_demographics_gr9.sav
module12_demographics_gr10.sav
module12_demographics_gr11.sav
module12_demographics_gr12.sav
module12_merge_9_10.sav
module12_merge_9_10_11.sav
module12_merge_9_10_11_12.sav
module12_cohort_456.sav

꒰ঌ

KEY LEARNING OBJECTIVES

The student will learn to

- make appropriate modifications to variables prior to creating a cohort file
- identify a cohort of students that attended the same school for 4 years
- create one file that contains all available data for students in the cohort

A. Description of Researcher's Study △

In this module, Dr. Salerno prepares data files to examine the third research question in her study: "For a cohort of students that attended the district's high schools in Grade 9 in 2008–09, Grade 10 in 2009–10, Grade 11 in 2010–11, and Grade 12 in 2011–12, what are the relationships between math achievement on a standardized test, total number of math courses taken, type of math courses taken, and overall cumulative math grade point average? Also, to what extent do results vary across schools and demographic subgroups?"

Operational definitions for a cohort vary depending upon the objective of the study. For the purposes of her research, Dr. Salerno will focus upon students who stayed in the school district from their freshman year in 2008–09 through their senior year in 2011–2012. With this subset of students, she will be able to examine high school math performance using multiple indicators. She can also investigate the trajectory of course-taking in mathematics over 4 consecutive years. Therefore, her cohort will not include students who (a) repeated a grade level, (b) exited for a period of time and returned later to the district, or (c) dropped out. This module describes the specific decisions she had to make and the process she used in order to obtain the file of cohort students.

△ B. A Look at the Data

The district's database contains a demographics file, a test file, and a math course file for each grade level. Fortunately, all files use the same conventions for naming variables and assigning values. This consistency across files is usually considered a necessity for large-scale longitudinal databases because it leads to efficient data preparation and analysis that is as error-free as possible.

Obtaining the cohort requires identifying the subset of students who were in the district files for Grades 9, 10, 11, and 12. Students who are in some, but not all, grade files are not in the cohort and will be called "noncohort" students in Dr. Salerno's study. This module shows how she used the demographic files for each grade to identify cohort students. These files have the variables shown in Table 12.1. You may recall them from Modules 10 and 11 in this section.

Table 12.1 Variables in the District Demographic Files for Each Grade From 2008–09 to 2011–12

Variable Name	Description
studentID	5-digit unique student identification number
grade	9, 10, 11, or 12 (this is actually a constant in each file, not a variable)
year	2009, 2010, 2011, or 2012 (this is also a constant in each file, not a variable)
school	2-digit unique school identifier
gender	1 = male; 2 = female
ethnicity	1 = Black; 2 = White; 3 = Other
SES	1 = free/reduced lunch; 2 = regular lunch

The school district had the foresight to ensure that every student has a unique 5-digit identifier (*studentID*). This allows for easily tracking students throughout their schooling in the district. Values in the *grade* and *year* variables identify the file by grade level and year. For example, a file with *grade* = 9 and *year* = 2009 contains all students in Grade 9 in the 2008–09 school year. The *school* variable lists the school attended by each student. If a student changed schools during the year, the school listed is the one recorded for that year based on accountability purposes. Three demographic variables describe students in terms of *gender*, *ethnicity*, and *SES*.

C. Planning and Decision Making △

Before proceeding, Dr. Salerno must make a few decisions. First, what path should she take to merge student information and identify the cohort? Second, are there any file modifications that are necessary to make before merging? Third, when planning her study, she defined the cohort as students who stayed in the district all 4 years. Some of these cohort students might have changed high schools within the district, whereas others remained in one school the entire time. How should she handle the two subsets of cohort students?

Path Taken to Merge Files

There are several ways in which files can be merged. One option is to merge the Grade 9 test file with the Grade 9 demographics file and then merge the Grade 9 math course file to the first merged file. This path will produce a Grade 9 file containing all variables needed in the study for all Grade 9 students in 2008–09. The process of merging demographics, test, and math course files must be repeated for all other grades. Finally, the four complete files would have to be merged and the cohort identified.

Dr. Salerno, however, decided to choose a second option that is more efficient and will not produce as much extraneous data (e.g., test and math course variables for non-cohort students). First, she will merge the Grade 9, 10, 11, and 12 demographics files to identify the cohort. Then, test and course files can be merged to the cohort file, producing a complete data file for cohort students in her study.

File Modifications Prior to Merging

Some variable names must be modified to retain yearly student information when files are merged. To do this, Dr. Salerno will add "*_gr9*," "*_gr10*," "*_gr11*," or "*_gr12*" (depending on the grade file) to the end of the

**1 Dr. Salerno says: "This information will be also useful when presenting the sample in the methodology section of my study. I can use it to describe how the cohort is demographically similar to, or different from, the entire population of students in the district high schools during the 4 years. If I do not create unique variable names for the demographic and school data, then I would not be able to describe yearly data in this way."

**2 Dr. Salerno says: "The main objective of my research question is to examine math performance from Grades 9 to 12. I am not conducting a mobility study, per se, so I don't want to go too far down the road in studying student movement. Mobility research typically investigates the amount and types of moves within and outside a district. This is not my focus. However, I want my results and conclusions about relationships between math test scores, math course-taking, and math grades to be as clean as possible. If I analyze cohort students who are not mobile within the district (i.e., stayed in the same school), portions of my analysis will be less prone to confounding factors such as potential differences in curriculum and instruction across district schools."

variable names for *school*, *gender*, *ethnicity*, and *SES*. These variables will become part of the merged file so that all students (cohort and non-cohort) will have demographic data and school data for each year. It is especially important that she be able to tell which school each student attended in Grades 9, 10, 11, and 12. **Dr. Salerno(1)

Similarly, Dr. Salerno will rename *grade* in each file by attaching "_gr9," "_gr10," "_gr11," or "_gr12" to the end. Recall that the variable contains a constant value that identifies the grade level students attended. In order to identify cohort students in the final merged file, she will need these four grade identifier variables. Another constant variable is *year*. It can be deleted because its information is redundant with *grade*, and it is not necessary for merging nor answering the research question.

The only variable that will retain its original name in all grade files is *studentID*. It will be the key variable used by SPSS to create the merged files, and therefore its name must be identical across files.

Further Specification of Cohort

Dr. Salerno expects that the cohort of students in district schools from Grades 9 to 12 will include those who stayed in the same high school the entire time as well as those who changed high schools at some point. To answer her research question, she decided to specifically analyze the cohort students who stayed in the same school. After merging, she will create a variable that indicates whether the cohort student was a "stable" student (attended one school) or a "mobile within the district" student (attended more than one school). **Dr. Salerno(2)

D. Using SPSS to Address Issues and Prepare Data △

Modify Variables

Dr. Salerno extracted the demographic files for Grades 9, 10, 11, and 12 from the district database. She deleted *year* in each file, then renamed *grade, school, gender, ethnicity,* and *SES* to include the grade level from which the data were obtained. Both actions were performed in the **Variable View** of the **Data Editor** for each file.

For example, the modified Grade 9 demographics file contains data in the following six variables for all students who attended during the 2008–09 school year.

- *studentID*
- *grade_gr9* (all cases have 9 as a value)
- *school_gr9*
- *gender_gr9*
- *ethnicity_gr9*
- *SES_gr9*

The demographic files for successive grade levels contain the same variables but with "*_10*," "*_11*," or "*_12*" added to the end of *grade, school, gender, ethnicity,* and *SES*. The four files are listed below. Note that the Grade 11 file is the same one used in Modules 10 and 11, except the variable names are modified.

- module12_demographics_gr9.sav (contains 576 students)
- module12_demographics_gr10.sav (contains 585 students)
- module12_demographics_gr11.sav (contains 568 students)
- module12_demographics_gr12.sav (contains 551 students)

Merge

The goal at the end of the merging process is to have one file consisting of all students in the district high schools from Grade 9 in 2008–09 to Grade 12 in 2011–12. To accomplish this, Dr. Salerno conducted three merges in SPSS. ****SPSS Tip(1)**

The process is similar to the one she performed in Modules 10 and 11 when she merged test and math course files to a demographics file. Here, she began by opening the Grade 9 file (*module12_demographics_gr9.sav*).

> SPSS Tip 1: Before merging, ensure that cases in each file are sorted by *studentID*. Select Sort under the Data menu. In the dialog box, sort by *studentID* in ascending order.

Under the **Data menu,** she selected **Merge Files** and **Add Variables**, and the dialog box shown in Figure 12.1 was obtained. She selected the Grade 10 data file (*module12_demographics_gr10.sav*), which was already an open data set.

Figure 12.1   Data → Merge Files → Add Variables

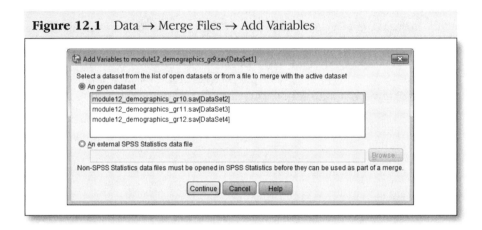

After she clicked the **Continue** button, another window opened (see Figure 12.2). A list of all variables included in the new merged file is shown under **New Active Dataset** on the right side of the window. Variables with an asterisk (*) are those that came from the first data file (Grade 9). Variables with a plus (+) are those that came from the second file (Grade 10). Notice that there are no variables listed in the **Excluded Variables** box on the left side. This means that all variables in both files will be included in the merged file. The variable *studentID* had been in **Excluded Variables,** but because SPSS will need it to match cases from both files, Dr. Salerno placed it in the **Key Variable** box and checked **Match cases on key variables in sorted files** box.

After she clicked **OK,** the warning shown in Figure 12.3 appeared as a reminder that cases must be sorted by *studentID* in both files.

After a final click on **OK,** the files were merged. Dr. Salerno did not want to overwrite her original Grade 9 file (*module12_ demographics_gr9.sav*), so immediately after merging, she selected **Save As** under the **File menu** and created a new file (*module12_merge_9_10.sav*. ****SPSS Tip(2)**

> SPSS Tip 2: There is no need to examine this file, except to make sure that the merge was successful (i.e., all variables from Grades 9 and 10 are included). The file has 616 cases, which include all students in Grade 9 plus students who were in Grade 10 but not Grade 9. Dr. Salerno, however, is interested only in the final merged file that will contain student data across all four grade levels.

Figure 12.2 Adding Variables in Merge

Figure 12.3 Warning in Merge

Next, Dr. Salerno merged the Grade 11 data (*module12_demographics_gr11.sav*) to *module12_merge_9_10.sav* using the process just described. The new file was saved as *module12_merge_9_10_11.sav*.

Finally, Dr. Salerno merged the Grade 12 data (*module12_demographics_gr12.sav*) to *module12_merge_9_10_11.sav*. The new file was saved as *module12_merge_9_10_11_12.sav*. ****SPSS Tip(3)**

SPSS Tip 3: If you did not make modifications to the newly merged files (e.g., *module12_merge_9_10.sav* and *module12_merge_9_10_11.sav*) after they were created, it is not necessary to sort on *studentID* again. Cases in the merged file will already be in ascending order based on *studentID*.

Dr. Salerno checked to ensure that the final merged file (*module12_merge_9_10_11_12.sav*) contained all the variables she wanted. There should be 21 of them; that is, one *studentID* and a set of *grade*, *school*, *gender*, *ethnicity*, and *SES* variables for Grades 9, 10, 11, and 12. There are 650 cases in the file. Some cases have missing data because not all students were in each grade level.

Identify Students in All Four Grades

To identify the cohort of students who stayed in the district all 4 years, Dr. Salerno made use of the grade identifier variables in *module12_merge_9_10_11_12.sav*. Under the **Data menu**, she chose **Select Cases** and clicked on the **If condition is satisfied** button (see Figure 12.4).

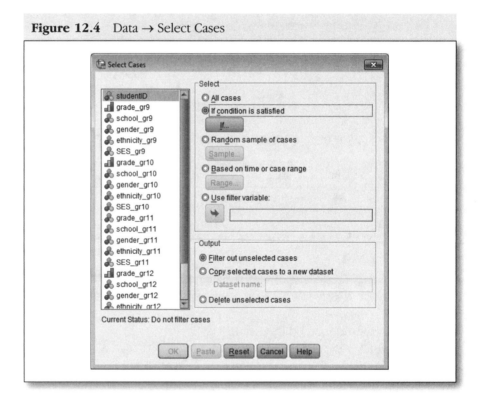

Figure 12.4   Data → Select Cases

The dialog box shown in Figure 12.5 opened, and she created a conditional expression that instructs SPSS to select only students who were in the Grade 9 file (*grade_gr9*=9), the Grade 10 file (*grade_gr10*=10), the Grade 11 file (*grade_gr11*=11), and the Grade 12 file (*grade_gr12*=12).

Figure 12.5 Creating the If Statement

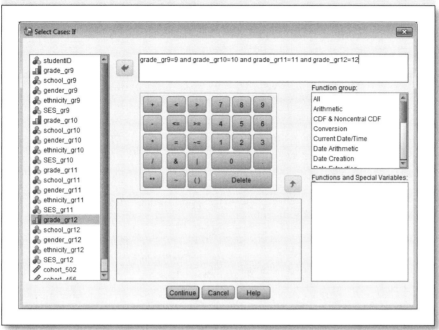

After she clicked **Continue** and **OK,** the **Select procedure** was conducted and a variable called *filter_$* was created. A frequency analysis on this variable (**Analyze → Descriptive Statistics → Frequencies**) showed that 502 students were in all four grades.

To make further data preparation easier and more efficient, Dr. Salerno renamed *filter_$* to *cohort_502* and recoded missing values as "0." The variable now contains two values: "1" to identify the cohort of students who stayed in the district all 4 years, and "0" to identify non-cohort students who did not stay in the district. ****SPSS Tip(4)**

Next, under **Select Cases**, she chose **All cases** and conducted a frequency analysis for *cohort_502*. It produced the output in Table 12.2. There are 502 cohort students (values of "1") and 148 non-cohort students (values of "0"). This sums to the total of 650 cases in *module12_merge_9_10_11_12.sav.*

> SPSS Tip 4: To recode *filter_$*, go to the Transform menu and select Recode into Same Variables. Assign a new value of "0" to the system-missing values, and keep the values of "1" the same.

Table 12.2 SPSS Frequency Output for Cohort and Non-Cohort Students in the Merged File

cohort_502		Frequency	Percent	Valid Percent	Cumulative Percent
Valid	0 Not Selected	148	22.8	22.8	22.8
	1 Selected	502	77.2	77.2	100.0
	Total	650	100.0	100.0	

Identify Students Who Attended the Same High School

SPSS Tip 5: You might think that a conditional expression that equates all variables could be used: *school_gr9=school_gr10=school_gr11=school_gr12.* However, this expression will produce missing values for all cases.

Because of Dr. Salerno's decision to analyze cohort students who attended the same high school all 4 years, she conducted another **Select procedure** under the **Data menu.** She selected all cases (in *module12_merge_9_10_11_12.sav*) for which the following conditional expression was true: ****SPSS Tip(5)**

(*school_gr9=school_gr10*) and (*school_gr10=school_gr11*) and (*school_gr11=school_gr12*)

The new *filter* variable indicates that 456 students have equal values for *school_gr9, school_gr10, school_gr11,* and *school_gr12.* Dr. Salerno renamed *filter* to *cohort_456.* Similar to the modifications she performed on the values for *cohort_502,* she recoded *cohort_456* so that system-missing values were "0" and values for students in the same high school were kept as "1." The output in Table 12.3 is from a frequency analysis on *school_gr9* and represents

Table 12.3 SPSS Output for Cohort Students Who Stayed in the Same School All Four Years

school_gr9		Frequency	Percent	Valid Percent	Cumulative Percent
Valid	31	141	30.9	30.9	30.9
	32	176	38.6	38.6	69.5
	33	139	30.5	30.5	100.0
	Total	456	100.0	100.0	

all students with a "1" for cohort_456. It should be noted that identical output would appear in frequency analyses for *school* variables representing Grades 10, 11, and 12. Approximately 31% of the 456 students attended school 31, 39% attended school 32, and 31% attended school 33. No students attended school 41 (alternative education center) across all 4 years.

Final Preparation

After the cohort of students who stayed in the same high school was identified, Dr. Salerno wanted to clean up the file so she has only what is necessary for answering the research question. She saved *module12_merge_9_10_11_12.sav* as *module12_cohort_456.sav*. In this new file, she deleted all cases except the 456 students. ****SPSS Tip(6)**

> SPSS Tip 6: There are two ways the deletion can be performed: Sort the file by *cohort_456*, highlight all cases with values of "0" for this variable, and press delete; or, under the Data menu, select If *cohort_456*=1 and check Delete unselected cases in the Output section of the dialog box.

Next, variables that helped identify the cohort but are no longer useful were deleted: *grade_gr9, grade_gr10, grade_gr11, grade_12,* and *cohort_502.* In addition, she deleted variables that were redundant with corresponding variables from the Grade 9 file: *school, gender, ethnicity,* and *SES* variables from Grades 10, 11, and 12. It is important, though, to keep *cohort_456* because of the role it will play in the last step of merging the test and math course files. Finally, she removed the "_gr9" portion of the demographic variables. After the cleanup, there are six variables and 456 cases in the *module12_cohort_456.sav* file. The variables are *studentID, school, gender, ethnicity, SES,* and *cohort_456.*

Merge Test and Math Course Data

Now that the cohort is identified, her last step is to merge the test and math course files to *module12_cohort_456.sav.* After each merge, she deleted cases in which the variable *cohort_456* was not equal to "1" because they represented students who are not in the cohort she will analyze. The procedures for merging the test and math course data are the same as those described fully in Modules 10 and 11 in this section. When the merging process is complete, Dr. Salerno will be ready to conduct analysis to investigate the nature of relationships among multiple indicators of math performance and to compare data across demographic subgroups.

△ E. Reflection and Additional Decision Making

From her research experience, Dr. Salerno understands the usefulness in thinking ahead to possible future analysis. Now is the best time to get the data ready for these purposes, while your head is still wrapped around all the variables, their meanings, and other details about the files. She decided to create two additional files: one for cohort students who remained in the district but changed schools (*n* = 46), and another for non-cohort students who moved in and/or out of the district schools (*n* = 148).

To create a new data file for cohort students who changed schools (*n* = 46), she deleted all cases from *module12_merge_9_10_11_12.sav* except the 46 students with values of "1" for *cohort_502* and values of "0" for *cohort_456*. She also deleted unnecessary or redundant variables. The four grade identifier variables were deleted as well as *gender, ethnicity,* and *SES* for Grades 9, 10, 11, and 12. She removed "_gr9" from the three remaining demographic variables. Then, she reordered the four *school* variables so that she could scroll through the file and visually examine student movement across schools. The final file contains 10 variables: *studentID, gender, ethnicity, SES, school_gr9, school_gr10, school_gr11, school_gr12, cohort_502,* and *cohort_456*. At a glance, she noticed that many of the 46 cohort students who moved among the high schools were listed as attending school 41 (alternative education center) one or more years. Further analysis of these data may be of interest to the district. In addition, it may be worthwhile at some point to summarize data according to the school to and from which students are moving.

The second file she created from *module12_merge_9_10_11_12.sav* contains the non-cohort students. She deleted all cases except the 148 students with a value of "0" for *cohort_502*. These are the non-cohort students who attended the district schools for some but not all years. All demographic and school variables for each grade were retained in this file. Dr. Salerno also reordered the variables in the file so that the four grade identifier variables would be at the beginning of the file. She sorted cases in descending order by *grade_gr9, grade_gr10, grade_gr11,* and *grade_gr12*. Visually, this allows her to scroll through the file and view students who were in Grades 9, 10, 11, but not Grade 12 (there were 22 of them). Likewise, she can see that there were 21 students in Grades 9 and 10 only, and 25 in Grades 10, 11, and 12 only. If questions arise at a later date regarding non-cohort student achievement in comparison to cohort students, she will have a file that is ready for merging additional variables.

F. Writing It Up △

The paragraph below includes Dr. Salerno's brief description of the process and her definition of cohort students.

"The definition of cohort students used to answer this particular research question was students who remained in the district from Grade 9 to Grade 12 and attended the same high school during the entire 4 years. The demographic files for each year of the study (2008–09 to 2011–12) were merged together and the school variable for each grade level was used to obtain the cohort. After identifying the set of 456 cohort students, math test scores and math coursework data were merged into the file."

Reflective Questions △

- What types of considerations must be taken into account when deciding how to identify a cohort of students?
- What modifications must be made to variables prior to merging files to create a cohort?
- What is the process for identifying the cohort after files have been merged?
- What is the process to create one file that contains only the cohort students?

Extensions △

- Create the two additional data files that Dr. Salerno talked about in the Reflection and Additional Decision Making section.
- Discuss other aspects of working with multiple data files that may surface in different research studies.
- Locate additional information in statistics or research books about cohort analysis. Discuss various definitions for cohorts and ways of identifying them.
- Obtain multiple data files and discuss the decisions that must be made before merging the data. If possible, practice some of the procedures Dr. Salerno used to obtain her final cohort file.

∆ Additional Resources for Section 5: Working With Multiple Data Files

Boslaugh, S. (2005). *An intermediate guide to SPSS programming using syntax for data management*. Thousand Oaks, CA: Sage. (See Chapters 14 and 16 on combining and restructuring data files.)

Holcomb, Z. C. (2009). *SPSS basics: Techniques for a first course in statistics* (2nd ed.). Glendale, CA: Pyrczak.

Huizingh, E. (2008). *Applied statistics with SPSS*. Thousand Oaks, CA: Sage. (See Chapter 11 on merging, aggregating, and transposing data files.)

IBM Corporation. (2011). *SPSS statistics 20 core systems user's guide*. Available: http://www-01.ibm.com/support/docview.wss?uid=swg27021213. (See Chapter 9, File Handling and File Transformations, for more information on merging, aggregating, and restructuring files.)

Kinnear, P. R., & Gray, C. D. (2009). *SPSS 16 made simple*. Sussex, UK: Psychology Press. (See Chapter 3 on aggregating data and merging files.)

Kulas, J. T. (2009). *SPSS essentials: Managing and analyzing social sciences data*. San Francisco: Jossey-Bass. (See Chapters 7 and 14 on collapsing, merging, and aggregating data files.)

Levesque, R., & SPSS, Inc. *Programming and data management for IBM SPSS statistics 17.0: A guide for IBM SPSS statistics and SAS users*. Chicago: SPSS Inc. A free pdf version can be obtained from http://www.spss.com/statistics/ under Downloads. (See Part 4: File Operations.)

References

Boslaugh, S. (2005). *An intermediate guide to SPSS programming: Using syntax for data management.* Thousand Oaks, CA: Sage.

Green, S. B., Salkind, N. J., & Akey, T. M. (2000). *Using SPSS for Windows: Analyzing and understanding data* (2nd ed.). Upper Saddle River, NJ: Prentice Hall.

Grissom, R. J. (2000). Heterogeneity of variance in clinical data. *Journal of Counseling and Clinical Psychology, 68,* 155–165.

Howell, D. C. (2002). *Statistical methods for psychology* (5th ed.). Duxbury, CA: Pacific Grove.

Huizingh, E. (2008). *Applied statistics with SPSS.* Thousand Oaks, CA: Sage.

McKnight, P. E., McKnight, K. M., Sidani, S., & Figueredo, A. J. (2007). *Missing data: A gentle introduction.* New York: Guilford.

Mertler, C. A., & Vannatta, R. A. (2005). *Advanced and multivariate statistical methods: Practical application and interpretation* (3rd ed.). Glendale, CA: Pyrczak.

Osborne, J., & Waters, E. (2002). Four assumptions of multiple regression that researchers should always test. *Practical Assessment, Research, and Evaluation, 8*(2). Available: http://pareonline.net/getvn.asp?v=8&n=2

Scariano, S., & Davenport, J. (1987). The effects of violations of the independence assumption in the one way ANOVA. *American Statistician, 41,* 123–129.

Stevens, J. (2009). *Applied multivariate statistics for the social sciences* (5th ed.). New York: Taylor & Francis.

Tabachnick, B. G., & Fidell, L. S. (2007). *Using multivariate statistics* (5th ed.). Boston: Pearson Education, Inc.

Tomarken, A. J., & Serlin, R. C. (1986). Comparison of ANOVA alternatives under variance heterogeneity and specific noncentrality structures. *Psychological Bulletin, 99,* 90–99.

Index

⑤SAGE research**methods**

The essential online tool for researchers from the world's leading methods publisher

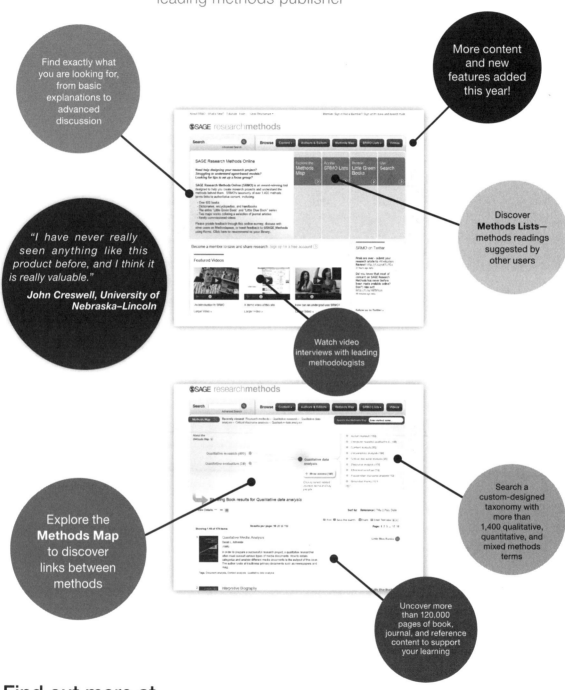

Find exactly what you are looking for, from basic explanations to advanced discussion

More content and new features added this year!

"I have never really seen anything like this product before, and I think it is really valuable."

John Creswell, University of Nebraska–Lincoln

Discover **Methods Lists**— methods readings suggested by other users

Watch video interviews with leading methodologists

Explore the **Methods Map** to discover links between methods

Search a custom-designed taxonomy with more than 1,400 qualitative, quantitative, and mixed methods terms

Uncover more than 120,000 pages of book, journal, and reference content to support your learning

Find out more at
www.sageresearchmethods.com